BEYOND BRUTALITY

HBI SERIES ON JEWISH WOMEN

Lisa Fishbayn Joffe, General Editor

Ronit Irshai, Associate Editor

The HBI Series on Jewish Women, created by the Hadassah-Brandeis Institute, publishes a wide range of work at the intersection of Jewish Studies and Women and Gender Studies by and about Jewish women in diverse contexts, disciplines and time periods.

The HBI Series on Jewish Women is supported by a generous gift from Dr. Laura S. Schor.

For the complete list of books that are available in this series, please see https://brandeisuniversitypress.com/series/hbi

Jane Kanarek, *Beyond Brutality: Reclaiming Female Presence in Bavli Sotah*

Janine P. Holc, *The Weavers of Trautenau: Jewish Female Forced Labor in the Holocaust*

Paula J. Birnbaum, *Sculpting a Life: Chana Orloff between Paris and Tel Aviv*

Susan Weidman Schneider and Yona Zeldis McDonough, editors, *Frankly Feminist: Short Stories by Jewish Women from Lilith Magazine*

Tamar Biala, editor, *Dirshuni: Contemporary Women's Midrash*

Marjorie Lehman, *Bringing Down the Temple House: Engendering Tractate Yoma*

Tamar Ross, *Expanding the Palace of Torah: Orthodoxy and Feminism*, Second Edition

Hadassah Lieberman, *Hadassah: An American Story*

ChaeRan Y. Freeze, *A Jewish Woman of Distinction: The Life and Diaries of Zinaida Poliakova*

Chava Turniansky, *Glikl: Memoirs 1691–1719*

Joy Ladin, *The Soul of the Stranger: Reading God and Torah from a Transgender Perspective*

Joanna Beata Michlic, editor, *Jewish Families in Europe, 1939–Present: History, Representation, and Memory*

Sarah M. Ross, *A Season of Singing: Creating Feminist Jewish Music in the United States*

Margalit Shilo, *Girls of Liberty: The Struggle for Suffrage in Mandatory Palestine*

Sylvia Barack Fishman, editor, *Love, Marriage, and Jewish Families: Paradoxes of a Social Revolution*

Cynthia Kaplan Shamash, *The Strangers We Became: Lessons in Exile from One of Iraq's Last Jews*

BEYOND BRUTALITY

RECLAIMING FEMALE PRESENCE IN BAVLI SOTAH

JANE KANAREK

BRANDEIS UNIVERSITY PRESS
WALTHAM, MASSACHUSETTS

Brandeis University Press

Manufactured in the United States of America
Designed by Richard Hendel
Typeset in Utopia and Monterchi by Passumpsic Publishing

Library of Congress Cataloging-in-Publication Data
NAMES: Kanarek, Jane L. author
TITLE: Beyond brutality : reclaiming female presence in Bavli Sotah / Jane Kanarek.
DESCRIPTION: Waltham, Massachusetts : Brandeis University Press, [2025] | SERIES: HBI series on Jewish women | Includes bibliographical references and index. | Summary: "Beyond Brutality draws on feminist analysis and gender studies to examine tractate Sotah of the Babylonian Talmud as a literary unit. By interrogating how, why, and where women are invisible within Bavli Sotah, Jane Kanarek brings to light a ubiquitous female presence throughout the text"—Provided by publisher.
IDENTIFIERS: LCCN 2025027682 (print) | LCCN 2025027683 (ebook) | ISBN 9781684582693 (cloth) | ISBN 9781684582990 (paperback) | ISBN 9781684583003 (ebook)
SUBJECTS: LCSH: Talmud. Sotah—Criticism, interpretation, etc.
CLASSIFICATION: LCC BM506.S73 K36 2025 (print) | LCC BM506.S73 (ebook) | DDC 296.1/2—dc23/eng/20250828
LC record available at https://lccn.loc.gov/2025027682
LC ebook record available at https://lccn.loc.gov/2025027683

5 4 3 2 1

For Andy

CONTENTS

TRANSLATIONS, TEXTUAL EDITIONS, AND MANUSCRIPTS

For ease of reader access to the original language, translations of the Babylonian Talmud in the main body of the text utilize the Vilna edition. I include significant manuscript variations in the endnotes, and when central to my argument, in the main body of the text. For Bavli manuscripts, I have utilized the Friedberg Project for Talmud Variants, the Saul and Evelyn Henkind Talmud Text Databank, and the critical edition of B. Sotah edited by Abraham Liss.[1] Where relevant, I have also consulted the dissertations of Gilad Landau and Abraham Cohen.[2] For the Yerushalmi, I utilize the transcription of the Leiden manuscript by the Academy of the Hebrew Language.[3] For Mishnah, I utilize the Kaufmann manuscript; for Tosefta, the Lieberman edition and, if not available, the Zuckermandel edition; for Sifrei Bemidbar, the Kahana edition. I base translations of the Tanakh on NJPS, modified as necessary in accordance with rabbinic context. All other translations are mine.

1. Abraham Liss, ed., *The Babylonian Talmud with Variant Readings Collected from Manuscripts, Fragments of the "Genizah" and Early Printed Editions* (Jerusalem: Institute for the Complete Israeli Talmud, 1977 [Hebrew]).

2. Cohen, "Edition and Comprehensive Commentary on Chapters II & III"; Landau, "An Edition and Comprehensive Commentary on Chapter IX." I also want to thank Moriah Shriki whose dissertation on the seventh chapter of B. Sotah is in progress as of this writing.

3. *Talmud Yerushalmi: According to Ms. Or. 4720 (Scal. 3) of the Leiden University Library with Restorations and Corrections* (Jerusalem: The Academy of the Hebrew Language, 2001 [Hebrew]).

BEYOND BRUTALITY

INTRODUCTION

And said R. Abbahu: "At first, I would say that I was humble.[1] *When I saw R. Abba from Akko, who said one reason and his speaker said one reason and he was not angry, I said, 'I am not humble.'"*[2]

And what was the humility of R. Abbahu?

That the wife of R. Abbahu's speaker said to the wife[3] *of R. Abbahu: "Behold! Ours does not need yours. And that he bends down and stands up before him is merely to do him honor."*

His wife went and told R. Abbahu.[4]

He said to her: "What do you derive from her? Through me and through him the Most High will be praised."[5]

—B. Sotah 40a (Vilna Edition)

On the surface, the Vilna edition of the Babylonian Talmud presents this story about two women and their husbands as a paradigmatic example of the humility to which a sage should aspire. The story opens with Rabbi Abbahu's declaration that although he is humble, Rabbi Abba from Akko is, in fact, the humbler sage because the latter did not anger when he heard his speaker—the person responsible for transmitting his words to the wider audience—alter his reasoning during the public lecture. Rabbi Abbahu's humility turns on a similar situation, although this time orchestrated by two women. The wife of Rabbi Abbahu's speaker informs the wife of Rabbi Abbahu that her husband (R. Abbahu's speaker) is conveying his own words to the larger audience rather than those of the sage. When the speaker bends down to listen to R. Abbahu and then stands up to speak, he does so only to show respect to the sage. Rabbi Abbahu's wife goes to inform her husband of this situation, and Rabbi Abbahu rejects her complaint. He tells her that regardless of whose words are heard by the public—sage or speaker—this public elucidation of Torah praises God. With these words of correction, and perhaps rebuke, from husband to wife, the Bavli appears to give Rabbi Abbahu the last word.

While we might focus our attention on positing some distinction between the types of humility that Rabbi Abbahu and Rabbi Abba each espouse, I instead invite us to shift our attention in another direction, away from these sages and toward the two women in this tale.[6] Despite the women's namelessness (as is often the case in the Talmud), this story nevertheless portrays them as having a stake in and knowledge of Torah's creation, transmission, and reception. Both women claim the importance of public knowledge; each wants who creates and transmits Torah to be accurately recognized by others. Both know the physical conventions of this public transmission of knowledge, that is the significance of posture, in this case who bends over to listen and who stands up straight.[7] The speaker's wife appears to have been present and attentive at the sage's lecture; she is able to describe her husband's movements and recognizes that his words differ from those of Rabbi Abbahu. As the speaker's wife claims both transmission and creation of original Torah for her husband, she questions and challenges the hierarchy of sage and speaker. Rabbi Abbahu's wife, by telling her husband about her conversation with this other woman, attempts to maintain and reinforce the hierarchy of sage over speaker. Indeed, the Talmud portrays these two women as speaking and competing directly with one another, apparently without male presence. They argue over social status, honor, authority, and pedagogy.

As we linger with these two women, I want to note another important detail about this story: its location in tractate Sotah of the Babylonian Talmud (hereafter Bavli Sotah or B. Sotah). The sotah ritual, as I will describe in more detail later in this book, is a proceeding initiated by a jealous husband upon suspicion of his wife's sexual intercourse with another man. In its biblical version, the accused woman drinks bitter waters into which a portion of the sotah text has been erased. If guilty, her belly distends and her thigh sags. If innocent, she becomes pregnant and bears a child. In its later mishnaic version, the ritual becomes a violent and voyeuristic spectacle that assumes the accused woman's guilt. Yet, in contrast to the jealous husband and the potentially cheating wife of the sotah ritual, this talmudic story depicts jealous women/wives and a male speaker who cheats his sage/master by presenting his own insights as the sage's. Instead of a husband competing with another man, here two women compete over Torah. Noticing this story's placement—or redaction—in B. Sotah enables us to see a ritual that places men in control of female bodies challenged by these two women who argue with one another and appoint themselves arbiters of Torah. We may even contend that this story destabilizes the sotah ritual itself by shifting the locus of jealousy from husband to wife and from sexual transgression to Torah transgression.

This story about these two women points to the central project of this book: a feminist analysis of Bavli Sotah as a literary unit. Through approaching the talmudic tractate as a unit of analysis, this book aims to make females visible by interrogating how, why, and where females have disappeared throughout B. Sotah and then exposing their presence. I argue four interconnected points about the tractate: First, that B. Sotah responds to and ameliorates the brutality of the mishnaic sotah ritual by teaching its audience that men, too, are sinful and making the sotah disappear. Second, that as B. Sotah attempts to disappear the sotah, it replaces her with a hypothetical model of the moral man and stories of mostly righteous women. Third, that the sotah ritual overflows the boundaries of the discussion of the ritual itself and weaves its way throughout the entire tractate, thus influencing and shaping a wide range of other topics in the tractate and resurfacing the sotah. Fourth, that B. Sotah engages in a process of mirroring, in which it inverts both the performative details of the sotah ritual and the notion of the destructive woman. Reading B. Sotah as a literary unit allows us to witness the ways in which the sotah herself and the judicial spectacle of the sotah ritual become pedagogical vehicles for conveying a vision for a pious society. Much as this process displaces women, B. Sotah's composition and content will resist this displacement, resurfacing women as integral to the formation and stabilization of rabbinic culture.

A LENS OF FEMALE PRESENCE

By choosing to begin this book with a tale of two women, I signal my commitment to reading the Bavli—and B. Sotah in particular—with assumptions of female presence rather than female absence. To speak somewhat facetiously, we know that the rabbis did not produce biological descendants through asexual reproduction—at the very least, they required women for childbearing.[8] Of course, this instrumental perspective is far too limiting. The physical presence of women (and not only in the world of rabbinic culture) means that women were an intrinsic part of that (and any) culture. Rather than debating whether women were part of a particular culture (because of course they were), we must shift and expand our lenses to see where women are present *and* how they are made to disappear. As Melanie Johnson-DeBaufre writes about Thessalonian wo/men, "First, the case that *wo/men were there* should no longer need to be made."[9] This noticing of presence works in tandem with noticing the ways in which our textual history, in which I include both rabbinic sources and academic scholarship, has obscured women.

The historian Tiya Miles writes about the project of recovering the histories of enslaved Black women: "In select moments where I encounter archival deficit, I imagine onto the page the figures of Rose, Ashley, and Ruth. At other times, I take an opposite approach of marking their absence in the record, so that we remain aware of how the real conditions of their lives precipitated not only physical and psychological trauma but also archival diminishment."[10] This book is not a work of history in which I try to reconstruct an ancient practice of the sotah ritual. Yet, I share with Miles the commitment to utilizing the evidence we do possess from B. Sotah to imagine women into presence. By making the processes of disappearance visible, I aim to denaturalize women's absence and restore their presence.[11]

Feminist analysis of B. Sotah as a literary unit reveals the ways in which the sotah and the sotah ritual leave their traces throughout the arc of the tractate. They intertwine with and shape rabbinic conceptions of language, empire, Torah study, and divine presence. In this sense, "thinking with" the sotah necessitates understanding women to function not only as literary devices that convey rabbinic ideologies but, equally crucial, as integral to the shaping of rabbinic culture.[12] As we read about the punitive sotah ritual and watch the sotah herself disappear, only to see her replaced by an ideal moral man and (even) a male sotah, we will also see the ways in which tales of other women abound and traces of the sotah are felt throughout this tractate. Reading B. Sotah through a feminist lens entails simultaneously holding absence and presence, brutality and grace.

A LENS OF THE TRACTATE

This book combines feminist analysis with an approach to talmudic analysis that treats individual tractates of the Babylonian Talmud as coherent literary units. I argue that much as Bavli tractates are composed of material from disparate chronological and geographical sources, anonymous editorial hands have intervened in these materials in such a way that in certain tractates, one can discern an overall theme and voice, even among materials that may initially appear disparate. What may appear on initial read as a digression may, in fact, be part of the tractate's thematic whole.[13] Thus, although this book relies on previous talmudic scholarship that has analyzed the source components of an individual sugya[14] and a sugya's place in its wider local literary context,[15] its methodological anchor lies with recent scholarship that returns to the talmudic tractate as a unit of literary analysis. In particular, I draw and build on the work of Mira Wasserman and Marjorie Lehman, who argue for the coherence of, respectively, tractates Avodah Zarah and Yoma of the Babylonian Talmud.[16] Wasserman brings B. Avodah Zarah into conversation with contemporary critical theory in order to read the tractate as a work of rabbinic anthropology. Lehman utilizes feminist theory to trace the theme of the house throughout B. Yoma, revealing the rabbis as deconstructing the Temple to differentiate themselves from priests and, in the process, replacing the Temple house with the rabbinic house. With Wasserman and Lehman, I share a conceptualization of the talmudic redactors as more akin to creative authors, that is, in Lehman's words, "as engaged in juxtaposing sources, arranging them, reformulating traditions, and adapting and integrating narratives into the larger context of the tractate."[17] Through this process, these redactor-authors form a tractate's narrative arc.

In conceptualizing B. Sotah as a coherent literary work, I also draw from—and differ with—the work of Jacob Neusner. Basing his analysis on the formal rhetorical techniques that the Bavli utilizes, Neusner argues that the entire Babylonian Talmud speaks with a unified, unique, and coherent voice that results from editorial work late in the process of the Bavli's final composition.[18] My analysis of B. Sotah leads me to agree with Neusner about the presence of a shaping editorial voice that intervenes in the tractate, likely later in the process of redaction, and provides coherence to the tractate. However, in contrast to Neusner, I contend that the content of the Bavli's statements should be given equal—if not greater—weight than its formal rhetorical structures. This emphasis on literary content rather than formal rhetorical structure results in two conclusions: first, that not all Bavli tractates possess an overarching theme (or themes); and, second, that those tractates that do exhibit an overarching theme (or themes) may differ ideologically from one another. From this vantage point, the Babylonian Talmud thus becomes a work of multiple coherent voices, many of which are evidenced on the level of the tractate.

An important corollary of this shift to the tractate as an analytical unit is the weight I give to the micro level of the talmudic sugya. While I build my argument through analysis of selected sugyot from B. Sotah, the crux of my argument rests on the ways in which these shorter passages are linked together literarily and thematically within the macro unit of B. Sotah. This emphasis on B. Sotah as a literary unit also enables us to see more clearly the work that B. Sotah does with its mishnaic inheritance, a picture that is obscured when focus lies primarily with the smaller unit of the sugya. Indeed, as we will see, while B. Sotah does not explicitly problematize the mishnaic version of the sotah ritual, it reacts to the Mishnah's violent vision of the ritual through constructing its version of idealized rabbinic masculinity and, at the same time, through positioning females as mostly righteous and males as responsible for society's breakdown. Unlike Mishnah Sotah (M. Sotah), B. Sotah is not concerned with reimagining the sotah ritual. Rather, as it examines the ritual, it often places it in conversation with other areas of rabbinic law, decentering the sotah as it shifts its focus to another topic.

My methodological choice to center one tractate as a literary unit of analysis also shapes the ways in which I utilize rabbinic sources found outside of B. Sotah. First, I cite parallel rabbinic sources—whether those found in earlier tannaitic compilations (Mishnah, Tosefta, Midrash Halakhah) or in other tractates of the Babylonian Talmud—only when they help highlight the particular project of B. Sotah. That is, I emphasize the thematic content of B. Sotah over posing a theory about the chronological development of a particular sugya. Similarly, I turn to the parallel tractate in the Palestinian Talmud—Yerushalmi Sotah (Y. Sotah)—when it helps bring to the fore and accentuate B. Sotah's particular ideology. This book does not aim to present a comprehensive comparison between B. Sotah and Y. Sotah, but rather to utilize Y. Sotah—a closely related but earlier document—as a tool to better help us understand B. Sotah. I contend that the ways in which B. Sotah departs from its textual inheritance, both in the ways in which it modifies and recontextualizes parallel sources and in its inclusion of otherwise unattested sources, marks this tractate as possessing its own ideology.[19]

Here I take note of a contention of one of the founders of modern Talmud scholarship, Jacob Nahum Epstein. Epstein observed a greater identity between Y. Sotah and B. Sotah, in both halakhah (law) and aggadah (narrative), than is usually common between tractates of the Bavli and Yerushalmi. Nevertheless, Epstein added to this observation the words, "Despite all of the differences and contrasts between them, of which it is not necessary to comment."[20] It is possible that Epstein's focus on the process of chronological composition and the sources involved in that process led him to decide that similarity outweighs difference. However, my choice to emphasize literary content leads me to accent difference (which Epstein also recognized) rather than similarity between Y. Sotah and B. Sotah. In this case, I agree with Lisa Grushcow's assessment that Y. Sotah is more concerned with "sexual behavior and marital relationships" than is B. Sotah.[21]

This book is thus simultaneously traditional and radical. It is traditional in its privileging of the tractate as a literary unit.[22] It is radical in its positioning of the editors of the tractate as creative authors.[23] The question of whether these interventions were conscious or unconscious is beside the point. The unconscious, embedded within a particular cultural context, may also produce literary work that is in concert with a more consciously produced theme. Combining feminist theory with analysis of B. Sotah as a tractate makes visible the ways in which responsibility for the disappearance of females from our conceptions of rabbinic culture lies not only with scholars and their scholarship but also with the compositional arc of B. Sotah itself.

STRUCTURE OF BAVLI SOTAH

Bavli Sotah is one of seven tractates that make up the Babylonian Talmud's order Nashim (Women).[24] It consists of nine chapters that, as is usual for the Bavli, conform to the topical division established by its predecessor, Mishnah Sotah. Because B. Sotah draws its topical organization from M. Sotah, I begin this section with some comments on M. Sotah's organization. In most general terms, M. Sotah's outline is as follows: chapters 1–4, 5:1, and 6 treat the sotah ritual;[25] the remainder of chapter 5 explicates a series of statements that begin with the words "on that day he interpreted"; chapter 7 treats language and ritual; chapter 8 the priest anointed for war; and chapter 9 the decapitated heifer (*ʿeglah ʿarufah*) and the downward trajectory of rabbinic society toward the end of the Second Temple period (as we would term it).

Noticing the departure from the sotah ritual in chapters 7–9 of M. Sotah, scholars tended to divide the tractate into two sections: chapters 1–6 and chapters 7–9, with earlier scholars positing a weak connection between these two sections. These earlier scholars argued for the inclusion of chapters 7–9 in M. Sotah as driven by 7:1's mention of the sotah ritual in a longer list of rituals that may be recited in any language (the sotah ritual is referred to first).[26] More recently, however, scholars have begun to argue for a stronger connection between these two sections, noting overlapping literary structures as well as recurring literary and legal motifs throughout M. Sotah.[27] I agree with those scholars who posit a stronger connection between these two sections of M. Sotah. B. Sotah, as we will see, is even more significantly and extensively integrated than M. Sotah.

Like all tractates of the Babylonian Talmud, B. Sotah is a composite document. It includes material found in a range of other sources —including Mishnah, Tosefta, tannaitic and amoraic midrashim, and the Palestinian Talmud (Yerushalmi)—that it then weaves into a larger composition. Chapters 1 and 7 are by far the longest of the tractate, composed, respectively, of twelve and a half (2a–14a) and ten and a half folio pages (32a–42a).[28] Keeping in mind the difficulty of precisely quantifying a tractate's aggadah,[29] chapters 1 and 7 also contain the most extensive aggadic sections of the tractate. Indeed, B. Sotah differs from other Bavli tractates in the significant amount of aggadah it includes. I hypothesize that the first and seventh chapters mark shifting pedagogical priorities of B. Sotah's editors, the former chapter responding more directly to M. Sotah and the latter transitioning more fully to the Bavli's own agenda.

B. Sotah is also notable for its dearth of medieval commentary. In contrast to tractates with an extensive tradition of medieval commentary, B. Sotah's is minimal: the only extant complete commentaries on the tractate are those of Rashi, the tosafists, and Menahem ben Meiri. This lack of commentary seems to indicate that B. Sotah was not widely studied in the medieval academies.[30] In contrast, it is difficult to assert with any certainty the place that B. Sotah, as a developing textual tradition, held in the ancient curriculum. However, the range of materials included in the tractate, particularly in the aggadic sections, leads me to hazard a guess that the tractate (or at least the tractate's concerns) did hold a more central place within amoraic and pre-geonic rabbinic culture than in the medieval academies.[31]

PREVIOUS SCHOLARSHIP AND TWO TALKING WOMEN

The title of this section intentionally elides whether its topic is previous scholarship on Mishnah Sotah, Bavli Sotah, or the sotah ritual itself. My lack of precision gestures toward the way that two trends in previous scholarship overlap with, inform, and diverge from this book's approach to B. Sotah. The first of these trends directs its analytical attention to the sotah ritual itself, interrogating the ritual's depiction in a chosen textual corpus—for example, Mishnah or Talmud. This perspective overlaps with my approach in its recognition of the unit of the tractate, whether M. Sotah or B. Sotah. However, it differs in its sole focus on those sections of the tractate that discuss the sotah ritual, to the exclusion of the larger textual unit. The second trend directs its analytical attention toward a particular topic, utilizing a sugya found in B. Sotah to investigate the chosen topic. These topics have included areas as diverse as language use,[32] angelology,[33] prophecy,[34] depictions of Jesus,[35] and definitions of halakhah and aggadah.[36] While this approach does look beyond the sotah ritual to other topics within the tractate, it ignores the potential analytical significance of a sugya's location within the larger unit of B. Sotah.

Two important monographs, one by Ishay Rosen-Zvi and one by Lisa Grushcow, exemplify the first trend.[37] As the title of Rosen-Zvi's *The Mishnaic Sotah Ritual: Temple, Gender and Midrash* indicates, the author's goal lies in interrogating M. Sotah's specific version of the ritual rather than interrogating the mishnaic tractate as a whole.[38] Rosen-Zvi argues that the Mishnah's ritual is best understood as punitive, "a latent midrash on the adulteresses' punishment in [the prophet] Ezekiel" that removes the possibility of the accused woman's innocence.[39] Rosen-Zvi thus recognizes the unit of the tractate as significant but does not extend his analysis beyond M. Sotah's depiction of the sotah ritual itself.

The title of Grushcow's monograph, *Writing the Wayward Wife: Rabbinic Interpretations of Sotah,* alludes to the author's synoptic approach to the sotah ritual. Tracing the ritual from Scripture through later aggadic midrashim, Grushcow argues that two overarching themes shape all rabbinic interpretations of the sotah: development of legal procedures and condemnation of adultery. These themes take different forms in the various rabbinic documents.[40] While, as I remarked earlier, I am in agreement with Grushcow's contention that B. Sotah has less of an interest in sexual temptation than does Y. Sotah, I am not convinced by her contention that B. Sotah has "a unique interest in the nature of jealousy and its consequences."[41] Indeed, although Grushcow recognizes B. Sotah as a coherent document, her focus only on the parts concerned with the sotah ritual (as well as the large textual corpus she analyzes) leads her to overstate both B. Sotah's thematic continuity with other rabbinic documents and some of the ways in which it is discontinuous.

The second trend, the analysis of a variety of topical sugyot without attention to their location in B. Sotah, is well illustrated through mention of another story found in proximity to the tale of two women with which I opened this book (B. Sotah 40a). Similar to the tale of two women, this story features R. Abbahu, but now teaching and talking with a different sage, R. Hiyya bar Abba. R. Abbahu expounds aggadah and R. Hiyya bar Abba expounds authoritative tradition (*shema'ta*). The word *shema'ta* is commonly understood to designate halakhah, with the story thus depicting a competition between the genres of halakhah and aggadah.[42] When R. Hiyya bar Abba's entire audience leaves him in order to go and hear R. Abbahu teach aggadah, R. Abbahu attempts to comfort his colleague through a parable comparing aggadah to shiny trinkets and authoritative tradition to precious stones; people, R. Abbahu declares, will always choose shiny trinkets over precious stones. He thus implies that R. Hiyya bar Abba teaches the more important material, that is, authoritative tradition. This story appears in a number of books and articles that treat the relationship between halakhah and aggadah, including ones by Steven Fraade, Marjorie Lehman, Jeffrey Rubenstein, and myself.[43] Yet none of these works (including mine) discuss the story's redaction within B. Sotah or even connect it with our tale of two women. Attention to the larger context of the tractate and the tale of two women highlights, once again, themes of competition and jealousy as well as brings to the fore the hidden presence of women. In fact, in his commentary on this other story, Rashi explains that "shiny trinkets" refers to "tools of women and the poor, such as spindles, needles, and hooks."[44] We may thus imagine people flocking to women's Torah.[45]

SOTAH AND HISTORICAL MEMORY

Discussions of the sotah ritual commonly engage two connected questions about its historicity. First, was the sotah ritual practiced during the Second Temple period? Second, does the Mishnah provide us with a historical record of the sotah ritual? Because the answers to these questions are connected to one of my central points about B. Sotah —its displacement of the sotah ritual—I discuss them in some detail below.

Rosen-Zvi has convincingly argued that although M. Sotah appears to narrate the sotah ritual as if it depicts Second Temple practice, it does not, in fact, provide a historical description of a now-defunct ritual. Rather, M. Sotah (and tannaitic literature in general) provides a rabbinically reimagined version of a possibly ancient practice. That is, even if M. Sotah does incorporate older traditions about the sotah ritual, it has reshaped these traditions according to the conventions of rabbinic writing and the tannaitic study house.[46] It conveys tannaitic ideologies about power, gender, sexuality, language, and ritual.[47] Crucially, M. Sotah reinforces a presumption of female guilt.

Like M. Sotah, B. Sotah shapes its discussion of the ritual in accordance with its own ideology and concerns. However, unlike M. Sotah, B. Sotah both decenters a historical Second Temple ritual and de-emphasizes female sexual transgression. Three mishnaic sources provide evidence for B. Sotah's lack of concern for female sexual transgression and its concomitant lack of interest in a historical sotah ritual. The three mishnaic sources are (1) the case of the freed slave Karkemit forced to drink the sotah waters (Mishnah Eduyot 5:6), (2) the gift of Queen Helene of Adiabene to the Jerusalem Temple of a golden tablet upon which the sotah portion was written (Mishnah Yoma 3:10),[48] and (3) the cessation of the sotah ritual because of the proliferation of adultery (M. Sotah 9:11).[49]

The traditions recorded in M. Eduyot and M. Yoma refer to named women who were involved in the practice of the sotah ritual, Karkemit through drinking the water potion and Queen Helene through gifting a tablet to the Temple as an aid to the ritual's performance. Yet B. Sotah nowhere integrates these two traditions or even alludes to these two women. On the other hand, Y. Sotah mentions both Helene's gift (Y. Sotah 2:2, 18a)[50] and Karkemit (Y. Sotah 2:5, 18b).[51] The Yerushalmi's inclusion of these two women highlights its greater interest in sexual transgression. It also highlights B. Sotah's choice to exclude historical memories of the sotah—however reshaped—whether of one forced to take part in the ritual (Karkemit) or another who facilitated it (Helene).

The final source, M. Sotah 9:11, is, at best, ambiguous about whether male adultery was a factor in the ritual's discontinuation.[52] However, B. Sotah utilizes this passage unambiguously, expanding the categories of people and types of behavior that render the bitter waters ineffective to include a husband's daughters *and* sons as well as a man's sexual intercourse with an unmarried woman (B. Sotah 47b).[53] The expansion of responsibility to include males and the exclusion of these two named women reinforce the idea that B. Sotah is not concerned with the preservation of historical memory about female sexual transgression. Rather, it utilizes the sotah ritual as a locus for constructing its own ideologies about a variety of other topics.

Despite B. Sotah's decentering of historical memory of the sotah ritual and female sin, other reimaginings of the sotah ritual testify to its continued presence within Jewish culture as a locus for amplifying and punishing female sin.[54] The sixth-century Palestinian liturgical poet Yannai dramatizes the sotah ritual in one of his sabbath *piyyutim* (liturgical poems).[55] A magical manual found in the Cairo Genizah that is likely dated to the post-talmudic period and entitled *ʿInyan Sotah* (Concerning the Sotah) provides instructions for a contemporary sotah ritual. This ritual includes the use of a series of divine magical names, spring water, and earth from the synagogue ark.[56] The eleventh-century *Chronicle of Ahimaʿatz* describes a revival of the sotah ritual, similarly utilizing dust from under the ark.[57] The more recent resurgence of interest in the rabbinic sotah ritual, and so its textual recordings, may be attributed to the rise of Jewish feminism and the concomitant desires to confront the more troubling elements of rabbinic Judaism and to seek out women's voices.

CHAPTER SUMMARIES

Each chapter in this book centers around analysis of a short base passage, or passages, found in a particular chapter of B. Sotah. I have chosen these sugyot from most chapters of the tractate. By and large, the book chapters follow the order of appearance of these base sugyot in B. Sotah. In each case, I build my argument by moving outward from these base sugyot, reading them in concert with other passages located throughout B. Sotah. This methodology enables me to illustrate and argue for my conception of B. Sotah's redactors as actively weaving the sotah and the sotah ritual throughout the tractate. Each chapter also treats a particular topic, further illuminating the editorial work necessary to create a coherent arc throughout the tractate. Finally, because B. Sotah is not primarily interested in recreating and elaborating the sotah ritual, I do not overly interrogate the specific details of the Bavli's version of the ritual. These details do not reach to the heart of B. Sotah's project or fully illuminate the work of this tractate.

Chapter 1 focuses on B. Sotah's opening sugyot and argues that these late—or saboraic—sugyot set the pedagogical stage for the tractate. They teach us how the tractate's editors, whomever they may be, want us to read and respond to M. Sotah. I argue that rather than amplify the biblical sotah ritual, as does M. Sotah, B. Sotah shifts our attention away from the sin of the sotah to a wider view of sinners that includes men and to envisioning an ideal rabbinic masculinity. These moves occur throughout the tractate. In the process, B. Sotah both ameliorates the sotah ritual and displaces women. This chapter also provides an overview of the biblical and mishnaic sotah rituals.

Chapter 2 continues to interrogate the ways in which B. Sotah responds to the mishnaic sotah ritual. It adds two other methodologies: first, a focus on male behavior rather than female; and second, a shifting of our attention back and forth from the sotah ritual to other rituals. Two sugyot serve as examples of this process, one from the tractate's first chapter and one from the second. The former interrogates the way in which B. Sotah delineates a time measurement for sexual intercourse and the latter details the *minhah* (grain) sacrifice. In the process, as we will see, B. Sotah once again ameliorates the mishnaic ritual but simultaneously displaces women as loci of knowledge within rabbinic culture. This chapter also presents the most detailed examination of the Bavli sotah ritual in this book. It acts as a bridge to chapter 3, which confronts the tractate's paradoxical erasure and displacement of women.

Chapter 3 exposes the ways in which the very redactional arc of B. Sotah displaces women. It focuses on two well-studied pericopes about familial knowledge transmission, one from the middle of the tractate (third chapter) and one from the end (ninth chapter). The former probes the type of merit that delays the punishment of an accused sotah, and the latter interrogates a prohibition against the teaching of Greek wisdom. Through the lens of Torah study as depicted in B. Sotah, I interrogate the process of female erasure within B. Sotah itself. This chapter argues that shifting our lenses to notice the ways in which the literary arc of B. Sotah has erased females enables us to restore females to the heart of rabbinic culture.

Chapter 4 marks this book's switch from a focus on the sections of the tractate that discuss the sotah ritual to a focus on the sections of the tractate that discuss other rabbinic rituals. I demonstrate the ways in which B. Sotah's understanding of the sotah ritual permeates even these seemingly disparate topics. In this chapter, rather than emphasizing the rabbinic family and Torah study, I turn to the Jewish people writ large and to ways that language is used. Two passages from the seventh chapter of the tractate—one about the wilderness spies and one about Joseph's name—anchor this section of the book. I argue that the attention the seventh chapter of the tractate devotes to language—written, oral, and aural—results from the concern with language that pervades the sotah ritual. In this instance, B. Sotah portrays language as a vehicle for knowledge transmission and as a medium for building or destroying human society.

Chapter 5 puts the sotah ritual in conversation with the deuteronomic ritual of the decapitated heifer (*ʿeglah ʿarufah*), rabbinically retold in the ninth chapter of B. Sotah. Focusing on the words that the elders recite at the conclusion of the *ʿeglah ʿarufah* ritual and two passages generated by those words, I argue that this section of the tractate once again evinces the theme of male potential for sin, once again with national implications. The first passage weaves together the necessity for accompaniment on a journey, the story of the prophet Elisha and the bears, and the birth of Ruth; the second passage portrays sage-teaching gone wrong, the care of a female innkeeper, and Jesus's heresy. Rather than portraying female sexual sin as responsible for the dissolution of rabbinic society, these passages depict sages as responsible for societal unraveling and females as the hope for future salvation.

Chapter 6 gives women the last word. Without erasing the sotah ritual's cruelty, I continue the constructive work of restoring female presence and voice. To do so, I move backward in B. Sotah, with two base passages from the tractate's eighth chapter and one from the first chapter. All of these passages stem from biblical texts about war. The first discusses laws about exemption from battle, intertwining the male battlefield with female sexual transgression and the possibility of female Torah study. The second retells the story of David and Goliath, including a violent scene of the rape of Orpah, Goliath's mother. The third tells the story of the righteous women for whose sake Israel was redeemed from slavery in Egypt, mirroring the sotah ritual through a tale of female rebellion against Pharaoh. I argue that as women thread their way throughout this tractate, they act as countertraditions to the sotah ritual, voicing the ritual's brutality as they subvert its power.

ONCE AGAIN, A TALE OF TWO WOMEN

I have translated the tale of two women that opens this introduction from the Vilna Talmud, the edition of the Bavli printed between 1880 and 1886 by the Widow and Brothers Romm.[58] As I remarked earlier, this version depicts two women talking with one another about their husbands' roles in a public lecture. The speaker's wife claims that her husband altered the reasoning of R. Abbahu when transmitting his lecture to the wider audience. In turn, R. Abbahu's wife goes and informs her husband about the other woman's claim. The story concludes with R. Abbahu's rejection of his wife's complaint; both his words and those of the speaker praise God. As the Vilna edition tells the tale, a conversation between two women quickly becomes a conversation between wife and husband. Yet two extant medieval manuscripts of B. Sotah (MS Munich 95 and MS Vatican 110) intimate a different possibility. I translate the end of the story as presented in MS Munich 95:

> That the wife of R. [Abbahu's speaker] said to the wife of R. Abbahu:
>
> "This one of ours does not need this of yours. And that he bends down and stands up before him is merely to do him honor."

> She [the wife of R. Abbahu] said to her [א״ל]: "What do you derive? Through me, through you the Most High will be praised."

Like the Vilna edition, MS Munich 95's version of the story presents a conversation between two women. However, while the Vilna edition shifts the scene to husband and wife, this medieval manuscript suggests that the two women continue talking with one another. Instead of R. Abbahu telling his wife that it makes no difference whether the audience hears speaker or sage, now R. Abbahu's wife makes that claim. Even more, she tells the speaker's wife that they—the two women—praise God.

I base my reading conjecture on two details: the missing sentence "his wife went and told R. Abbahu," and the ambiguous scribal abbreviation for direct speech in the story's final line (א״ל). While I might focus on adjudicating between these two versions, once again I want to shift our attention elsewhere, to these two women.[59] We may consider MS Munich to make visible women talking with one another and, through this conversation, claiming their place within B. Sotah. These two women—who do not talk about the sotah ritual but *do* discuss authority, Torah's transmission, and their place within rabbinic society—serve as a fitting introduction to tractate Sotah of the Babylonian Talmud.

CHAPTER ONE

THE DISAPPEARING SOTAH AND THE MORAL MAN

The opening sugya of Bavli Sotah declares that temptation to sexual sin belongs as much in the realm of men as it does in that of women. In reply to a seemingly technical question about why tractate Sotah follows tractate Nazir, B. Sotah provides counsel to men: any male who sees the sotah "in her disgrace" should distance himself from wine. Drinking wine, the sugya implies, leads men to sin much as the sotah did. Although Mishnah Sotah 1:1 presents the suspicious husband as the grammatical subject of the pericope ("a man who warns his wife") and describes how *he* should proceed with sotah litigation, the topic of the opening mishnah and, indeed the mishnah's discussion of the sotah ritual, is *female* sexual transgression. B. Sotah's switch to the potential for male sin in its opening sugya is thus striking.

Many of these opening sugyot—and B. Sotah 2a among them—have long been classified as late additions to the Bavli. This project of classification began in the eleventh century with Sherira Gaon's declaration that the beginning of B. Kiddushin (2a–3b) was the provenance of a group of post-amoraic scholars called saboraim.[1] While Wissenchaft scholars of the nineteenth and twentieth centuries largely focused on establishing formal criteria for identifying these late sugyot, and thus their chronological relationship to the Bavli as a whole, more recent scholarship has turned away from chronological questions and toward literary and conceptual questions. It assumes the late date of these sugyot.[2] Charlotte Fonrobert has proposed that instead of using the term "opening" for these late sugyot, we should rather think of them as introductory forewords, framing devices that introduce a tractate's conceptual, intellectual, and theoretical concerns. In other words, they provide a framework for study of that tractate.[3]

Although the Wissenchaft scholar Avraham Weiss categorized the opening of B. Sotah as among those late passages that act as formalistic notes to their respective mishnah,[4] following in Fonrobert's footsteps I contend that we should understand the introductory sugya of B. Sotah to have a larger pedagogical function. Through asking a question about the order of mishnaic tractates, the introductory sugya of B. Sotah teaches us how the final editors of B. Sotah want us to read or respond to the Mishnah's version of the sotah ritual. This process extends from the introductory sugya through the next two sugyot.[5] As we will see, M. Sotah rewrites the biblical sotah ritual in a way that amplifies the ritual's humiliation of the accused woman. In contrast, B. Sotah, in beginning the tractate with a shift of emphasis to male sexual sin, signals that it will not further amplify the woman's humiliation. Instead, B. Sotah will shift its attention away from the sin of the sotah to both a wider view of who sins and its own vision of ideal rabbinic masculinity. In so doing, B. Sotah implicitly reveals its recognition of the problematics of the sotah ritual. What was once women's proclivity to sin becomes men's as well. As Rosen-Zvi has observed in regard to the opening four pages of B. Sotah, whereas earlier rabbinic literature places men in supervisory and punitive roles over women, now men also become the subject of warning against sexual sin, a widening of the discursive framework in which material once specific to the sotah is now used to discuss sexual sin in general.[6] As we will see, the themes found in the first three sugyot thread their way through the entire tractate.[7]

In noting the Bavli's refocusing of M. Sotah, I do not aim to chart a vision of either progress ("better than") or regression ("worse than")[8] but rather to examine two thematic trends—changing conceptions of who sins and constructions of rabbinic masculinity—in B. Sotah and to read them, in concert with the introductory sugya, as the Bavli's reframing of the mishnaic sotah ritual.[9] This argument about pedagogical purpose and B. Sotah 2a intersects with the larger feminist question of what it might mean to cope with the sotah ritual. In the opening sugya, B. Sotah de-emphasizes women's sin and refocuses its rhetorical energy on constructing rabbinic masculinity. In other words, the Bavli ameliorates the sotah ritual while displacing women themselves. Whether this response is conscious or unconscious is immaterial; what is important is that B. Sotah departs from M. Sotah's interpretive path and takes another route.[10]

To make this case, this chapter begins with a description of the biblical and mishnaic sotah rituals. In each instance, I summarize and highlight the elements of the ritual that are crucial for understanding B. Sotah's project. While M. Sotah is not the sole tannaitic text that explicates the sotah ritual, it is the only extant tannaitic text that renders a narrative of the ritual similar in scope to the biblical depiction.[11] It is also the base text upon which the Bavli comments. After presenting the biblical and mishnaic rituals, I turn to the first three sugyot of B. Sotah, integrating these sugyot with a wider lens on the tractate. This wider lens illustrates the ways in which these opening passages are intertwined with and draw their interlocutors toward other passages within B. Sotah. In declaring that the Mishnah chooses to order tractate Sotah after tractate Nazir, B. Sotah shifts our attention away from female sexual sin to male sin, then to sin in general, and finally to the construction of rabbinic masculinity.

THE BIBLICAL SOTAH RITUAL (NUMBERS 5:11–31)

Tractate Sotah is named for what has come to be known as the sotah ritual. The ritual takes its name from the verb *s.t.y.* that appears in Numbers 5:12: "Any man whose wife has turned aside [*ki tisteh ʾishto*] and acted treacherously against him" (Numbers 5:12).[12] It is an unusual and detailed ritual carried out in response to a crisis of uncertainty in the judicial system: a lack of knowledge about whether a crime has been committed, although at least one of the potential "criminals" is known.[13] A husband may impose this ritual on his wife if he suspects her of engaging in sexual relations with another man but has no definitive proof that she has done so.[14] Assuming that either guilt or innocence is a possible verdict for the accused woman (Numbers 5:12–14), the biblical verses stage a private ritual between priest and accused woman through which God judges the woman's guilt or innocence. Thus, while the ritual's rabbinic name centers the accused woman, the biblical ritual centers two men: the husband and the priest. It is the husband who instigates the ritual after being overcome by jealousy (*kinʾah*),[15] and it is the priest who carries out the ritual. Indeed, the biblical ritual may be conceptualized as an instruction manual for the priest, teaching him what to do with and to this woman whose husband has accused her of sexual intercourse with another man.[16] Since this crime cannot be "solved" by the regular legal procedures, the Bible mandates this unusual ritual procedure to resolve the crisis of knowledge and the perceived threat to the moral fabric and purity not only of the patriarchal family but also of Israelite society.[17] As Bonna Haberman observes, the larger literary context of the sotah ritual—descriptions of the choreography for the transportation of the Israelite camp in the wilderness—emphasizes the theme of holiness and the need to keep impurity outside of the Israelite camp.[18]

The biblical description of the sotah ritual is confusing, containing repetitions, inconsistencies, and unique vocabulary. While the authors of the Mishnah and the Bavli likely would have noticed many of these ambiguities, they also would have considered this passage to be a single literary unit, whatever its textual prehistory.[19] The summary description of the ritual that I give here is not meant to erase these ambiguities but rather to set the stage for understanding the interpretive projects of M. Sotah and B. Sotah.[20]

The manual opens with the circumstances of the ritual: an allegation by a jealous husband of his wife's infidelity. His allegation may be based either on probable cause (vv. 12–14a) or jealousy alone (v. 14b), but in either case there are no witnesses to the alleged offense.[21] The husband must initiate the ritual, bringing his wife to the priest at the tabernacle along with an unusual barley offering (v. 15). The priest prepares the woman by bringing her to the altar, baring her head, and making a special potion from sacred water and earth taken from the floor of the tabernacle (vv. 16–18).[22] The priest adjures the woman orally, declaring that if she is innocent, the bitter waters will not harm her. If, on the other hand, she is guilty, God will make her a curse among her people and cause her belly to distend and her thigh to sag (vv. 19–22a).[23] After the woman answers "amen," the priest writes the adjuration/curse and then rubs it off into the bitter waters (vv. 22b–23). Finally, the priest presents the meal offering on the altar and makes the woman drink the bitter waters. If she is guilty, her belly will distend and her thigh fall. If innocent, she will conceive a child (vv. 24–28). The final verses circle back to the beginning of the passage, recapitulating the circumstances under which the ritual is to be performed and providing a post-ritual resolution (vv. 29–31).[24] The biblical ritual makes clear that verdict and punishment lie with God who, through the potion, will either cause the woman's reproductive organs to fail (if guilty) or cause her to become pregnant (if innocent).[25]

The biblical ritual is surely an instance of patriarchal control: a husband—without fear of punishment—may accuse his wife of sexual intercourse with another man based solely on his jealousy and then subject her to a ritual that can result in her bodily injury. Indeed, the very performance of the ritual, regardless of verdict, validates the man's expression of jealousy.[26] However, much as the biblical sotah ritual inscribes male control, that control is not absolute. The biblical ritual remains a private performance between priest and woman; it holds out the possibility of the woman's innocence. When combined with the passage's sevenfold repetition of the root *k.n.*ʾ. (jealousy) in reference to the husband, this possibility of female innocence fractures the husband's control. The husband's accusation may be viewed as transgressive and thus the husband himself as transgressing.[27] As we will see, the Bavli will pick up this thread of male transgression.

THE MISHNAIC SOTAH RITUAL

As I remarked earlier, the biblical ritual is simultaneously private and inquisitive: it takes place primarily at the tabernacle altar between priest and accused woman and presents an equivalent possibility for the woman's innocence or guilt. The ritual procedure centers on the bitter waters, the minhah offering, and the process of the oath. In contrast, the mishnaic sotah ritual is simultaneously public and punitive. That is, M. Sotah expands the sotah ritual beyond the confines of the altar, transforming it both into a rabbinic judiciary procedure[28] and also, as Sarra Lev argues, into a voyeuristic, pornographic, and punitive ritual.[29]

In the biblical version of the ritual, the husband's jealousy alone is sufficient for him to activate the ritual, and he alone brings his wife directly to the priest (Numbers 5:14–15). In contrast, M. Sotah imagines an extended journey in which the number of people involved gradually multiply from husband, wife, and witnesses, to the local court, to two sages who accompany husband and wife to Jerusalem, to the great court of seventy-one, and finally to the entire rabbinic community. Now, even to initiate the sotah procedure, a husband must warn his wife against being alone with a particular man in the presence of two witnesses (M. Sotah 1:1). If she violates his warning and then again is witnessed going into a secret place with the warned-against man,[30] remaining there for sufficient time to have sexual intercourse (M. Sotah

1:1–2), the husband brings her to the local court. The local court adds two more people to the mix: two sages who accompany the husband and wife on their journey to Jerusalem (M. Sotah 1:3).[31] Once in Jerusalem, these three men bring the woman to the great court, the Sanhedrin composed of seventy-one,[32] whose members try to cajole and threaten the woman into a confession of guilt (M. Sotah 1:5). If she refuses to confess, they then bring the woman to the Temple courtyard's Nicanor gate.[33] There a priest rips her clothes, revealing her breasts, and then undoes her hair (M. Sotah 1:5).[34] If the woman is wearing white clothes, she is dressed in black ones; jewelry is removed from her—all of this, in M. Sotah's words, "to degrade her" (*kedei le-navelah*).[35] The priest then ties a rope made of palm-twigs above her breasts (M. Sotah 1:6).[36] M. Sotah 1:6 concludes with a declaration of the entire community's voyeurism: "And all who want to see come to see, except for her male and female slaves since with them she feels no shame. And all the women are permitted to see her, as it says, 'All the women shall take warning not to imitate your wantonness' [Ezekiel 23:48]." While the audience for the biblical ritual consisted of priest and possibly husband, M. Sotah invites the community to witness the accused woman's degradation. Yet, besides the need for the husband to initiate the procedure, the sotah ritual described in Numbers 5 has yet to begin![37]

M. Sotah 1:6's demand for the woman's humiliation and degradation occurs in response to her declaration of innocence; it is the *prelude* to the barley offering, oath, and drinking of bitter waters detailed in the biblical ritual. Indeed, as I remarked in the introduction, Rosen-Zvi has convincingly argued that the mishnaic sotah ritual is best viewed as a punitive ritual that follows after prophetic descriptions of punishment against adulterous women, with the details of the sotah ritual echoing those of Ezekiel's punishment for adulteresses.[38] While the biblical ritual assumes that the woman could be innocent, M. Sotah excludes that possibility and presumes the woman's guilt.[39] One way in which M. Sotah does this is by positing a binary of either immediate death or suspended punishment for the accused woman rather than a binary of guilt or innocence (M. Sotah 3:4–5).[40] The Mishnah's exclusion of the possibility of a woman's innocence is highlighted by the fact that other works, such as the tannaitic Sifrei Bemidbar and the later Bavli, *do* record tannaitic opinions that consider the woman's innocence an option.[41]

Although the rest of M. Sotah's description of the ritual is not identical to that in Numbers, the most striking differences are those that I described previously.[42] For the most part, M. Sotah turns to the types of questions and explications that we might expect from the Mishnah about any biblical ritual that it seeks to make rabbinic. For example, M. Sotah delineates which accused women lose their *ketubah* (marriage contract) payment and which do not (1:5; 4:1–4; 6:2), on what type of material the priest may write the oath and with what type of ink (2:4), the details of the barley sacrifice (3:1–2, 6–7), and the legal consequences of contradictory witnesses (6:4). M. Sotah's most significant innovation lies in the ritual it creates as a prelude to the altar ritual described in Numbers 5; it is here that the sotah ritual becomes not only an act of androcentric and patriarchal control (as is the case in the biblical ritual) but also a visual spectacle of brutal degradation.[43] With this background in mind, I turn now to the passage that opens B. Sotah.

REFRAMING SIN: BAVLI SOTAH 2A, PART 1

B. Sotah opens with a question about the order of tractates: Why does tractate Sotah follow tractate Nazir (A)?[44] B. Sotah's answer will, eventually, displace the sotah and replace her with a conception of the moral man.

A. Since the tanna finished [tractate] Nazir what is he teaching such[45] that he teaches [tractate] Sotah?
B. According to Rabbi, as it is taught [in a baraita]:
C. Rabbi says: Why is the portion of nazir adjacent to the portion of sotah? To say to you that any man[46] who sees the sotah in her disgrace should separate himself from wine.
D. Let him [the tanna] teach [tractate] Sotah and return and let him teach [tractate] Nazir![47]
E. Because he taught [tractate] Ketubot and he taught "a man who vows that his wife [shall derive no benefit from him],"[48] he taught [tractate] Nedarim. And because he taught [tractate] Nedarim he taught [tractate] Nazir which is similar to Nedarim. And he [then] taught [tractate] Sotah according to [the statement] of Rabbi.

This opening question presumes that a pedagogical choice lies behind the mishnaic recomposition of Scripture.[49] That is, whereas in its biblical home, the sotah passage (Numbers 5:11–31) precedes that of the nazir (Numbers 6:1–21), in the Mishnah, and the Bavli following it, the order of topics is reversed.[50] In this opening passage, B. Sotah answers its own question about why tractate Sotah follows tractate Nazir by citing a baraita in the name of Rabbi Yehudah ha-Nasi: "Rabbi says: Why is the portion of nazir located adjacent to the portion of sotah? To say to you that any man who sees [*kol ha-roʾeh*][51] the sotah in her disgrace should separate [*yazir*] himself from wine" (B–C). In using the verbal root *n.z.r.*, B. Sotah alludes to the nazirite vow, a pledge through which a male or a female restricts his or her behavior in three areas —abstaining from any grape product, avoiding contact with the dead, and letting one's hair grow—in order to attain greater holiness.[52] A question about the redaction of the Mishnah becomes an opening for a pedagogical statement: the mishnaic sotah ritual grants men supervisory and coercive power over female behavior;[53] in contrast, in B. Sotah's opening sugya the sotah ritual functions as a caution to men to control their own behavior. If men refrain from drinking wine as does the nazir, the sugya teaches, they will not go astray with sexually immoral behavior. For B. Sotah, the order of the mishnaic tractates points toward how men could be led to sin; its explanation of that order leads men away from sin.

As Rosen-Zvi points out, in light of the way in which M. Sotah portrays the judges describing wine's behavioral effects to coerce the accused woman to confess ("And they say to her: 'My daughter, wine causes much . . .'"; M. Sotah 1:4) and directs the pedagogical power of the disgraced sotah toward other women (see below in M. Sotah 1:6), B. Sotah's shift from a female to a male pedagogic target is particularly significant.[54] In contrast to the mishnah, the opening sugya cautions men against wine rather than women.

B. Sotah's explication of the conclusion of M. Sotah 1:6—found further on in the tractate—highlights the way in which the opening sugya moves from female sin to male sin. The Bavli's version of M. Sotah 1:6 reads as follows: "And anyone [*ve-khol*] who wants to see comes to see except for her male and female slaves, since with them she feels no shame [*libah gas bahen*].[55] And[56] all the women [*ve-khol ha-nashim*] are permitted to see her, as it is said, 'And all the women [*kol ha-nashim*] shall take warning not to imitate your wantonness' [Ezekiel 23:48]."[57] B. Sotah (8b) notices a contradiction between the mishnah's first and second sentences: the former implies that with the exception of the sotah's male and female slaves, all men and women may come to see her on display; the latter specifies that *only* women are permitted to see her. Rava resolves this contradiction by reading the mishnah to teach that while both free men and women *may* come and see the sotah, women are *obligated* to do so (B. Sotah 8b).[58] That B. Sotah records Rava as understanding this mishnah to require women to see the sotah emphasizes the dramatic way in which this introductory sugya has shifted its emphasis away from women's sin to men's. The potential to emphasize women's sin and the need for all women to learn from the sotah—as Rava does later in the tractate—is open to the redactors of B. Sotah's first sugya. Yet the tractate turns away from the possibility of emphasizing female sin at its very beginning. According to the introductory sugya, if *men* see the sotah, they should refrain from wine. B. Sotah appears to have picked up the biblical fracture that holds out the possibility of male transgression.

To be sure, B. Sotah does not erase the brutal aspects of the mishnaic ritual. However, it does attempt to shift our attention elsewhere. Note, however, that while the sotah ritual enlists men as supervisors over women, when B. Sotah turns to men's sin, they remain their own guardians. The target, but not the fact of patriarchy, is different.[59]

However, while Rabbi's answer shifts the rhetorical emphasis from female to male, it does not really answer the question of why tractate Sotah follows tractate Nazir. As the anonymous voice objects, "Let him teach [tractate] Sotah and return and let him teach [tractate] Nazir" (D). In other words, even if tractate Sotah were to precede tractate Nazir, the lesson that men ought to guard against intoxication would remain the same. Hidden in the Bavli's answer that the order is driven by tractate Ketubot's placement in the chain of tractates (E) is yet another inversion of Scripture: biblical laws about vows occur even later in the book of Numbers (30:2–17) than do the laws of sotah and nazir. If the order of biblical passages is the driving factor behind B. Sotah's question, then the Bavli could have also asked a question about the placement of tractate Ketubot—with its section about vows—before tractates Nazir and Sotah. It could have questioned why B. Ketubot does not follow the biblical order and appears after tractates Sotah and Nazir. The fact that B. Sotah does not ask this question points to another pedagogical purpose of this opening sugya beyond formulaic matters of order.

Indeed, B. Sotah's use of the seventh chapter of M. Ketubot as a proof text for the mishnaic and talmudic order of, respectively, Ketubot, Nedarim, Nazir, and Sotah again displaces women and hints at the consequences of unreasonable male action. Although eight of the thirteen chapters of M. Ketubot have women as the opening subject of the chapter, B. Sotah focuses on a chapter with a male subject.[60] Through its use of the seventh chapter of M. Ketubot, the opening sugya of B. Sotah also alludes to a list of unreasonable vows that a husband might make concerning his wife and the penalty for doing so—he must divorce her and pay her *ketubah*.[61] Similar to the way in which Rabbi's explanation displaced women through an emphasis on male sin and hinted at the consequences of unrestrained masculine drinking (B–C), B. Sotah's final answer both displaces women by choosing a chapter with a male subject ("a man who vows that his wife") and hints at the consequences of unreasonable male action ("he must divorce her and give her her *ketubah*") (E).[62] In framing this shift from female to male as a question about tractate order, B. Sotah both hides the change and normalizes it. The possibility of male sin and the need for men to prevent it is, as it were, bound to the normative or right order of the Bavli.

SAMSON AND THE SOTAH

In connecting the tractates Ketubot, Nedarim, Nazir, and Sotah, the editors of this introductory sugya also remind us to take note of the ways in which gender, family, power, voice, and piety are interconnected. They point us forward to, and draw on, the aggadic traditions about the biblical character Samson, also found in the first chapter of B. Sotah (9b–10a). The Samson traditions connect the themes of marriage, parental relations, nazirite vows, and sexual transgression embedded in tractates Ketubot, Nedarim, Nazir, and—in particular—Sotah.

As I have mentioned, the introductory sugya recommends that men behave as if they were nazirites—refraining from drinking wine—in order to counteract the ways in which their eyes might lead them sexually astray. Rava expresses this point later on in the same chapter of the tractate: "The evil inclination [*yetzer ha-ra*] only rules over that which his eyes see" (B. Sotah 8a).[63] B. Sotah reimagines Samson—a nazirite from the time of his conception (Judges 14:3–5)—as the paradigmatic example of the male nazirite gone sexually astray through the gaze.[64] It hypersexualizes the character of Samson while portraying his mother as following the tenets of Jewish law.[65] Samson willfully follows his eyes to sexually transgressive behavior, is blessed as a child by having sperm comparable to a flooding river, and has the ability to impregnate multiple women.[66] In contrast, Samson's mother eats only foods permitted by rabbinic law and refrains from those forbidden to a nazirite.

B. Sotah even makes explicit the connection between Samson and the sotah ritual. The section on Samson in B. Sotah 10a includes a statement in the name of R. Yohanan that proclaims husbands as bearing responsibility for their wives' adultery:

A. And said R. Yohanan: Any man who whores, his wife will whore against him. As it is said, "If my heart has been seduced by a woman, and I have lain in wait at my neighbor's door" [Job 31:9], and it is written, "May my wife grind for another, may others kneel over her" [Job 31:10].
B. This corresponds to what men say:[67] He is among the gourds and his wife is among the plants [indicating that a husband who transgresses will have a wife who similarly transgresses].

R. Yohanan's statement is part of a longer chain of five dicta recorded in his name. It is the only one of these five that does not mention Samson, an omission that suggests that this statement's inclusion in the chain results from its claim of male responsibility for female sexual transgression.[68]

The parallel section in Y. Sotah (1:8, 17a–b) highlights the ways in which the Samson traditions found in B. Sotah are shaped by and are appropriate to their location in this Bavli tractate. Y. Sotah does not mention Samson's status as a nazirite or hypersexualize him to the same extent as does B. Sotah.[69] Rather, the Yerushalmi is more interested in contextualizing Samson's behavior within rabbinic prohibitions of exogamy. For example, Samson's mother and father try to convince him not to marry a Philistine woman by comparing Philistine sexual practices to rabbinic laws concerning *kil'ayim*, in this case likely extending laws prohibiting the mixing of plants in a vineyard to boundary-crossing sexual behavior.[70] Since Y. Sotah in general is more concerned with sexual behavior and marital transgression than is B. Sotah, the unusual hypersexualization of Samson and the law-abiding portrait of his mother in B. Sotah should be understood within the context of its particular ideology of expanding male potential for sin.

LESS-THAN-IDEAL RITUAL: BAVLI SOTAH 2A, PART 2

A. A man who warns [his wife not to seclude herself with a particular man]:
B. Ex post facto—yes [he may warn her]; ab initio—no [he should not warn her].
C. Our tanna [the sage who teaches M. Sotah 1:1] thinks: it is forbidden [for a man] to warn [his wife].

Through a remark on the opening word (*ha-mekanei*, "a man who warns") of M. Sotah 1:1, this second anonymous—and late—sugya recasts the Mishnah's sotah ritual as a less-than-ideal judicial procedure. Focusing on the descriptive formulation of the word *ha-mekanei*, B. Sotah posits that the mishnah describes an after-the-fact scenario: if a man has already entered the judicial process of the sotah ritual through warning his wife not to secret herself with a particular man, his action is permitted ex post facto. However, ab initio, he is forbidden to begin the process (A–C).

While the first sugya discussed the sotah within a moralistic context, the rabbinic judiciary is the context of this second sugya. The turn from ethics to law parallels two main themes of the post-tannaitic sotah: a moralistic approach that uses the sotah to condemn all adulterous behavior—not just that of women—and a legalistic one that moves the sotah ritual out of the realm of priestly procedure and into that of the rabbinic judiciary.[71] The opening sugya exemplifies the former theme; this sugya exemplifies the latter. B. Sotah's utilization of the rabbinic judiciary is not an innovation: the tannaitic version of the sotah has already recomposed the ritual within a rabbinic judicial framework. B. Sotah's innovation lies in locating its declaration of the ritual as less than ideal at the very beginning, thus setting the stage for how we read the sotah ritual whose description follows.

The Bavli's emphasis on the ritual as less than ideal at the outset of the tractate is particularly striking in light of its later citation on B. Sotah 3a of a debate between the tannaitic sages Rabbi Ishmael and Rabbi Akiva. These sages debate whether a husband's warning to his wife is a permissible or an obligatory action, that is something he may choose to do ab initio or something he must do ab initio.[72] In contrast to B. Sotah's reading of the anonymous voice of the mishnah, neither R. Ishmael nor R. Akiva imply that the sotah ritual is a less-than-ideal option by permitting its performance only ex post facto. Both condone the husband's initiation of the ritual, and R. Akiva even requires the husband to initiate the ritual. Y. Sotah, however, does not mention an ab initio prohibition on the ritual. Rather, it only records a similar debate about whether the husband's warning is permissible or obligatory (Y. Sotah 1:1, 16b).[73] The absence of an ab initio prohibition in the Yerushalmi passage and the presence of R. Ishmael and R. Akiva's debate later in B. Sotah combine to highlight the multiple options available to begin the tractate. B. Sotah chooses to use one which, at the very outset of the tractate, stages the sotah ritual as unfavorable.

YOU GET WHAT YOU DESERVE: BAVLI SOTAH 2A, PART 3

A. Said R. Shmuel bar Rav Yitzhak: When Reish Lakish[74] would interpret [the Torah portion of] sotah, he would say this: One only matches a man with a woman according to his actions, as it says, "The scepter of the wicked shall never rest upon the land allotted to the righteous, [that the righteous not set their hand to wrongdoing]" [Psalms 125:3].

B. Said Rabbah bar bar Hannah in the name of R. Yohanan: And it is as difficult to match them as was the splitting of the Sea of Reeds, as it says, "God restores the lonely to their homes, sets free the imprisoned, safe and sound, [while the rebellious must live in parched land]" [Psalms 68:7].

C. Is that so?

D. But did not Rav Yehudah say in the name of Rav:[75] Forty days before the creation of the fetus, a heavenly voice [*bat kol*][76] goes out and says: "The daughter of *ploni* to *ploni*, the house of *ploni* to *ploni*, the field of *ploni* to *ploni*."[77]

E. This is not difficult. This [second statement by Rav] refers to the first marriage; this [first statement by R. Yohanan] refers to the second marriage.

This third opening passage of the tractate, amoraic in provenance, returns to the moralizing tone of the first introductory passage and once again lays blame for marital misconduct on men as much as women.[78] The sage Reish Lakish would, when interpreting the biblical sotah passage, proclaim that marriage operates under the principle of measure-for-measure:[79] men are paired with women whose actions match their own. Psalms 125:3 provides the reason that the wicked marry the wicked and the righteous marry the righteous: if a wicked man were to marry a righteous woman, *he* would lead *her* astray (A). Rather than interrogating whether the husband may initiate the sotah ritual and so punish his wife for her alleged misbehavior, the sugya recasts the man's role as one of responsibility for his wife's actions.[80] Although the sugya continues with a homily attributed to R. Yohanan that shifts the emphasis of Reish Lakish's statement from criticism of males to a statement about the difficulty of finding the correct marital match (B–E),[81] Reish Lakish's statement of male responsibility nevertheless retains its continuity with the first two passages as implicit criticism of the mishnaic sotah ritual. It also overlaps with R. Yohanan's statement, redacted in the midst of the Samson traditions, of male sexual sin causing female sexual sin.

These different statements by R. Yohanan may also be part of a larger chain of marriage traditions—in the name of R. Yohanan—preserved and recontextualized in B. Sotah. An aggadic tradition redacted later in the first chapter about the marriage of the biblical characters Caleb and Miriam (B. Sotah 11b–12a) inverts the Samson traditions of male sexual sin causing female sin and instead emblematizes the idea of righteous marrying righteous and the difficulty of making these matches. Part of an extended aggadic sugya on the Exodus narrative, this passage portrays Caleb as a man who rules over and controls his *yetzer*, fasts until his face becomes blackened, and has the ability to turn away from the evil counsel of the spies reporting on the land of Israel.[82] He marries Miriam despite the fact that all other men turn away from her. Fittingly for such a man, Miriam is an ancestor of the Davidic line. After she marries Caleb, she becomes so beautiful that her face is comparable to noontime; any man who sees her brings a gift of a prostitute's wage (*ʾetnan*) to his wife. Rather than leading men to sexual sin, Miriam causes men to desire their wives, in the process transforming illicit desire for a prostitute into licit sex. In the midst of this explication of Miriam and Caleb, B. Sotah redacts yet another statement of R. Yohanan: "Said R. Yohanan: Any man who marries a woman for the sake of heaven, Scripture accounts it to him as if he had given birth to her." Similar to the R. Yohanan tradition redacted in the context of Samson, this dictum does not mention Caleb or Miriam, again reinforcing the idea that this is an independent tradition intentionally redacted into the longer exegetical passage. And again like the Samson traditions, these traditions about Miriam and Caleb testify to the ways in which the opening sugyot reflect and are interwoven with later sugyot in the tractate.

THE DISAPPEARING SOTAH AND THE MORAL MAN

As B. Sotah turns away from the alleged crime of the accused sotah to condemn male sexual sin and sin in general, the tractate also becomes a locus for the presentation of a picture of the idealized moral rabbinic male. Intertwining condemnations of male sexual sin with a wider ethical message, B. Sotah instructs men in proper conduct that extends beyond sex and sexuality. In shifting its lens from the sotah to the sinning and to the moral man, B. Sotah signals its implicit criticism of the mishnaic sotah ritual. However, this focus on male behavior simultaneously disappears the sotah herself. Turning to sugyot from the first (B. Sotah 4b–5b), third (B. Sotah 21–22a), and eighth chapters (B. Sotah 44a), we witness this process of amelioration and disappearance threading its way throughout the tractate.

B. Sotah 4b–5b opens with a homiletical explication of Proverbs 6:26 ("The last loaf of bread will go for a harlot; a married woman will snare a man of honor") that likens a man who eats bread without first ritually washing his hands to a man who has sexual intercourse with a prostitute. While the three homiletical explications of Proverbs 6:26 turn to male sexual sin with either prostitutes or married women,[83] the larger portion of the sugya conveys a broader ethical message: the sugya condemns the characteristic of arrogance (*gasut ruah*) and praises that of humility (B. Sotah 4b–5b).[84] B. Sotah declares that a man who acts haughtily is considered as if he had committed idolatry and built an unauthorized sacrificial altar (*bamah*); even if this man were to give charity secretly,[85] he would still receive the judgment of *gehinnom*.[86] An arrogant man will not be resurrected at the time of the resurrection of the dead; conversely, a man who repents from his arrogance will, at the time of his death, be gathered in with the patriarchs Abraham, Isaac, and Jacob. A humble man imitates the way God revealed himself on the lowly Mount Sinai and in the modest burning bush; a humble man's prayers are heard and he is accounted as one who offered all the sacrifices in the Temple.[87] As Richard Lewis observes, in contrast to biblical literature where arrogance stems from a man's high societal status and results in behavior that oppresses those of lower status, in rabbinic literature any man may be guilty of the sin of arrogance and should be cautioned against the resultant behavior.[88] While declaring the value of humility for men in general, the sugya even raises the possibility that sages may differ from other men and that a bit of arrogance may protect them.

Just as the first sugya of the tractate inverts the "everyone" (*ha-kol*) in M. Sotah 1:6 from women to men, this sugya on 4b–5b performs a similar inversion with the word *gas*. In the mishnah, the phrase *gas libah bahen* (with them she feels no shame) refers to the accused sotah; here B. Sotah uses the concept of *gas ruah* to condemn men. The secrecy mentioned in each sugya supplies an additional inversion: The sotah commits her crime in secret; the arrogant man's giving charity in secret does not mitigate his punishment, and he is punished by *gehinnom*. This extended sugya on B. Sotah 4b–5b becomes a meditation on masculinity and the correct behavior for any man aspiring to the rabbinic community: humility and modeling oneself after God. This counsel is reinforced at the end of the tractate's first chapter, where B. Sotah advises people to become like God by following in God's ways: clothing the naked, visiting the sick, comforting mourners, and burying the dead (B. Sotah 14a).[89]

Torah study, of course, lies at the heart of the rabbinic enterprise. In its discussion of the mishnaic premise that merit (*zekhut*) will protect or defer punishment of the accused sotah (M. Sotah 3:4), B. Sotah's search for the precise type of merit to which the mishnah refers centers on this cultural value of Torah study (B. Sotah 21a). Rather than an extended analysis of the sotah, the sugya presents us with an extensive analysis of the protective powers of Torah study and of the performance of commandments.[90] In consonance with this shift, when B. Sotah explicates R. Eliezer's statement in the same mishnah that "any man who teaches his daughter Torah teaches her lasciviousness [*tiflut*],"[91] it turns not only to a statement about how wisdom (*hokhmah*) can mislead any person (*ʾadam*) to sin but also to a more general statement about how Torah endures only through a sage who practices self-abnegation (B. Sotah 21b).[92] The sotah's sin becomes secondary to rabbinic counsel of how a man may become a sage.

When B. Sotah turns to R. Yehoshua's list of people that destroy the world, another quote from M. Sotah 3:4, that sugya again identifies behaviors that run counter to rabbinic ideals of Torah study (B. Sotah 21b–22a). For example, a pious fool (*hasid shoteh*) does not apply common sense to his practice of Jewish law: he sees a woman drowning in a river and does not save her because it is not proper to look at her. As Moulie Vidas argues about the evil and cunning person (*rasha ʿarum*), the list of seven behaviors that the Bavli condemns have a pedagogical purpose that is not limited to the particulars of the laws mentioned but extends to a more general interpretation of the mishnah:[93] "The 'cunning and evil' person is someone who has mastered significant amounts of Torah knowledge (therefore he is 'cunning' or 'wise'), but abuses this knowledge or otherwise conducts himself badly (therefore, he is evil)."[94] That the last behavior in this list names discipleship as central to becoming a sage ("Ulla said: [An evil and cunning person] is one who reads [Scripture] and recites [Mishnah] but does not serve the sages") reinforces the pedagogical nature of this list and the way in which a conversation about the proper way a man becomes a sage has become a main topic of the tractate.[95] B. Sotah even goes on to bring a statement in the name of R. Elazar[96] that identifies a man who reads Scripture and recites Mishnah but does not serve the sages as an *ʿam ha-ʾaretz*, an outsider to the rabbinic community.[97] In this context of the shift to male sages and the disappearing female sotah, it is also worthwhile to point out that the term *ʿam ha-ʾaretz* does not refer to females.[98] In this instance of delineating who is inside and who is outside the community of sages, women do not factor.[99]

Even when B. Sotah discusses exemptions from war, it turns to the ethical life and the rabbinic curriculum. B. Sotah 44a cites a toseftan baraita that utilizes the biblical prescription that a man who has "built a house," "planted a vineyard," or "betrothed a woman" returns from the battlefield (Deuteronomy 20:5–7) as a model for both the proper way in which a man should conduct his life (*derekh ʾeretz*) as well as the rabbinic curriculum.[100] The baraita opens by reading this verse about leaving battle as a prescriptive verse about the stages in which a man should create a household: first build a house, next plant a vineyard, and only afterward marry a woman.[101] The baraita continues to map Proverbs 24:27 onto the rabbinic curriculum, presenting three different possible programmatic orders:

A. Another interpretation: "Prepare your labor outside"—this refers to Scripture. "Get ready what you have in your field"—this refers to mishnah. "And afterwards build yourself a home"—this refers to gemara.[102]
B. Another interpretation: "Prepare your labor outside"—this refers to Scripture and mishnah. "Get ready what you have in your field"—this refers to gemara.[103] "And afterwards build yourself a home"—these are good deeds [*ma'asim tovim*].
C. R. Eliezer the son of R. Yosi ha-Galili said: "Prepare your labor outside"—this refers to Scripture, mishnah, and gemara.[104] "Get ready what you have in your field"—these are good deeds [*ma'asim tovim*]. "And afterwards build yourself a home"—interpret and receive a reward [*derosh ve-kabeil sakhar*].

The first proposal (A) refers to knowledge of rabbinic learning, whether that be content (Scripture and mishnah) or methodology (gemara). The second and third proposals (B–C) refer both to content and methodology but also add a behavioral category (performance of good deeds). The third proposal adds yet another element: interpretation for its own sake.[105] Moving from the battlefield to marriage to a rabbinic curriculum of learning and ethics, B. Sotah's inclusion of this toseftan baraita (something that Y. Sotah does not do) illustrates, yet again, the ways in which this tractate has become a location through which the rabbis consider what it means to be a male rabbinic Jew. In this case, it means marriage to a woman, rabbinic knowledge, and ethical behavior.

While it may sound trite to state that B. Sotah teaches about the proper way for a man to become a sage—this, after all, could be seen as the larger project of the entire Bavli—it is crucial to note that not all tractates engage in this project in an identical manner. Thus, for example, Marjorie Lehman has demonstrated the ways in which B. Yoma depicts the (male) rabbis as distinguishing themselves from the (male) priests by contrasting the all-male beit midrash or study house with that of the all-male Temple and contrasting Temple purity with rabbinic purity.[106] B. Sotah does not seek to differentiate the rabbinic male from the priestly male; rather, it engages in a discussion of ethics that might apply to any person and that differentiates members of the rabbinic community from idolators and outsiders to the rabbinic community (*'am ha-'aretz*).

CONCLUSION: RESPONDING TO THE MISHNAH

As I remarked earlier, the sugyot discussed in this chapter are taken from the beginning, middle, and second-to-last chapters of the tractate. Although the beginning and middle chapters are ostensibly centered around the sotah ritual, the end of the tractate, like the war passage, is not structured as commentary on the sotah ritual. Nevertheless, the tractate's conclusion similarly declaims the makings of the ideal moral man, that is, a sage (B. Sotah 49a). R. Eliʿa bar Yiverekhyah proclaims that two sages on a journey who do not speak words of Torah are fit to be burned in fire.[107] If two sages live in the same city but do not support one another in halakhah, one will accidentally kill the other and then be exiled to a city of refuge. R. Yehudah the son of R. Hiyya declares that any sage who occupies himself with Torah despite his poverty will have his prayer heard. R. Abbahu says that this sage will be satisfied through God's presence (*shekhinah*). R. Aha bar Hanina goes a step further and declares that the heavenly curtain (*pargod*) will not be closed before him. Even the final line of the tractate may be read through this lens of the elevation of the ideal sage. Presented as a response to the mishnaic dictum, "When Rabbi died humility and the fear of sin disappeared" (M. Sotah 9:15), B. Sotah teaches, "Rav Yosef said to the tanna [reciter and transmitter of rabbinic traditions]: Do not teach humility[108] because there is me. Rav Nahman[109] said to the tanna: Do not say fear of sin because there is me" (B. Sotah 49b). Much as B. Sotah opened with shifting the possibility for sin away from women and toward men, the tractate closes with a sage proclaiming that fear of sin, that is distancing oneself from any sin, is a key element of the ideal sage.

As we have seen, M. Sotah is surely about the sotah ritual. However, B. Sotah, while discussing the sotah ritual, responds to the brutality of the mishnaic ritual by teaching its audience that men are also sinful and by identifying the key elements of an ideal (male) sage. In the process, B. Sotah ameliorates the sotah ritual but leaves the sotah herself as an afterthought. The opening sugyot of the tractate proclaim this ideological program. In the next chapter we will see two other strategies that B. Sotah utilizes to respond to the mishnaic ritual: making the male the normative measure of behavior and changing the topic.

CHAPTER TWO
CHANGING THE TOPIC

Reading B. Sotah necessitates negotiating multiple interpretive perspectives simultaneously. As we have seen, M. Sotah focuses our gaze on an elaborate and brutal spectacle antecedent to the biblical ritual, one that the biblical ritual does not necessitate and that is unique in its assumption of the woman's guilt. In contrast to the Mishnah, B. Sotah does not produce a new spectacle. Rather, it examines and delineates the existent mishnaic ritual, often in conversation with earlier tannaitic traditions and other areas of rabbinic law. Of course, some of this process of examination and delineation is simply the literary way of the Bavli. Yet, I contend that in order to properly understand the project of B. Sotah, we must pay attention to the ways in which this particular tractate engages in the recomposition of earlier material and the addition of new material. In other words, we should notice how a specific tractate utilizes and deploys the Bavli's familiar literary modes.

B. Sotah shifts between a direct focus on sotah ritual procedure, to extended aggadic passages, to questions about ritual procedure connected with but not identical to that of the sotah. This editorial composition moves the reader's attention back and forth from the sotah ritual itself. This, then, is yet another way in which B. Sotah responds to the mishnaic ritual: It shifts our attention from the ritual and the sotah herself. In addition, as the Bavli refines the sotah ritual, it evinces an interest in doing so through a focus on male behavior rather than female. In other words, the male rather than the female becomes the normative measure.

This chapter turns to two sugyot: B. Sotah 3b–4b and B. Sotah 14a–15b. The former, a passage that tries to define a time measurement for sexual intercourse, exemplifies the way in which B. Sotah refines the sotah ritual while establishing the male as the measure of the norm. The second, detailing the minhah (grain) sacrifice, exemplifies B. Sotah's shifting attention from the sotah ritual to another priestly ritual. On the one hand, this lessening of emphasis on the sotah ritual itself, and certainly on the mishnaic spectacle, may be read as a positive trend, an amelioration of M. Sotah's misogyny. On the other hand, this lessening of emphasis also displaces women as loci of knowledge within rabbinic culture. Reading the Bavli on the sotah ritual requires holding both of these truths simultaneously.[1]

MEASURING SEX: BAVLI SOTAH 3B–4B

Although ostensibly further defining the circumstances under which a woman can be said to have violated the prohibition of seclusion with a designated man (*setirah*), B. Sotah 3b–4b reveals itself as concerned with knowledge production more generally and the tensions generated through this desire for knowledge. As we will see, the sugya opens by establishing the necessity for two witnesses to observe the woman and the prohibited man engaging in sexual intercourse in order for her to become permanently forbidden to her husband. It concludes with propositions about the source of the sage Ben Azzai's knowledge about sexual intercourse. In moving from the male and female gaze (both men and women may testify to the accused woman's guilt or innocence)[2] to the male sage, the case of the sotah becomes a location for interrogating both the legitimate sources of rabbinic knowledge and the tensions between Torah study, on the one hand, and marriage and procreation on the other.

The opening passage of this sugya, citing M. Sotah 6:3, turns on a comparison between what it terms "first testimony" (*ʿeidut ha-rishonah*) and "last testimony" (*ʿeidut ha-ʾaharonah*). While B. Sotah concludes that both "first testimony" and "last testimony" require two witnesses, it does not, at the outset, clearly define either term.[3] Only after the Bavli concludes that both first and last testimony require two witnesses does it cite a baraita that defines first testimony as testimony of hiding or seclusion (*ʿeidut setirah*)[4] and last testimony as testimony of impurity (*ʿeidut tumʾah*).[5]

A. Our sages taught: What is first testimony?
B. This is testimony of hiding [*ʿeidut setirah*].
C. [What is] final testimony?
D. This is testimony of impurity [*ʿeidut tumʾah*].[6]

That is, in order for a husband to bring his wife to Jerusalem, he must have warned her not to be alone with a particular man, she must have secluded herself with that prohibited man, and then she must have remained there with him for sufficient time to become "impure," all before witnesses. In defining the measure of time required for "hiding," the redactional arc of the Bavli foregrounds male experience and male perceptions of female experience. The baraita continues:

E. And what is the measure of [time required for liability for] hiding?[7]
F. Sufficient for impurity.
G. Sufficient for sexual intercourse.
H. Sufficient for the first stage of sexual intercourse [*haʿaraʾah*].

The baraita moves through a three-step definition of hiding, each step further specifying the time requirement (F–H).[8] By the time the baraita has reached the last item in the list (H), the measure of time required for liability for hiding has become synonymous with the time required for *haʿaraʾah,* a term that refers to the initial insertion of the penis into the vagina.[9] As we will see in chapter 6, B. Sotah will return to the concept of *haʿaraʾah* when it discusses the circumstances of Goliath's conception. However, for this baraita, *haʿaraʾah* itself is a sufficiently indeterminate term such that it now cites nine sages, each of whom provides an example of a different physical action[10] whose length of time would correspond to that of *haʿaraʾah*—and by extension the time measurement for hiding:

I. Sufficient [time] for walking around a palm-tree, the words of R. Ishmael.
J. R. Eliezer says: Sufficient [time] for mixing the cup [of wine with water].
K. R. Yehoshua says: Sufficient [time] to drink it [the cup of wine].
L. Ben Azzai says: Sufficient [time] to roast an egg.
M. R. Akiva says: Sufficient [time] to swallow it [the egg].
N. R. Yehuda ben Beteira says: Sufficient [time] to swallow three eggs one after another.[11]
O. R. Eliezer ben Yirmeyah says: Sufficient [time] for a weaver to knot the threads of a fringe.
P. Hanin ben Pinhas says: Sufficient [time] for her to extend her hand into her mouth to take a wood-chip.

Q. Peleimo says: Sufficient [time] for her to extend her hand into a basket and take bread. Even though there is not proof for the matter, there is a hint:[12] "The last loaf of bread will go for a whore; [a married woman will snare a person of honor]" [Proverbs 6:26].

The measures of time provided by the first seven sages (I–O) certainly may correspond to either male or female actions (men and women both, presumably, swallow eggs). However, since R. Eliezer ben Yirmeyah refers to a male weaver (O) and the last two opinions (P–Q) attempt to measure time through specifically female action, we should consider the former opinions (I–N) as corresponding to what the baraita perceives as male action.[13] Certainly, this is B. Sotah's perspective. For, as the Bavli analyzes this baraita it makes two moves: the first interrogates why the baraita lists three different time measurements for hiding (F–H), and the second puts the baraita in conversation with its toseftan version. In both instances, the male becomes the measure of the norm. In the first instance, B. Sotah explains that all three measurements (impurity, sexual intercourse, and *haʿaraʾah*) are necessary to prevent us from reaching mistaken conclusions. That is, if the baraita had only taught the case of time sufficient for impurity, we might have mistakenly concluded that a more extended period was required: that necessary for both her impurity and her seduction (*kedei tumʾatah ve-ʾartzutah*). Therefore, the Bavli declares, the baraita also taught time sufficient for sexual intercourse. Similarly, had the baraita only taught the example of sexual intercourse, we might mistakenly have thought the measurement to include time sufficient for the conclusion of sexual intercourse. To prevent this conclusion, the baraita taught the example of *haʿaraʾah*. However, had the baraita only taught the case of *haʿaraʾah*, we might mistakenly have thought the required time to be that sufficient for seduction. Therefore, the baraita also taught the case of impurity. In other words, rather than each measurement mapping directly onto another, with each delineating the same amount of time, the Bavli understands the various measurements as pointing to different times. Each measurement prevents a mistaken conclusion. B. Sotah ends this section by defining the time necessary for *haʿaraʾah* as the amount of time needed to walk around a palm tree.

The logic of the Bavli's proof is of secondary concern; what interests me is the way B. Sotah has again raised male action—and male sin—as an inextricable part of the sotah's sin. While she becomes impure, the forbidden man is the one who might seduce her. Although B. Sotah ultimately excludes his seduction from its delineation of the required time, it nevertheless understands seduction as something the man does to the woman. This interpretive move contrasts with the baraita's conclusion, where Peleimo cites Proverbs 6:26 as a proof text for females as responsible for ensnaring otherwise honorable males (Q). Yet B. Sotah's interrogation of the beginning of the baraita has again emphasized male action over female.

This centering of the male, despite two sages' attempt to measure time by female action, becomes even more explicit as B. Sotah puts the first baraita in conversation with its toseftan version. The Bavli's discussion of these two baraitot focuses on the fact that although the content of T. Sotah 1:2 largely corresponds to that of the Bavli baraita (T. Sotah 1:2 mentions the same tradents and the same physical actions), the toseftan baraita attributes a number of these actions to different sages.[14] In the process of reconciling these two traditions, B. Sotah might have chosen to determine which physical action best corresponds to the time necessary for *ha'ara'ah*. Instead, it turns to affirming the accuracy of each sage's two varying statements.

Here is one instance of this phenomenon from the larger sugya, an example that foregrounds the sage Ben Azzai:

A. There [in the first baraita] Ben Azzai said: Sufficient [time] to roast an egg.
B. Here [in the second toseftan baraita] he said: Sufficient [time] to drink it [a cup of wine]!
C. Both refer to one measurement [of time].

The anonymous voice of the Bavli points out a potential contradiction between Ben Azzai's statements: did he say "sufficient [time] to roast an egg" or "sufficient [time] to drink [a cup of wine]" (A–B)? Then it goes on to resolve that contradiction by positing that the difference between the egg and the wine is not crucial: they both refer to the same time measurement (C). That B. Sotah provides five of these examples indicates that it is not concerned with articulating a definitive answer to the sugya's question about the length of time necessary for a woman to have engaged in "hiding." The reliability of male speech rather than the definition of this aspect of sexual intercourse (or female guilt) becomes B. Sotah's main interest.

As the sugya progresses, it moves even further from the sotah. Although the statements of Hanin ben Pinhas and Peleimo, each of which measures time through female action (a woman's taking a wood splinter from her mouth or bread from a basket), might have provided an opening for further discussion of female activity, B. Sotah's questions focus on the status of the object and not how the woman might handle that object. For example, the Bavli wonders whether Peleimo's statement refers to bread squeezed into the basket or easily accessible, old or new, warm or cold, barley or wheat, soft or hard.[15] While establishing the type of bread would more precisely delineate Peleimo's imagined time of hiding, it nevertheless yet again represents a turning from the female.

The sugya's conclusion clearly renders this turning from female experience to male experience:

A. Said R. Yitzhak the son of Yosef[16] in the name of R. Yohanan: Each man calculated [the time measurement for hiding] through himself.
B. But there is Ben Azzai who never married!
C. If you want, say that he was married but sexually abstained [*neseiv u-feirash havah*].
D. And if you want say: He heard from his teacher.
E. And if you want say: "The secret of the Lord is for those who fear Him" [Psalms 25:14].

B. Sotah cites an amoraic tradition in the name of R. Yohanan that each man's own experience with sexual intercourse provides the basis for his measurement (A), a statement that it then goes on to problematize. Referencing a tradition that Ben Azzai never married (B), the Bavli posits that he did not engage in sexual intercourse and thus could not have provided a time measurement. In this move, B. Sotah both delineates sexual intercourse as the provenance of marriage and moves us far away from its initial concerns with witnessing and hiding.

To solve the "problem" of Ben Azzai, B. Sotah proposes a number of solutions: he married and then abstained from sexual intercourse (C), he learned from his teachers (D), or he received divine knowledge (E). Both the problem (celibacy) and the three solutions allude to a central tension within rabbinic culture: that of the competing demands of Torah study and marriage and procreation.[17] Although the tradition of Ben Azzai's celibacy first appears in T. Yevamot 8:7 as part of a discussion about the commandment to procreate (according to Ben Azzai, one who does not procreate is a murderer who also diminishes the divine image), B. Sotah has redeployed it as part of a discussion about the sources of knowledge. In so doing, it links the sotah ritual not only to questions of sexual transgression but also to those of the transmission of male knowledge of bodily experiences more generally. A similar tradition found on B. Sotah 10b demonstrates that these ideas about the transmission of male knowledge of the male body are a trope within the tractate. B. Sotah 10b explains Rav Nahman's description of gout (*pedagra*) as comparable to the sensation of a needle in one's flesh: he either felt it himself, learned from his teacher, or—again citing Psalms 25:14—received his knowledge from God.[18] In our sugya about hiding, that Ben Azzai rather than Rav Nahman becomes the problematic character should not surprise. Ben Azzai is, as we will see, the sage who proposes the permissibility of a father teaching his daughter Torah in order that she not think she has evaded punishment when she drinks the bitter waters without immediate physical consequences. She will instead know that merit has deferred her punishment (M. Sotah 3:4).

The Yerushalmi's version of this sugya highlights the ways in which the Bavli has shifted from questions of female sexual transgression to ones about male knowledge acquisition. Rather than a context of witnesses, Y. Sotah (1:2, 16c) cites the above baraita about time measurements for hiding in the context of a discussion of M. Keritot 2:6.[19] That mishnah distinguishes between a man who has sexual intercourse with a person included in the biblical lists of forbidden sexual relations (*'arayot*; Leviticus 18, 20) and a man who has sexual intercourse with a female slave designated for another man (Leviticus 19:20–22). Y. Sotah interrogates the section of the mishnah that states that in the case of *'arayot*, a man is liable for transgression from the moment of the initial insertion of the penis into the vagina rather than the later act of ejaculation (*'asah bah et ha-me'areh ka-gomer*). The ruling implies that in the case of a female slave, a man would be liable only after ejaculation. A statement in the name of Rav interrogates the appearance of the phrase *shikhvat zera* (a flow of semen) in Leviticus 19:20 (the female slave) and in Numbers 5:13 (the sotah), questioning why different rulings stem from the same words. In the case of the slave, a man is liable only after ejaculation; in the case of the sotah, she is liable after initial insertion of the penis. The answer, in the name of R. Yosi, distinguishes between the two cases. In the instance of the sotah, her act of seclusion with the prohibited man suffices to place her in the category of impure. The same does not hold true for the female slave.[20] Y. Sotah then turns to ask after the purpose of the phrase *shikhvat zera* in Numbers 5:13. If it is understood contrary to its common meaning of ejaculation, why then does the verse utilize these words?[21] The Yerushalmi's response —time measurements—brings us to our baraita.

Opening by quoting Numbers 5:13, Y. Sotah's version of the baraita (largely parallel to T. Sotah 1:2) similarly presents a number of physical actions as possible understandings of the time necessary for *ha῾ara᾽ah*.[22] B. Sotah, in its characteristic dialectical way, as I have described previously, extensively interrogates the baraita; Y. Sotah, in its characteristic way, does no such thing. Instead, after the baraita concludes, Y. Sotah cites a statement about female clothing: "Said R. Yosi, all of these measurements are after untying the *sinar* [a garment associated with females]."[23] It concludes with a similar discussion of the source of Ben Azzai's knowledge about sexual intercourse. Intriguingly, Y. Sotah's version includes the possibility of Ben Azzai's knowledge through sexual excitement and excludes the possibility of his receiving knowledge from his teacher.

On the one hand, the divergence between the Bavli and Yerushalmi may be explained through the formal compositional differences and chronological time span between these two documents. However, difference in form or time of composition does not render a particular content choice as inevitable. The context in which Y. Sotah embeds the baraita is one of sexual transgression more generally. This is consonant with Y. Sotah's greater interest in sexual transgression. In addition, Y. Sotah's inclusion of untying the *sinar*—the beginning of undress —focuses our attention on the act of sex and the establishment of measurements rather than knowledge more generally. Further, the language of "untying the sinar" (*hatarat ha-sinar*) leaves ambiguous who does the untying, opening the possibility that either the woman or the man—or both—bear responsibility for sexual transgression.

Connected through the mention of bread and Proverbs 6:26, B. Sotah follows its extensive discussion of this baraita with the sugya about humility and arrogance discussed in the previous chapter (B. Sotah 4b–5b). That is, from measuring male experience and the meaning of male speech, B. Sotah turns to the measure of the moral man. Y. Sotah, however, remains with the topic of the sotah, continuing with a discussion that differentiates the sotah from a raped woman and interrogates the intersection of the laws of the sotah, levirate marriage, and incest (*ʿarayot*) prohibitions. In this instance, Y. Sotah creates an interconnected web of questions about the sotah and other sexual relations. B. Sotah's move from the sotah to the moral man illustrates its programmatic difference: the sotah becomes a vehicle through which B. Sotah can construct its vision of masculinity. In our Bavli sugya, a man may learn through his own experience, through his teachers, or even from heaven. What he does not do is learn from or ask a woman.

TOPICAL DIVERSIONS: BAVLI SOTAH 14A–15B

When B. Sotah turns away from the sotah ritual in favor of other topics, it does not completely displace the sotah. Instead of disappearing, she is marginalized. In the sugya that follows, the sotah will bookend a discussion of the regular minhah offering.[24] While the Bavli will remind us that its topic is ostensibly the sotah ritual and that the sotah has sinned, it will continuously turn away from that ritual to others. This process of topic-switching should not be understood as the Bavli engaging in connected but tangential discussions. Rather, this process should be understood as one of the methods that B. Sotah utilizes to neutralize the mishnaic version of the ritual.[25] We should read B. Sotah 14a–15b, a passage that begins with the sotah's minhah offering (described in M. Sotah 2:1), within this framework.

M. Sotah 2:1 describes the sotah's minhah offering and also describes the normative minhah procedure. However, it is clear that it does so in order to sharpen the contrast between the sotah's offering and other offerings. M. Sotah 2:1 opens by informing us that the husband brings his accused wife's minhah offering in an Egyptian basket[26] and then places this basket upon her hands in order to tire her.[27] This mishnah then presents a series of comparisons between the normative minhah offering and that of the sotah, listing the ways in which the sotah's minhah offering differs from the everyday minhah. It concludes with a statement in the name of Rabban Gamliel: "Just as her actions are the actions of an animal, so too her offering is the food of an animal." That is, according to Rabban Gamliel, the mishnah utilizes details about the common minhah offering in order to teach us how and why the sotah's minhah offering differs from the norm. The sotah's offering is primary and the normative minhah offering secondary. However, when the Bavli comments on this mishnah, it quickly turns from the sotah to an extended explication of the standard minhah offering.

B. Sotah 14a opens its commentary on M. Sotah 2:1 by citing a baraita (also found in Sifrei Bemidbar)[28] that links the husband placing the Egyptian basket onto the accused woman's hands with God's care for the sotah and then God's care in general:

A. It was taught [in a baraita]: Abba Hanin says in the name of R. Eliezer: (All of this why?)[29] In order to tire her so that she will retract [her claim of innocence].
B. If the Torah protects those who transgress His will, all the more so [will the Torah protect] those who do His will.

The emphasis on godly care in this baraita is striking, particularly in light of the comparison that later midrashim such as the Tanhuma and Numbers Rabbah[30] draw between the husband's jealousy of his wife and God's jealousy at Israel's apostasy with the golden calf (Exodus 32).[31] The baraita, in contrast, does not depict God as jealous but the opposite: the goal of tiring the woman by having her hold the minhah offering is to convince her to recant and admit her guilt so that she will not drink the bitter waters (A).[32] Rather than suffering death—M. Sotah's punishment for a guilty woman who drinks the water (M. Sotah 3:4, 6)[33]—a woman who admits her guilt loses the money promised in her *ketubah* and exits her marriage (M. Sotah 1:5). Of course, this form of care is problematic: the woman is being forced to admit guilt rather than being presumed innocent. Nevertheless, the consequences of guilt admission (divorce) appear preferable to death. Finally, the Bavli's version of the baraita presents R. Eliezer as extrapolating from the particulars of the sotah to the rewards for correct behavior in general (B).[34] The baraita is yet another example of the ways in which the sotah is a springboard for discussing ethical behavior writ large.[35]

B. Sotah goes on to interrogate the baraita, questioning whether the reason for having the woman hold the minhah is actually due to consideration for the woman. Instead, B. Sotah proposes that the reason for placing the minhah offering on her hands is to prevent the sotah scroll, and thus God's name, from being erased:

C. And from where is your proof that [the Torah wants to][36] protect her?
D. Perhaps it is so that the scroll will not be erased.
E. [R. Eliezer] thinks[37] that he [the priest] makes her drink [the potion] and afterwards [he] offers the minhah. Because if [the reason for placing the minhah on her hands was] because of the scroll, it has [already] been erased.

In this view, instead of God's care for the sotah, the minhah procedure would demonstrate human care for God by preventing the erasure of the divine name (C–D). Alluding to M. Sotah 3:2, the Bavli rejects this proposal by asserting that according to R. Eliezer the woman first drinks and then afterward the priest offers her minhah sacrifice (E).[38] Since the priest would have already erased God's name to make the drinking potion, the reason for her holding the minhah cannot be attributed to a concern for God's name but instead to a concern for the accused woman. Furthermore, as the water only ascertains whether she is innocent or guilty once the sacrifice is offered,[39] a confession of guilt would prevent further bodily punishment. In contrast, the similar passage in Y. Sotah 2:1, 17d, does not mention an ethic of care either for the sotah or for the erasure of God's name. Instead, Y. Sotah proposes that the sotah holds the minhah offering in order to induce fear in her. B. Sotah, in this short section, evinces two elements that characterize its approach to the ritual: the reconciliation of multiple earlier sources and the extrapolation from the sotah to a more generalized ethics.

The Bavli's shift of emphasis from the topic of the sotah becomes more pronounced in the next portion of the sugya when the Bavli presents an extended analysis of the regular minhah offering. Although the Bavli's interrogation has a basis in M. Sotah 2:1's mention of other minhah offerings, the Bavli's discussion minimizes the minhah of the sotah in favor of the standard minhah. Again illustrating the difference between the Bavli and Yerushalmi, Y. Sotah stays with the topic of the sotah's minhah for longer. It interrogates in whose name the priest must sanctify the minhah offering (whether just her or her and her husband), and whether the husband or another man may separate the minhah offering without the woman's consent.

The Bavli's shift away from the sotah begins with the citation of an extended toseftan baraita that, among other details, challenges M. Sotah 2:1's description of the standard minhah offering (T. Menahot 1:16–17).[40] M. Sotah 2:1 declares that at the outset and at the conclusion of the standard minhah offering, the offering must be brought in a vessel consecrated for Temple service (*keli sharet*).[41] The baraita, however, prescribes that a person first bring the offering in gold or silver baskets (*kelatot*)[42] and afterward place the offering in a *keli sharet*. B. Sotah resolves the contradiction by citing Rav Pappa, who proposes that we understand the mishnah's dictum requiring service vessels to mandate the use of vessels *appropriate* for service vessels. Gold and silver vessels, such as those required in T. Menahot 1:2, would fall into this category of vessels that can be consecrated for Temple service. By juxtaposing two tannaitic texts, B. Sotah has refined, or perhaps reinterpreted, the initial steps of the sacrificial procedure for the standard minhah offering. Crucially, it does not refine the sotah's minhah offering.

Although the Bavli's next move appears to bring us back to the sotah ritual, the sugya's question about Egyptian baskets (used for the sotah's minhah offering) sets the stage for a concern to establish what types of wooden vessels may be consecrated as Temple service vessels in general:

A. It follows by implication that an Egyptian basket is not fitting [for Temple service].[43]
B. According to whose opinion [is this true]?
C. It is not according to R. Yosi the son of R. Yehudah, as it is taught [in a baraita]: service vessels that are made from wood, Rabbi [Yehudah ha-Nasi] invalidates them [for Temple service], and R. Yosi the son of R. Yehudah validates them [for Temple service].[44]
D. You may even say that [Egyptian baskets are not fitting for Temple service] according to R. Yosi the son of R. Yehudah.
E. Say that R. Yosi the son of R. Yehudah [thinks that baskets made from wood are valid when they are of] superior [quality]. In the [case of baskets of] lesser [quality] would he say [they are valid]?! Does he not agree [with the principle stated in Malachi 1:8]: "[When you present a blind animal for sacrifice—it doesn't

> matter! When you present a lame or sick one—it doesn't matter!] Just offer it to your governor: [Will he accept you? Will he show you favor?—said the Lord of Hosts]."[45]

Opening with a statement that extrapolates from Rav Pappa's previous comment the principle that Egyptian baskets, as they are made from wood,[46] would not be considered appropriate Temple service vessels, B. Sotah wonders which sage would agree with that ruling (A–B). Paradoxically, it proposes the name of a sage who would *not* agree with that ruling, R. Yosi the son of R. Yehudah. In support of this proposition, B. Sotah cites a baraita about all Temple service vessels, one in which R. Yosi permits these vessels to be made of wood (C). Yet, in a move characteristic of the Bavli, the sugya then goes on to propose that R. Yosi might agree with the proposition that Egyptian baskets are not fitting for Temple service (D). The editorial voice does so by asserting that R. Yosi considers only baskets made from superior wood to be permitted; baskets made from inferior types of wood, such as Egyptian baskets, he would consider forbidden. In support of this assertion, B. Sotah cites a verse from the prophet Malachi that intimates God's refusal of blemished sacrificial animals (E). In so doing, the Bavli contextualizes the earlier baraita in which R. Yosi permitted the use of wooden vessels to refer only to a situation of superior wooden vessels. This passage's discussion of the sotah's Egyptian baskets becomes a vehicle through which the Bavli can discuss the use of permitted and forbidden wooden implements in Temple ritual in general rather than a means for discussing the specific contours of the wooden implement utilized in the sotah ritual.

The Bavli's greater interest in the standard minhah ritual rather than the sotah can also be seen in the sugya's continuation. The toseftan baraita cited earlier by the Bavli as an objection to M. Sotah 2:1 presents a detailed description of the procedure for the standard minhah sacrifice:

> A. What is the order of the minhah offering?
> B. A man brings the minhah from his house in baskets of silver or gold.
> C. He places it within a service vessel and sanctifies it within a service vessel.
> D. And he puts its oil and frankincense on it and brings it to a priest.

E. And the priest brings it to the altar and brings it near the southwest corner opposite the point of the horn of the altar. And this is sufficient.

F. And he removes the frankincense to one side and takes a handful [of the minhah offering] from the place where its oil has increased.

G. And he puts it in a service vessel and sanctifies it in a service vessel.

H. And he gathers its frankincense and puts it on top [and brings it up to the altar].[47]

I. And he brings it up and offers it in a service vessel.

J. And he salts it and puts it on the fires.

K. After the handful is sacrificed, its remnants are eaten.

L. And the priests are permitted to put in it wine, and oil, and honey.

M. And they are forbidden only from [letting the remnants] become leavened.

The continuation of the Bavli sugya presents a line-by-line analysis of the baraita, in most cases matching the relevant line in the baraita with its corresponding biblical proof text from Leviticus 2, the biblical description of the standard minhah offering.[48] The Bavli does not link the standard minhah with that of the sotah. Instead, B. Sotah turns from the baraita to analyze the next line of M. Sotah 2:1 ("all minhah offerings require oil and frankincense, but this one [of the sotah] does not require either oil or frankincense"); it even brings four other offerings into the sugya's conversation. B. Sotah turns to the *minhat hotei* (the meal offering of the inadvertent sinner), the sin and guilt offerings of the *metzora* (the person with skin disease), and the sin offering of the nazir.[49] Since tannaitic texts do list the sotah's minhah together with these other offerings,[50] the Bavli's omission of the case of the sotah is all the more striking; it yet again points to the way in which B. Sotah turns our attention away from the sotah ritual itself to other topics. B. Sotah only returns to a clearly delineated discussion of the sotah when it examines Rabban Gamliel's statement at the end of the mishnah ("Just as her actions are the actions of an animal, so too her offering is the food of an animal").

In this instance, the Bavli presents Rabban Gamliel's statement in the mishnah as a response to another measure-for-measure declaration by the sage R. Meir:

A. It was taught [in a baraita]: Said Rabban Gamliel to the sages: Scholars, allow me and I will interpret it like a jewel.[51]
B. Since he heard R. Meir who said: She fed him the delicacies of the world, therefore her offering will be the food of an animal.
C. He said to him: That would be appropriate for a rich woman, but [in the case of] a poor woman, what is there to say?
D. Rather, just as her actions are the actions of an animal, so too her offering is the food of an animal.

While R. Meir explains the sotah's austere minhah as mirroring the accused woman's feeding her lover fine food (B), Rabban Gamliel presents the sotah's minhah as corresponding to her actions: "animal" behavior deserves animal food (D).[52] Although the Bavli bookends this sugya with a discussion of the sotah, the lengthier middle turns away from that topic to explore the standard minhah offering. While the Bavli certainly could have focused its attention on the sotah's minhah, as does the mishnah, its choice not to do so is instructive. Rather than viewing the middle of the sugya as a digression from the main topic, we should instead understand it as illustrative of one of the ways in which B. Sotah approaches the sotah ritual. In place of directly challenging the mishnaic procedure, B. Sotah shifts our attention elsewhere without completely leaving the sotah behind. She disappears only to resurface once again.

CONCLUSION

B. Sotah conveys its message through its form and content. When B. Sotah moves back and forth from the sotah and the sotah ritual to other topics, it embeds the sotah and the sotah ritual within other topics. This embedding shifts our eyes from the accused woman and the brutal ritual to other topics of rabbinic discourse. While we might view this literary act as normalizing the sotah ritual by framing it as just another topic of rabbinic discourse, I claim that we should better understand it as a rhetorical strategy through which B. Sotah hides from and attempts to neutralize the mishnaic ritual's brutality. Yet, this act of neutralizing the mishnah's brutality also has negative consequences.

In the process of making the male the measure of the norm and of switching topics, we run the risk of losing sight of the sotah herself and therefore participating in the process of displacing women from B. Sotah's discourse. The next chapter confronts this issue of disappearing women through the lens of Torah's transmission, arguing that the Bavli's own redactional arc amplifies the disappearance of women.

CHAPTER THREE

ERASED WOMEN AND TALMUDIC REDACTION

In contrast to M. Sotah, which opens with a debate about judicial procedure—the correct way for a husband to warn his wife—B. Sotah begins with a question about rabbinic study: "Since the tanna finished [tractate] Nazir, what is he teaching such that he teaches [tractate] Sotah?" Instead of centering the ritual procedure of the sotah with its concomitant interest in the family and control of female sexuality, B. Sotah signals with this opening that rabbinic teaching and learning—and not the female sotah, as one might have thought—will be a crucial interest of this tractate. As we have seen, B. Sotah is not primarily concerned with defending or even defining the contours of the marital and biological family. Instead, it teaches a man how to become a member of the rabbinic family. Yet much as rabbinic literature commonly frames the transmission of Torah as a particularly male enterprise, B. Sotah also reveals that this process of male discipleship does not unequivocally displace women or the family.[1] Accordingly, this chapter asks what we might surface about women, family, Torah study, and knowledge transmission when we pay closer attention to the literary arc of B. Sotah.[2]

Rather than interrogate the question of women's presence (were women there?), I assume women's presence at the heart of rabbinic culture and, through the lens of Torah study, interrogate the process of their erasure in B. Sotah itself.[3] Studying B. Sotah as a textual unit enables us to not only uncover isolated moments of erasure within a sugya but also to notice the ways in which the redactional arc of the tractate as a whole has contributed to a perception of women's absence. As B. Sotah shifts its emphasis away from purely female responsibility for sexual sin and attempts to frame Torah study and its transmission as a particularly male enterprise, it nevertheless reveals females—as daughters, wives, wetnurses, and mothers—as vital to the creation and replication of rabbinic culture. I contend that attention to B. Sotah as a tractate enables us to restore women's presence.

This chapter focuses on two sugyot, the first from the middle of the tractate and the second from the end. The former passage, B. Sotah 21a, interrogates the type of merit that might delay the punishment of an accused sotah. The latter, B. Sotah 49b, interrogates the prohibition against the teaching of Greek wisdom. Each of these sugyot acts as commentary on mishnaic passages that discuss knowledge transmission from father to child, whether Torah (father to daughter; M. Sotah 3:4) or Greek language (father to son; M. Sotah 9:17).[4] As we will see, B. Sotah obscures the (female) sotah by figuring Torah study as protecting a male from penalty for sexual sin and obscures the family by transforming parental teaching into the academy.[5] Examining each of these sugyot as a unit and then putting them in conversation with one another enables us to notice female presence *and* absence—and, through this process—restore females to the heart of B. Sotah.

FATHERS, DAUGHTERS, AND TORAH: SETTING THE STAGE—MISHNAH SOTAH 3:4

Daniel Boyarin has argued that, for rabbinic Judaism, the exclusion of women from the study of Torah—the core of the rabbinic enterprise—is the central moment of the subjection of women.[6] M. Sotah 3:4, with its discussion of merit (*zekhut*) suspending the accused sotah's punishment and of fathers teaching their daughters Torah, has become a primary text for the conversation—academic as well as practical—about female exclusion from Torah study.[7] In presenting and discussing this mishnah, I do not seek to recapitulate these conversations nor to take a definitive stand on the debates surrounding the referent of the words "merit" or "Torah." Rather, I want to notice the gaps that lay the foundation for the Bavli's discussion. Because my focus lies with the Bavli's discussion of merit and Torah study, I cite the portions of M. Sotah 3:4 most relevant for understanding the Bavli sugya:

A. She [the accused sotah] has hardly finished drinking when her face grows pale and her eyes protrude and she is filled with tendons. And they say, "Take her out, take her out, so that she does not make impure the Temple courtyard."

B. If she has merit, it suspends [punishment][8] for her.
There is merit that suspends for one year.
There is merit that suspends for two years.
There is merit that suspends for three years.

C. From here said Ben Azzai: A man [*ʾadam*] is obligated to teach his daughter Torah [*torah*] so that if she drinks [the bitter waters] she will know that merit suspends [punishment; *teida she-ha-zekhut tolah lah*].

D. R. Eliezer says: One who teaches his daughter Torah teaches her lasciviousness [*ha-melameid*[9] *ʾet bito torah melamedah tiflut*].[10]

In declaring that merit has the power to delay a guilty sotah's punishment (A–B) and connecting that declaration (*mikan ʾamar*; "from here he said") with a debate about the necessity of and permissibility for a father to teach his daughter Torah (C–D),[11] M. Sotah 3:4 opens the question of the nature of this merit and the place of the family in Torah's transmission and reception. According to Ben Azzai, a man (*ʾadam*)[12] must teach his daughter Torah so that if she were to drink the bitter waters and suffer no immediate effect, she would not—if guilty—think she has evaded punishment. Rather, she would recognize that merit (whether of Torah study or more generally)[13] suspends her punishment (C).[14] Rabbi Eliezer, on the other hand, contends that a man who teaches his daughter (*ha-melameid ʾet bito*) Torah teaches her lasciviousness (*tiflut*) (D). Torah may refer here more narrowly to the biblical sotah passage or more broadly to the Pentateuch or, more broadly still, to the entire corpus of Oral Torah;[15] one sage obligates a father to teach his daughter Torah and the other forbids it. Nevertheless, both sages connect teaching of Torah from father to daughter with sexual transgression. Ben Azzai links it with the prevention of sexual transgression and R. Eliezer with influencing such transgression.[16]

Much as M. Sotah 3:4 stages a pedagogical relationship between father and daughter and thus points us toward the household as a location for Torah study, it simultaneously de-emphasizes the father's status as a father. In Elizabeth Shanks Alexander's words, when this mishnah imagines fathers teaching daughters, it "does not represent Torah study here as an act that serves the interests of the father in his role as father. It is an act he performs as an *ʾadam* (man), rather than as a father. What is important in this teaching is that daughters receive certain information."[17] Of secondary importance is the fact that the father is the one teaching his daughter. Although both sages depict Torah study as "an interaction between a father and his offspring,"[18] a common pattern in the Mishnah, the father does not teach (or refuse to teach) his daughter as a way to replicate his status as *pater familias* or to induct her into the covenantal community of sages. Rather, he teaches her as a man in general.[19] This terminological blurring of the lines between father and any man is one way that M. Sotah 3:4 obscures learning as a familial enterprise. Indeed, Alexander also speculates that because *ʾadam* can refer to males and females, Ben Azzai may indicate that both fathers *and* mothers are obligated to teach their daughters Torah.[20] We need not adjudicate Alexander's speculation but rather utilize it to notice that much as the word *ʾadam* blurs the line between father and any male, it also blurs the line between paternal and maternal instruction. This blurring will be crucial for the Bavli sugya to come.

STUDIOUS MEN AND TEACHING WOMEN: BAVLI SOTAH 21A

M. Sotah 3:4 emphasizes that merit protects the daughter; Torah study enables her to understand why her punishment was not (or would not be) immediate, despite her transgression. However, when B. Sotah 21a discusses the mishnaic premise that merit will protect or defer punishment of the accused sotah, in the process of determining the referent of that merit, it makes two moves. On the one hand, it frames Torah-studying men as potential sotahs; on the other hand, it positions women as teachers of Torah. The first serves to disappear the sotah and thus women in general; the second resurfaces women, positioning them as crucial to the formation and transmission of rabbinic culture. Although the sugya begins with a question about what type of merit might delay the sotah's punishment—Torah study or the performance of commandments—it quickly turns away from the particular question of the sotah to a more abstract discussion that implicates male behavior. This discussion of merit and male behavior will also surface the biblical characters of Doeg, Ahitofel, and David. When the sugya does return to female merit in particular, the sotah will have been replaced by the faithful mother and wife.

The Male Sotah and Righteous Women

With its inquiry into the protective powers of female engagement in Torah study and the performance of commandments, B. Sotah 21a initially frames its topic as female behavior and the rabbinic curriculum:

A. There is merit that delays [punishment] for three years etc.
B. Merit of what?
C. If we say merit of Torah [study], she is not in the category of one who is commanded and does.
D. Rather, it is the merit of [performing a] commandment.

Because, like all women, the accused sotah is not commanded to study Torah,[21] the merit of Torah study cannot be the referent of the mishnah's merit and the reason for the delay of her punishment (A–C). Instead, the Bavli proposes that the merit that defers the sotah's punishment must refer to her previous performance of commandments (D). To this point, it appears that the Bavli has engaged in its familiar process of demoting female Torah study. Yet, as the Bavli goes on to challenge this assertion in the next section of the sugya ("But does the merit of commandment protect to this extent?!"), it leads us into a baraita that changes the topic from female Torah study. This baraita depicts the superior protective powers of Torah study over performing commandments and includes a parable about a (male) traveler in the dark of night. With its move from the question of delay of punishment to the overarching protection offered by Torah study, B. Sotah signals a shift of topic from the sotah and her merit to an exploration of the hierarchy of male Torah study versus male commandment performance.[22]

At the conclusion of the baraita, B. Sotah turns to the voices of two amoraic sages (Rav Yosef and Rava),[23] each of whom weighs in about the relative protective powers of Torah study and commandment performance. Although both sages agree that Torah study protects males, they disagree about the extent of its apotropaic powers. Rav Yosef proposes that commandments do have a modicum of protective power: when a man is in the midst of performing a commandment, it both protects and saves him. In contrast, Torah study protects and saves regardless of whether a man is currently engaged in that study. The precise meaning of "protect" and "save" is ambiguous; what is clear is that saving is higher on the hierarchical ladder.[24] Rava's objection to Rav

Yosef surfaces the characters of Doeg and Ahitofel—the former who killed the priests of Nob at Saul's bidding (1 Samuel 22:17–19) and the latter who advised David's son Absalom to have sexual intercourse with his father's concubines (2 Samuel 16:20–23) as well as to assassinate his father (2 Samuel 17:2). "Rava attacked it [the statement of Rav Yosef]: But from here [there is the case of] Doeg and Ahitofel.[25] Did they not occupy [themselves] with Torah [study]?! Why did it [Torah study] not protect them?" Rava's rejection of Rav Yosef's opinion through the case of Doeg and Ahitofel alludes both to their tragic end (according to M. Sanhedrin 10:2, Doeg and Ahitofel are counted among those who have no share in the world to come)[26] and to rabbinic traditions about their excellence as Torah scholars.[27] In utilizing Doeg and Ahitofel as challenges to Rav Yosef's statement, B. Sotah once again centers male sin and male Torah study. After all, if Torah study possessed complete apotropaic powers, surely it would not have failed to protect Doeg and Ahitofel! Instead, Rava posits that while a man is engaged in Torah study, that study protects and saves him; when he stops studying, that study protects him but no longer saves him. Commandment performance, on the other hand, always protects but never saves.[28]

Doeg and Ahitofel will resurface a bit later in the Bavli's analysis of the baraita. When they return, B. Sotah frames them as paradigmatic examples of men who misinterpret Torah rather than men who study Torah. As the Bavli does so, it also positions David as a male version of the sotah:[29]

A. Said Rav Yosef: R. Menahem bar Yosi interpreted this verse like Sinai. And if only Doeg and Ahitofel had interpreted it thus, they would not have chased after David. As it is written, "Saying: God has forsaken him [so chase him and capture him, for no one will save him]!" [Psalms 71:11]

B. What [verse] was interpreted?

C. "Since the Lord your God moves about in your camp to protect you and to deliver your enemies to you, let your camp be holy;] let Him not find any matter of sexual prohibition [*ʿervat davar*] [and turn away from you]" [Deuteronomy 23:15].[30]

D. And they [Doeg and Ahitofel] did not know that a sin extinguishes a commandment but a sin does not extinguish Torah [study].

This portion of the sugya opens with Rav Yosef referencing an unnamed verse interpreted incorrectly by Doeg and Ahitofel. Their mistaken interpretation leads them to assume God's abandonment of David and their concomitant ability to kill David (A). The missing verse —provided by the sugya's anonymous voice as Deuteronomy 23:15— suggests that God protects only those people who do not engage in prohibited sexual relations (B–C). The pericope closes with a statement that Doeg and Ahitofel did not realize the power of Torah study to protect a person from the consequences of sin (D).

Through the use of a verse that mentions sexual prohibitions, B. Sotah hints at David's guilt of the sin of sexual intercourse with a married woman, in this case Batsheva (2 Samuel 11–12).[31] David's sin thus overlaps with that of the sotah, albeit with a reversal of gendered culpability. Much as the merit of Torah study protects the guilty sotah, suspending her punishment, the merit of Torah study protects David from Doeg and Ahitofel's attempt to kill him. Following the thread of David as the sotah, we may also conceptualize the death of David and Batsheva's baby (2 Samuel 12:15–24) as parallel to the sotah's miscarriage and David's bodily deterioration at the end of his life (1 Kings 1:1) as a form of suspended punishment.[32]

This framing of the male biblical character of David as a sotah is not solely an act of gender reversal or appropriation of the female for the male. It is part of B. Sotah's larger project of shifting sinfulness to males. In contrast to the example of David as a sotah, B. Sotah does not name or position specific females as potential sotahs, even in cases when it might have done so. To provide one example, the biblical story of Tamar (Genesis 38) depicts Tamar's seduction of her father-in-law Yehudah when he fails to properly follow the laws of levirate marriage.[33] Although Genesis 38:26 does proclaim Tamar's righteousness (Yehudah declares, "She is more righteous than I"), it would not have been outside the realm of B. Sotah's midrashic imagination for it to condemn Tamar for her ruse.[34] Yet, B. Sotah not only depicts Tamar as free of guilt for seducing her father-in-law Yehudah but enhances her righteousness (B. Sotah 10a–b).[35] Much as B. Sotah renders David as a sotah, it presents Tamar as possessing some of the characteristics that it elsewhere associates with the ideal male rabbinic Jew. Tamar follows after the patriarch Abraham (sitting at the place where Abraham once pitched his tent),[36] utilizes halakhah to seduce Yehudah (making a number of legal claims about her personal status),[37] models modesty by covering her face in her father-in-law's house (as a result she merits that prophets and kings descend from her),[38] and warrants angelic interference in her fate (Gabriel steps in to ensure that signs she gave to Yehudah are recognized).

B. Sotah's depiction of Tamar as knowing a number of laws concerning her eligibility for marriage also contrasts with the Mishnah and Bavli's ambivalence about female Torah study. In this case, Tamar not only knows rabbinic law but deploys it to achieve her goal of pregnancy and familial continuity. B. Sotah even interprets her treatment of Yehudah as the basis for a rabbinic maxim about the crucial importance of not humiliating another person: "It is better for a person to cast himself into a fiery furnace rather than to whiten the face of [i.e., humiliate or shame] another person publicly" (B. Sotah 10b).[39]

On the one hand, we may view this hyperrighteous presentation of Tamar and hypersexualized positioning of King David as sotah as "positive" for women. Men become the primary sexual sinners and thought of as the sotah. On the other hand, we may also view it as part of B. Sotah's larger displacement of females in the face of constructing rabbinic masculinity. Indeed, much as B. Sotah depicts Tamar as knowing Jewish law, it also depicts her displaying that knowledge as she is interrogated by her father-in-law, an interrogation echoing that of the priest's questioning of the accused sotah (M. Sotah 1:4).[40]

The larger passage within which the discussion of David, Doeg, and Ahitofel is embedded is striking for the way it opens with a discussion of the sotah, turns to a more general philosophical discussion about the relative protective powers of Torah study versus performance of commandments, and then locates sexual sin in males. The latter strategies serve to effectively "disappear" the accused sotah. As B. Sotah plays with gender and sin, it both hides and surfaces women.

Mothers as Teachers

The portrayal of Tamar as knowledgeable of Torah intersects with another trope in this longer passage on B. Sotah 21a. B. Sotah 10a–b depicts Tamar as knowing Torah for the sake of achieving a familial goal: having a child. That is, knowledge of Torah does not position Tamar as a sage but as a mother. Yet B. Sotah also views knowledge that is transmitted in a familial context—and by mothers in particular—as central not only to the founding of a royal and messianic line but also to the reception of Torah and the continuity of the rabbinic community itself.

B. Sotah 21a interrupts its discussion of Doeg and Ahitofel and the hierarchy of the protective powers of male Torah study versus commandment performance to return to its question of what might suspend the sotah's punishment. As the sugya returns to the idea that the merit of Torah study *is* what protects the accused sotah, it describes female Torah study through a relational lens. B. Sotah turns away from a more philosophical discussion as well as from biblical precedent and depicts the anonymous every-woman as wife and mother, one who is enmeshed in care for her family, where part of that care is ensuring that her sons[41] and husband engage in the rabbinic curriculum.[42]

A. Ravina said: In all cases, the merit of Torah [protects].[43]
B. And as to what you said that she [is in the category of one who] is not commanded and [nevertheless] performs [the commandment]: Granted that they [women] are not commanded—
C. however for the reward of teaching their sons[44] to read Scripture and to learn the oral tradition[45] and for waiting for their husbands until they come from the house of study, do they not split [the reward for Torah study] with them?!

The amoraic sage Ravina declares that the merit of Torah study is, in fact, what consistently protects a woman (A). He accepts the premise that women are categorized as those who are not commanded to fulfill (certain) commandments but nevertheless may perform them (B). But he counters the idea that this designation implies that Torah study does not protect women. Ravina declares that women are protected through the reward they receive for teaching their sons Scripture and Oral Torah (*be-ʾagra de-makreyan u-matneyan benaihu*) and for waiting for their husbands to return from the study house. These mother-wives divide with their sons and husband the merit that the male relatives receive as ones who are commanded to study Torah (C).

Ravina's statement about mothers and sons (C) is commonly understood and translated following Rashi's commentary, that is, differently than I have done above.[46] Rashi explicates this clause as referring to mothers exerting themselves to bring their sons to school in order that they may study Scripture and Mishnah.[47] This reading leads us down the usual road of women being at least once removed from the teaching and study of Torah, or, in more contemporary language, serving as facilitators but not practitioners. Yet the *ʾafʿel* form of the verbs (*makreyan u-matneyan*), the causative, opens the possibility that these mothers taught their sons Scripture and Oral Torah themselves.[48] Intriguingly, the Munich manuscript leaves out the direct object "sons," enabling us to understand these women as teachers of Scripture and Oral Torah to an uncertain audience, perhaps including their daughters and perhaps including children outside of their immediate household. Certainly, papyri from first- to sixth-century Greco-Roman Egypt testify to the presence of female teachers who provided literary instruction to students other than their own children.[49]

While the historical veracity of this claim of mothers as teachers of Torah is difficult to ascertain, it is also likely that our assumptions about Torah and rabbinic culture have led us to overlook instances where women not only received but also transmitted Scripture and Oral Torah. In a culture that was both mimetic and textual[50] and where texts were transmitted and created orally,[51] it is possible that mothers shaped rabbinic culture both through mimesis—how they behaved—and through textual literacy—teaching Scripture and Oral Torah. That rabbi-disciple teaching also took place in the household and not solely in the male study house renders it more likely that mothers taught Torah to their sons and perhaps even their daughters.

Judith Hauptman has collected a number of talmudic passages in which rabbinic traditions are transmitted to women and then these women challenge, modify, or clarify these rules based on their experiences. Most of these passages occur in the context of the household, often (but not only) to do with the kitchen and food preparation. These women are described as wives, sisters, and daughters of rabbinic sages and portrayed as teaching their husbands, sons, daughters, and fathers about rabbinic law.[52] Here in B. Sotah, however, Ravina specifies the more general subject matter of Written and Oral Torah rather than any specific topic. This use of Torah writ large speaks to the way in which B. Sotah is concerned with Torah as the central ideological frame of rabbinic culture and mothers as crucial to its transmission.[53] This frame of Torah as central and mothers as critical to its transmission can also be seen in B. Sotah's depiction of Moses as refusing to nurse from an Egyptian woman and the connection it draws between his refusal to nurse and his future intimate and oral relationship—through speech—with God. According to B. Sotah, only the ingestion of milk from an Israelite woman, in this case his mother, will prepare Moses for receiving the Torah (B. Sotah 12b).[54]

Returning to Ravina and the second half of phrase (C) (merit refers to the practice of wives waiting for their husbands until they return from the house of study) brings us to what Daniel Boyarin has called a culture of "married monks," the Babylonian tendency for males to marry first and then leave for extended periods of time to study.[55] It is difficult to know whether B. Sotah alludes to a study house in the same town or one far away. It is similarly difficult to know the length of time of the husband's absence.[56] Yet since the wife is most likely also a mother, this second clause combines with the first half of the statement to create an impression of mothers teaching their children in the absence of fathers.[57] Even if depicted as outsiders to the more formal scholastic culture, B. Sotah nevertheless imagines mothers as crucial to the creation, transmission, and perpetuation of rabbinic culture—not simply through the biological act of having children (B. Sotah also depicts males as biological fathers) but through what they *do* in the absence of fathers.

When M. Sotah 3:4 discusses teaching that takes place in the family, it marginalizes the father by calling him an *ʾadam*. B. Sotah 21a, on the other hand, turns clearly to mothers and sons. Perhaps we may understand the Bavli's conception of maternal care to include not only the vital embodied obligations[58] of food preparation, laundry, making the beds, wool-work,[59] and breastfeeding but also the provision of rabbinic education, both mimetically and more formally.[60] Surely B. Sotah 21a, with its contrast between absent fathers and present mothers who teach Scripture and Oral Torah, holds out this tantalizing possibility.

FATHERS, SONS, AND GREEK: SETTING THE STAGE—MISHNAH SOTAH 9:17

We may trace an arc throughout B. Sotah about Torah study. B. Sotah opens with a question about the teaching and learning of mishnaic tractates (B. Sotah 2a), in the middle turns to David as the Torah-studying sotah and to mothers as teachers of sons (B. Sotah 21a), and then concludes with the academy of Rabban Gamliel (B. Sotah 49b).

Tracing the shift from Jewish knowledge transmission and reception (Torah) to foreign knowledge transmission and reception (Greek/Greek wisdom) reveals the editorial process that conceals females and the family as central to the formation and sustaining of rabbinic Judaism. As we will see, much as the opening sugya erased the sotah and turned to male sin, the story of Rabban Gamliel's academy erases father and daughter, replacing them with an elegy for a lost world of a thousand male students.

The story of Rabban Gamliel's academy is found as commentary on M. Sotah 9:17, one of the final mishnayot in the tractate.[61] While M. Sotah 3:4 discussed fathers, daughters, and Torah instruction, M. Sotah 9:17 discusses fathers, sons, and Greek-language instruction:

A. During the war against Vespasian, they decreed against the crowns of bridegrooms and against the *ʾeirus* [a musical instrument used at weddings].[62]

B. During the war against Kitos,[63] they decreed against the crowns of brides and that a man [*ʾadam*] should not teach his son Greek [*yevanit*].

C. During the final war, they decreed that a bride should not go out in the palanquin in the city.

D. But our sages permitted the bride to go out in the palanquin in the city.

The mishnaic (and tannaitic)[64] ban against a father teaching his son Greek language is embedded within a list of other conflict-driven bans against certain festive wedding practices, such as wearing a crown.[65] Although the sotah ritual is not ostensibly the object of concern in this mishnah, as the ritual is, at least partially, a response to a wedding gone wrong, this topical conjunction is striking. If we understand the specific ways in which weddings are performed—and not just the existence of weddings—as essential to cultural transmission, this mishnah's prohibitions intimate that something has gone deeply wrong. The ban against a father's transmission of Greek language and the implication that he may only teach Hebrew language is part of M. Sotah's larger signaling of the ways in which cultural transmission has gone awry.[66] Notable in this mishnah's description of rabbinic culture gone wrong is the fact that it, much like M. Sotah 3:4, describes a father as a teacher while simultaneously marginalizing his status as father by calling him an *ʾadam*. However, in contrast to M. Sotah 3:4, M. Sotah 9:14 depicts the father as teaching his son rather than his daughter, and Greek rather than Torah.

DISAPPEARING FEMALES AND THE FAMILY: BAVLI SOTAH 49B

When B. Sotah discusses this mishnah, it turns from a prohibition against teaching Greek language (*yevanit*) to a prohibition against teaching Greek wisdom (*hokhmat yevanit*). The prohibition against a father teaching his son Greek wisdom is unique to the Bavli and, in the case of B. Sotah, first appears in a baraita found on the final page of the tractate (B. Sotah 49b).[67] The baraita describes a siege during the Hasmonean civil war in which an informant's knowledge of Greek wisdom results in the desecration of Jerusalem by a pig and, as a result, a subsequent curse against both a man raising pigs and a man teaching his son Greek wisdom. Moulie Vidas has convincingly argued that this baraita and the Bavli's ensuing debate about it do not represent a theoretical discussion about the validity of the teaching and study of Greek wisdom.[68] Rather, noting the prominent place that the study of Greek philosophy in translation held in the Syriac curriculum, part of the larger cultural world in which the literature of the Bavli was embedded,[69] he contends that "Mesopotamian Jews, like their Christian neighbors, were debating the limits, value, and legitimacy of their engagement with Greek letters."[70] Vidas's assertion about this passage in B. Sotah is another instance of the current scholarly trend to view rabbinic literature's representation of the past not as historical record but as a reflection of contemporaneous cultural issues, struggles, and anxieties.[71] In this mode, we can also view B. Sotah's dialectical discussion of the baraita as an attempt to elevate a particular type of teaching—the rabbinic academy (*yeshivah* or *metivta*)—and to hide another type of teaching—familial teaching that occurs in the home.

B. Sotah's discussion of this baraita opens by questioning the validity of the baraita's claim of a prohibition against Greek wisdom. It cites a statement attributed to the patriarch Rabbi Yehudah ha-Nasi who, questioning the use of the Aramaic language (*leshon sursi*) in the land of Israel, instead encouraged the use of Hebrew or Greek. The Bavli rejects this objection by distinguishing between the study of Greek language and Greek wisdom: the former is permitted and the latter (mentioned in the baraita) is forbidden. Discontent with this resolution, B. Sotah questions whether the study of Greek wisdom is truly forbidden:

A. But is Greek wisdom forbidden?
B. Did not Rav Yehudah say in the name of Shmuel who said in the name of Rabban Shimon ben Gamliel: What is the meaning of that which is written, "My eyes have brought me grief over all the daughters of my city" [Lamentations 3:51]?
C. There were one thousand children in the house of my father [*be-veit ʾabba*]. Five hundred studied Torah and five hundred studied Greek wisdom. And only I and the son of my father's brother in Asia remain of them.
D. The house of Rabban Gamliel is different because they were close to the government.
E. As it is taught [in a baraita]: Trimming the front of the hair, this is of Amorite ways. They permitted Avtulus ben Reuven to trim the front of his hair because he was close to the government.
F. Those of the house of Rabban Gamliel they permitted Greek wisdom because they were close to the government.[72]

In questioning the prohibition against the study and teaching of Greek wisdom (A), this pericope portrays a golden age of rabbinic learning that existed prior to the destruction of Beitar during the Bar Kokhba rebellion,[73] in which the patriarch Rabban Gamliel headed an academy of a thousand students. Five hundred of these students studied Torah and five hundred studied Greek wisdom (B, C). The study of Greek wisdom on such a scale would indicate that, contrary to the baraita, its study is permitted. B. Sotah, however, rejects this claim by presenting yet another distinction: the house of Rabban Gamliel was exceptional because of its close political relationship with the government (D). It goes on to support this claim by citing an earlier tradition that permitted Avtulus ben Reuven to cut his hair in the style of a Roman haircut. Despite the violation of the prohibition against following in the foreign ways of the Amorites,[74] the rabbis permitted Avtulus ben Reuven to do so because of his close political relationship to the government (E).[75] The sugya concludes with the citation of a modified toseftan tradition (T. Sotah 9:15) that the learning of Greek wisdom was similarly permitted to the house of Rabban Gamliel because of their close relationship with the government; for others, by implication, Greek wisdom would be forbidden (F).

As Vidas has demonstrated, this depiction of a large academy in Beitar during the tannaitic period is a later editorial literary creation that retrojects the stammaitic academy onto the rabbinic past.[76] Study in the earlier tannaitic and amoraic periods likely took place primarily in smaller disciple circles that met within the physical space of households (*bei rav*).[77] In retrojecting the academy into the rabbinic past, this sugya thus elides earlier traditions that emphasize the ways in which learning took place in the more intimate space of the family. That is, M. Sotah 9:14 forbids a *father* teaching his *son* Greek language; in B. Sotah 49b, Rabban Shimon ben Gamliel describes the way in which his father taught *one thousand* students. Indeed, the toseftan version from which the sugya's final line (F) is derived emphasizes the paternal teaching of sons and not other students: "They permitted the House of Rabban Gamliel to teach their sons Greek as they were close to the rulers" (T. Sotah 15:8). This toseftan tradition imagines fathers teaching their sons Greek language because of their need to interact with the government; when B. Sotah includes and reshapes this tradition, it does not make explicit mention of fathers and sons. As Vidas writes about the larger sugya, "The exception allowed for a single family becomes a full-fledged program with hundreds of students; the practical study which accommodates political duties becomes something that can parallel Torah study."[78] Instead of the father primarily teaching his son as he does in the mishnah, the sugya depicts Rabban Shimon ben Gamliel as lauding his father for teaching Torah to a great number of unrelated students.

This move from family to academy is also gendered. In Lamentations 3:51, the verse that provides the exegetical anchor for this portion of the sugya (B), the poet laments the destruction of the daughters of Jerusalem. In the sugya, the daughters of Lamentations 3:51 become the thousand male students who once studied together in the school of Rabban Gamliel. This disappearance of daughters is similar to the disappearance of daughters in our earlier sugya on Torah study (B. Sotah 21a), where the Bavli concerns itself with the hierarchy of male Torah study versus male commandment performance.

The shift from family to academy in B. Sotah 49b is all the more striking in light of the Yerushalmi's earlier version of this passage, which does not mention the academy (Y. Sotah 9:14, 24c). Y. Sotah's version of the sugya instead emphasizes paternal teaching of Greek language, from fathers to sons and fathers to daughters.

A. They asked R. Yehoshua: What is the ruling [concerning whether] it is permissible for a father to teach his son Greek?
B. He said to them: Let him teach him at a time that is not day and not night. As it is written, "And you shall meditate on it [Torah] day and night" [Joshua 1:8].
C. From here it would be forbidden for a man to teach his son a profession because it is written, "And you shall meditate on it day and night."
D. But did not R. Ishmael teach, "And you shall choose life" [Deuteronomy 30:19]—this refers to a profession.
E. R. Ba the son of R. Hiyya bar Ba in the name of R. Yohanan: Because of informants [it is prohibited to teach Greek].
F. R. Abbahu in the name of R. Yohanan: It is permitted for a man [ʾ*adam*] to teach his daughter Greek because it is jewelry for her.
G. Shimon bar Ba heard and said: Because R. Abbahu wants to teach his daughter [Greek] he attributes this [statement] to Rabbi Yohanan?! Let [punishment] come upon me if I have heard this from R. Yohanan![79]

Contrasting the study of Greek language with Torah study, Y. Sotah builds its sugya around a tradition from T. Avodah Zarah 1:20 in which R. Yehoshua is asked whether it is permissible for a man to teach his son a Greek book (A). R. Yehoshua replies that the father, in keeping with Joshua 1:8 ("And you shall meditate on it [Torah] day and night"), should teach his son at a time that is "neither day nor night." The teaching of a Greek book is forbidden as it would conflict with the requirement for continuous Torah study (B). The Yerushalmi objects that if the ban on Greek were due to a conflict with the requirement for continuous Torah study, that requirement would make it impossible for a father to teach his son a trade (C), yet another mandate (D). Thus, the passage continues, the reason for the ban against the study of Greek cannot be ascribed to Joshua 1:8 and the conflict with Torah study. Instead it has a political basis, the need to prevent informants who could speak with the government in Greek (E). The passage concludes with a debate about whether a father is permitted to teach Greek to his daughter, with R. Yohanan permitting such a practice (F–G).[80]

Vidas observes that this Yerushalmi passage frames the ban against Greek as a pragmatic solution to a political problem. In so doing, it rejects the initially proposed cultural tension between Torah study and Greek. As a consequence, in cases where there is less political danger in the study of Greek—for example, with females—such an activity may "even be recommended."[81] Reading the Yerushalmi and Bavli passages through the lens of uncovering the differing cultural tensions between Torah and "foreign knowledge" is an important move. Yet, we need not overlook the ways in which this Yerushalmi sugya understands knowledge transmission as a relational act that occurs in the family. Whether it is Torah, a trade, or Greek, teaching happens between father and child. The isolation of Greek as the subject that a father may teach his daughter and the exclusion of Torah reinforces the idea of father-son Torah study as ritual, that is, a mode of study through which a father inducts his son into the covenantal community.

Much as B. Sotah suppresses familial learning in favor of the academy, for Y. Sotah, learning remains within the family. Indeed, the Yerushalmi sugya that immediately precedes the Greek-language sugya concerns itself with the family of R. Akiva. After defining the Mishnah's bridal crown as a city of gold (*ʿir shel zahav*), Y. Sotah (Y. Sotah 9:14, 24c) goes on to tell a story about the dedication of Rabbi Akiva's wife to her husband's learning Torah:

A. R. Akiva made for his wife a city of gold [*ʿir shel zahav*].
B. And the wife of Rabban Gamliel was jealous of her.
C. He [Rabban Gamliel] said to her [his wife]: If you had done that which she had done [I would also have made you one]. She sold the braids of her hair and gave him [the money] and he studied Torah.[82]

This passage idealizes the relationship of Rabbi Akiva and his wife. She is willing to sell her hair to enable her husband to study Torah; in return, he gifts her with a gold diadem.[83] Rabban Gamliel's wife, on the other hand, has not made a similar sacrifice. In contrast, when the Bavli similarly defines the bridal crown as a city of gold (B. Sotah 49b), it does not cite this tradition about R. Akiva and his wife. The Yerushalmi, by describing Greek learning as jewelry for the daughter, connects it with the jewelry with which R. Akiva gifts his wife.[84]

The literary arc of Y. Sotah in which learning remains in the family—the ideal wife provides financial support to her husband, fathers teach sons Torah and daughters Greek; much as the gift from husband to wife, the Greek that fathers teach daughters is jewelry—sharpens our ability to see the literary arc of B. Sotah. At the conclusion of B. Sotah, the mishnah's ban against a father teaching his son Greek and the Yerushalmi's possibility of a father teaching his daughter Greek has become a discussion of an imagined golden age of learning in the academy. Instead of the intimacy of any father teaching his son or daughter, B. Sotah laments the loss of the teaching of one father—the patriarch Rabban Gamliel—to a thousand male students.

CONCLUSION

Our tendency to conflate the development of the post-amoraic rabbinic academy with earlier study spaces and to center the homosocial space of the beit midrash has obscured the many different locations in which rabbinic learning occurred. In particular, it has obscured the learning that took place in the family—whether between mother and son, wife and husband, father and daughter, or father and son. Responsibility for this oversight should not be laid solely at the feet of modern scholarship.[85] B. Sotah itself engages in this obfuscation through its grammatical ambiguities and regendering of the sotah: Does the word "sons" refer to just sons or daughters too? What does it mean for mothers to "cause" their children to study? Will David's Torah study protect him from punishment for sexual transgression? Even more so, B. Sotah engages in this obfuscation through its literary arc—from beginning to middle to end of the tractate.

B. Sotah begins with a question about the content of rabbinic learning in general (why are the talmudic tractates in a particular order?), turns to learning in the family (may a father teach his daughter Torah?), and concludes with learning in the academy and an elegy of loss: of rabbinic leadership, wisdom, humility, and learning. This litany of loss foregrounds "great men" and a great academy. Whether this redactional ordering of the tractate was intentional or unintentional is not my concern here. Rather, I am interested in the fact that a reader of this tractate will experience this trajectory. In concluding with a memory of the golden age of the academy, B. Sotah's larger literary framework has become part of the process through which the family—mothers and daughters in particular—has become hidden from sight, marginalized in its contributions to the formation of rabbinic culture. By shifting our lens to notice what the literary arc of B. Sotah has obscured, we are better able to notice the ways in which women, as wives, mothers, and daughters, should be conceptualized as creators and transmitters of rabbinic culture.

CHAPTER FOUR
LANGUAGE AND NATIONAL CATASTROPHE

The previous chapter focused on the smaller unit of the biological family and Torah study. It argued that attention to the larger literary arc of B. Sotah enables us to notice the ways in which the tractate obscures mothers and daughters as transmitters of rabbinic culture. This chapter shifts its focus from the rabbinic family to the Jewish people writ large, and from Torah study to language use. Focusing primarily, but not only, on the depiction of spoken languages in the seventh chapter of B. Sotah, I argue that the attention the seventh chapter devotes to language—written, oral, and aural—results from the concern with language that permeates the sotah ritual itself. B. Sotah's extensive discussions of language do not simply stem from an associative tie to the Mishnah's declaration that the portion of the sotah may be recited in any language (M. Sotah 7:1). Rather, as the sotah ritual prescribes and necessitates the use of written, spoken, heard, and consumed language, B. Sotah's attention to language should be viewed as an example of the ways in which the sotah ritual overflows the boundaries of the ritual itself to inform a range of seemingly tangential topics. The intertwining of language's ability to construct power, authority, and relationship within the sotah ritual shapes B. Sotah's concern with what language comes out of a person or divine being's mouth, what people or divine beings hear, *and* what those words accomplish.

I contend that the seventh chapter of B. Sotah portrays language in two ways: first, as a vehicle for knowledge transmission and reception (between people and between the divine realm and the human); and second, as a medium for building or destroying human society. In the former case, B. Sotah explores which language should be spoken, whether *leshon ha-kodesh* (Hebrew)[1] or *leshonam* (their language).

In the latter, B. Sotah uses *lashon ha-ra* (slander) to examine how language is utilized and what words accomplish, regardless of which language (or tongue) is spoken. Language becomes a mode through which to negotiate difference, show fealty to Israel's God, resist empire, and internalize rabbinic ideologies. Rather than focusing on individual sin and the construction of the moral man, B. Sotah here shifts its emphasis to national sin and the righteous nation. The sinning man becomes the sinning nation and the moral man the righteous nation. As the sotah ritual overflows its bounds and intersects with these discussions, the sotah herself—appearing and disappearing—becomes a way to think about and with rabbinic concerns and rabbinic rituals rather than those of the priestly Jerusalem Temple. To explore these claims, this chapter turns, yet again, to the biblical sotah ritual, then to certain mishnaic precedents, and finally to three passages within B. Sotah. The first of these passages focuses directly on the sotah ritual (B. Sotah 32b), the second on the wilderness spies (B. Sotah 34b–35a), and the third on Joseph's name (B. Sotah 36b).

SPEAKING THE SOTAH RITUAL: BIBLICAL AND MISHNAIC ANTECEDENTS

While my earlier treatment of the sotah ritual emphasized the transition from private ritual (biblical) to public spectacle (mishnaic), and then B. Sotah's concomitant retreat from that spectacle, I turn here to another crucial component of the ritual—language. As we have seen, the biblical ritual describes the priest's recitation of an imprecation to the woman, the woman's response, the priest's writing and erasing of the imprecation in the bitter waters, and the woman's drinking of these bitter waters.[2] In this process, language is oral (the priest recites a curse; the woman responds "amen, amen"),[3] aural (the woman hears the curse; the priest hears the woman respond "amen, amen"), written (the priest writes the curse), and consumed (the woman drinks the waters). Echoing the prophet Ezekiel's consumption of a divine scroll (Ezekiel 3:1–3), the woman's physical consumption of these textualized waters[4] not only tests her innocence or guilt but also signals the successful transmission of the ritual between priest and woman.[5]

Following in these biblical footsteps, even before its mention of ritual language in the seventh chapter, M. Sotah is replete with references to language use. Some specify the legal contours of the sotah ritual itself while others shift focus to related cultural concerns. Although M. Sotah surely discusses the writing and erasure of the sotah portion (M. Sotah 2:3–5),[6] the verbal root *ʾ.m.r.* (speak, say) also threads its way through the tractate, a subtler way that M. Sotah indicates its concern with language use.[7]

M. Sotah's interest in speech begins at its very opening, where it presents a debate about the number of witnesses in front of whom the husband must warn his wife (M. Sotah 1:1) and then legislates the words the husband must utilize to initiate the legal procedure of the sotah ritual: "How does he warn her? He says to her [*ʾamar lah*] before two [witnesses]: 'Do not speak with this man'" (M. Sotah 1:2).[8] Speech also proves crucial to a woman's self-incrimination: a woman who states that she is impure as a result of sexual intercourse with another man ("a woman who says: 'I am impure for you'") or who states that she refuses to drink ("and a woman who says: 'I refuse to drink'") is, if she is married to a member of the priestly class, forbidden to eat *terumah*, the tithe reserved for priests (M. Sotah 1:3).[9] Conversely, a woman who states she is pure ("if she says: 'I am pure'") is forced to drink the bitter waters (M. Sotah 1:5). Women's speech may even be used to incriminate another woman: R. Yehoshua considers the gossip of spinning women to be sufficient evidence of a woman's seclusion with the forbidden man to require the husband to divorce the secluding woman/wife and provide her with her *ketubah* payment (M. Sotah 6:1).[10] In addition, M. Sotah infers speech when it discusses whether a father may teach his daughter Torah (M. Sotah 3:4), when it prohibits a father teaching his son Greek language (M. Sotah 9:17), and, crucially, when it mentions R. Shimon's contention that merit does not delay punishment (M. Sotah 3:5). Merit delaying punishment would result in aspersions (*motzi sheim ra*) being cast even on pure women who have undergone the ritual (*ha-tehorot she-shatu*). Finally, much as M. Sotah opens with speech, it also concludes its focus on the sotah ritual with a passage about speech. Replete with the verb *ʾ.m.r.*, the final mishnah in the sixth chapter of M. Sotah (6:5) legislates cases of contradictory witness testimonies—male and female—concerning whether the woman did, in fact, seclude herself with the forbidden man.[11] This pericope functions as a bridge between the mishnah's discussion of the sotah ritual and the discussion that follows in M. Sotah's seventh chapter of those rituals that may be recited in any language and those that must be recited in Hebrew.

M. Sotah 7:1–2 lists a series of fifteen rituals, seven of which may be recited in "their tongue"—that is, any language—and eight of which must be recited in the "holy tongue"—that is, Hebrew.[12] Fittingly for this mishnah's location in tractate Sotah, the sotah ritual is mentioned first. It is included in the list of rituals that may be recited in any language:

> A. These are said in their tongue [*ʾeilu neʾemarim bilshonam*]:[13] the portion of the sotah, the tithe confession, the recitation of the shema, prayer [*tefilah*], grace after meals, the oath of the witnesses, and the oath of deposit.[14]
> B. And these are said in the holy tongue [*ʾeilu neʾemarim bilshon ha-kodesh*]: the recitation of the first fruits, release from levirate marriage [*halitzah*], blessings and curses, the priestly blessing, the blessings of the high priest,[15] the portion of the king,[16] the portion of the decapitated heifer [*ʿeglah ʿarufah*],[17] and the one anointed for war at the time he speaks to the people.[18]

While the mentions of speech, ritual language, and procedure in the seventh chapter of M. Sotah surely provide some of the foundation for B. Sotah's discussion, they do not adequately explain its discourse. As we will see, when B. Sotah elucidates these mishnayot, and the mishnayot that follow them, the concerns of speech, knowledge transmission, and authority that permeate the sotah ritual in its biblical and mishnaic forms will combine with B. Sotah's more expansive notion of sin. B. Sotah's concerns with individual wrongdoing—male and female—will become concerns about national wrongdoing, again writ through the lens of speech gone wrong.[19]

FOREIGN LANGUAGES, SPEECH GONE WRONG, AND INSTRUCTING THE SOTAH: BAVLI SOTAH 32B

As we have seen, the sotah ritual becomes a locus for debates about the teaching and transmission of Torah by and to females and the teaching and transmission of Greek language/Greek wisdom by and to sons and daughters. When B. Sotah 32b provides an explanation for the permission M. Sotah 7:1 grants the priest to conduct the sotah ritual in any language, it includes a rewritten toseftan baraita (T. Sotah 2:1).[20] Fittingly, the Bavli's rewritten version links teaching, female behavior, foreign languages, and gossip. The subtle changes that B. Sotah introduces to the toseftan baraita begin to move us from the particulars of the accused sotah toward the larger nation of Israel. These changes shift subjectivity from the accused woman to the bitter waters. They also begin to connect the sotah ritual to languages of instruction and to speech gone wrong on the national level.

Evil Talk: Bavli Sotah 32b

A. Our rabbis taught [in a baraita]: One announces[21] to her in whatever language that she understands why she drinks and how she drinks, why she is impure and how she became impure.

B. Why she drinks?—concerning matters of warning and hiding [*kinui u-setirah*]. How she drinks?—from a piece of an earthen vessel. Why is she impure?—concerning matters of laughter and childishness [*yaldut*].[22] And how does she become impure?—unintentionally or intentionally, through compulsion or willfully.

C. And all of this why? In order not to bring forth evil talk [*le-hotzi la ʿaz*] concerning the bitter waters.

While the toseftan version of the baraita similarly declares the necessity for the woman to understand why she drinks, how she drinks, why she is impure, and how she became impure (A),[23] B. Sotah expands the baraita in two important ways. It broadens the field of the priest's instruction to include details of the circumstances under which the waters are efficacious (B) and provides a reason for this broader instruction: to prevent the bringing forth of evil talk (*le-hotzi la ʿaz*) concerning the bitter waters (C).[24] If drinking the bitter waters does not result in the expected punishment, the accused sotah—and perhaps the larger audience as well[25]—is instructed not to attribute this lack of punishment to the bitter waters' malfunction. Rather, the sotah's particular sexual transgression lies outside the boundaries of those transgressions tested and punished by the waters.[26]

The phrase *le-hotzi la ʿaz* likely has mishnaic precedent. When R. Shimon declares that merit does not delay punishment, he reasons this would result in a "bad name" (*u-motzi ʾatah sheim ra*), that is, rumors of presumed guilt, for innocent women (M. Sotah 3:5).[27] Thus, similar to questions about merit delaying punishment (M. Sotah 3:5), the Bavli baraita emphasizes linguistic aspersions.[28] In this case, though, the baraita shifts its emphasis from aspersions on innocent women to aspersions on the bitter waters.

The phrase "to bring forth evil talk" (*le-hotzi la'az*) occurs a total of four times in B. Sotah. The first three occurrences are found in regard to the bitter waters (B. Sotah 9b, 28a, 32b) and the last in regard to the Torah scroll (B. Sotah 41a).[29] In the first three instances, the phrase evinces a concern for correct knowledge of the bitter waters' workings. However, on B. Sotah 9b and 28a, correct knowledge refers to a more limited context than in the passage cited above. In these two instances, correct knowledge refers to the priest instructing the woman about the order in which the waters will affect her body—first the thigh and then the belly.[30]

In contrast to these passages, the sugya found on B. Sotah 41a turns to the public reading of the Torah scroll by the high priest on Yom Kippur, a ritual depicted in M. Sotah 7:9.[31] The mishnah instructs the high priest that, after reading the two required portions from the book of Leviticus (16:1–34; 23:26–32), he roll the Torah scroll, place it on his lap, and then state, "More than I have read before you is written here."[32] B. Sotah 41a explains the necessity of this procedure with the words, "so as not to bring forth evil talk upon the Torah scroll [*she-lo le-hotzi la'az 'al sefer torah*]."[33] In this case, the priest's words are meant to protect the sanctity of the Torah scroll rather than the sanctity of the bitter waters. Instead of the woman, or the larger community, misunderstanding the workings of the bitter waters, here the priest tries to protect the community from a mistaken understanding of the contents of the Torah scroll.

Given the textualized nature of the sotah ritual, it is fitting that the phrase *le-hotzi la'az* appears in both the context of the bitter waters and the Torah scroll. Sarit Kattan Gribetz observes that the mishnaic debate over whether females can study Torah is embedded within a passage that depicts the accused sotah's consumption of the textualized waters.[34] Similarly, when B. Sotah interrogates whether the merit of Torah study or of commandment performance protects a person (discussed in the previous chapter), it also explores which kinds of ink may be used to write entire Torah scrolls, which to use in the sotah portion within those scrolls, and how to transmit this knowledge about ink from one sage to another (B. Sotah 20a–b). B. Sotah connects its expanded discussion of merit and Torah study to the production of Torah scrolls in their entirety and the sotah scroll in particular.

The multiple appearances of the phrase *le-hotzi laʿaz* in B. Sotah thus connect the waters of the sotah ritual to debates about female Torah study, rumors about innocent individuals, and rumors about the Torah scroll itself. Crucially, as the semantic range of the noun *laʿaz* includes foreign languages and evil talk,[35] the phrase *le-hotzi laʿaz* surely links the sotah ritual to the study of the Greek language and to national questions of speech gone wrong. The sotah ritual threads its way through this tractate's discussions of language, Israel, and foreign empires.[36]

LASHON HA-RA: NATIONAL SPEECH GONE AWRY (BAVLI SOTAH 34B–35A)

B. Sotah 34b–35a retells the biblical story of the twelve spies sent out to scout the land of Canaan in advance of Israel's entry and who, with the exception of Joshua and Caleb, return with evil reports about the land (Numbers 13–14). Numbers 13:32 and 13:37 describe the spies' speech as *dibat ha-ʾaretz* (evil reports about the land). B. Sotah, following in the footsteps of M. Arakhin 3:6,[37] recasts *dibat ha-ʾaretz* as *lashon ha-ra* (evil tongue/language).[38] In so doing, B. Sotah adds a third type of speech—*lashon ha-ra*—to the two already mentioned in M. Sotah 7:1–2—*leshonam* and *leshon ha-kodesh*. While the use of the word *lashon* (tongue or language) marks these three languages as overlapping, the phrase *lashon ha-ra* diverges from its mishnaic predecessors in its emphasis on the content of that speech—the misuse of language—rather than the language in which that speech is said.[39] *Lashon ha-ra* is a "tongue" that has gone wrong regardless of the language spoken. In B. Sotah 34b–35a, evil speech about the bitter waters becomes evil speech uttered by the desert spies. Much as the sotah's punishment manifests in the brutal disfiguration of her body, the spies' punishment will manifest in the brutal disfiguration of their bodies and even in the bodily punishment of the entire nation. Reversing the erasure of God's name in the sotah ritual, the ability of Caleb and Joshua to resist the evil speech of the spies will result in God's name being encoded in these men's names. Themes of the sotah ritual will weave their way throughout B. Sotah's retelling of misused—and properly used—language in the spies episode.

B. Sotah retells the spies episode as part of an extensive exegetical passage found on B. Sotah 33b–37a. This lengthy passage expounds[40]

M. Sotah 7:4–7's description of the covenantal ceremony Israel must conduct upon crossing the Jordan and entering the land of Canaan (Deuteronomy 27).[41] The mishnaic version of the ceremony includes the recitation of blessings and curses on Mount Gerizim and Mount Ebal,[42] the erection of stones into an altar,[43] and the inscription of the Torah in seventy languages upon that altar.[44] The Bavli's long exegetical narrative is threaded throughout with references to the sotah. The ark of the covenant containing some part of the written biblical revelation passing through the overflowing Jordan represents yet another form of textualized waters (B. Sotah 33b–34a);[45] Joseph, tempted by and resisting the temptation of Potiphar's wife (to be discussed later) is imagined as a partial sotah (B. Sotah 36b); and the blessings and curses are said in reference to male and female adulterers (B. Sotah 37b).[46]

The literary link that B. Sotah makes between the spies and the covenantal ceremony is not original to this tractate. Rather, T. Sotah 8:6 — a passage that B. Sotah will integrate, reshape, and comment upon — first proposes the extrapolation from the weight of the covenantal stones to the weight of the grape cluster carried by the spies (Numbers 13:23).[47] When B. Sotah 34a comments on this earlier tradition, it introduces an amoraic tradition that only ten of the twelve spies carried produce out of the land of Canaan;[48] Joshua and Caleb did not carry anything. B. Sotah's anonymous voice suggests two reasons for this privileging of Joshua and Caleb: first, they were more important, and, second, they did not participate in the advice or counsel of the spies (*she-lo hayu be-ʾotah ʿeitzah*). Although T. Sotah provides the textual impetus for the link between covenantal ceremony and spies episode, B. Sotah's narrative about the spies turns the conversation toward speech gone wrong.

Bavli Sotah 34b–35a: From Names to Lashon Ha-Ra

B. Sotah next mentions counsel gone wrong (*ʿeitzah*) when it cites an amoraic tradition that details how Caleb and Joshua successfully resisted the words of the spies. This section of the spies narrative introduces us to names as symbolizing resistance to misleading speech.

A. "They went up to the Negev and he came to Hebron" [Numbers 13:22].

B. "They came" it should have said.

C. Said Rava:[49] It teaches that Caleb separated himself from counsel/advice of the spies [*'atzat meragelim*][50] and went and prostrated himself on the graves of the patriarchs. He said to them: "My fathers, plead for mercy for me that I be saved from counsel/advice of the spies [*'atzat meragelim*]."

D. Moses had already pleaded for mercy on behalf of Joshua, as it says: "And Moses called Hoshea the son of Nun Yehoshua" [Numbers 13:16]—May Yah save you from counsel/advice of the spies [*'atzat meragelim*].[51]

E. And this is what is written: "And my servant Caleb, because he was imbued with a different spirit [and remained loyal to Me—him I will bring into the land that he entered, and his offspring shall hold it as a possession]" [Numbers 14:24].

Turning on a seeming grammatical paradox in Numbers 13:22 (the use of the plural verb phrase "they went up" followed by the singular verb phrase "he came"), B. Sotah proposes that Caleb separated himself from the larger group and journeyed to Hebron, the burial place of the patriarchs, where he pleaded for their help in resisting the words of the spies (A–C). Joshua, on the other hand, had already been saved from the counsel of the spies through Moses's intercession. Adding the divine name *yah* to Joshua's original name (*hoshea* becomes *yehoshua*), Moses intervenes on Joshua's behalf. He encodes within Joshua's name a plea that God prevent his succumbing to the spies' words (D). This passage concludes with a verse that confirms Caleb's successful resistance to the spies and his subsequent reward of entrance to the land of Israel (E).

B. Sotah makes a similar move earlier in the tractate when it explains the name Caleb the son of Yefuneh (*kaleiv ben yefuneh*; Numbers 13:6). Playing on the root *p.n.y.* (to turn), Caleb is a son who "turned aside" from the counsel of the spies (B. Sotah 11b). In B. Sotah, names are a type of language that signals attunement to misleading speech and a hope for the ability to resist that misleading speech. Names also come to represent the power of the colonized to resist empire. In the case of Joshua, the addition of the divine name to *hoshea* mirrors the erasure of scriptural text—including God's name—that occurs within the sotah ritual. We may thus view the language of the spies as a counterpart to the use of language in the sotah ritual but now reimagined as a nation gone wrong rather than an individual.

Within this framework of men who must plead to be saved from evil speech, the appearance of Rahav the Prostitute (*rahav ha-zonah*)[52] in a baraita found earlier in this same exegetical passage is particularly noteworthy. Speaking to another set of spies, those whom Joshua sent to reconnoiter Jericho (Joshua 2), Rahav the Prostitute informs them of God's power to dry up the Reed Sea and the Canaanites' subsequent fear of Israel's one God (B. Sotah 34a). Since the toseftan version of this baraita (T. Sotah 8:4) does not include the descriptor "the prostitute" (*ha-zonah*), B. Sotah's addition of this word simultaneously renders Rahav as overlapping with the sinning sotah and aligns her with Caleb and Joshua. However, in contrast to Caleb and Joshua, Rahav does not need immediate intercession to resist the speech of her king and articulate God's power. Rather than turn over the spies, she hides them, enabling them to complete their mission successfully and thus become instrumental to Joshua's successful invasion of Canaan. The straightforwardness of Rahav's speech contrasts with the Bavli's portrayals of the spies' more convoluted speech as well as the difficulties that Caleb and Joshua have in convincing the people to ignore the spies' counsel. In the former, as we will see, B. Sotah overlays the drama with a pedagogical principle about *lashon ha-ra*. In the latter, it points us back to the sotah ritual.

In explaining why the spies begin their report by praising the land ("it does indeed flow with milk and honey"; Numbers 13:27) and only then turn to the overwhelming power of its inhabitants and cities ("the people who inhabit the country are powerful, and the cities are fortified and very large"; Numbers 13:28), B. Sotah introduces an aphorism that utilizes the terminology *lashon ha-ra*: "Said R. Yohanan [a mnemonic: truth, alone, borrowing][53] in the name of R. Meir: Any evil tongue [*lashon ha-ra*] that does not have a matter of truth at its beginning will not endure at its end."[54] Much as B. Sotah signaled at its beginning how a man might distance himself from sexual sin by abstaining from wine, here R. Yohanan implicitly signals how a man might protect himself against sin caused by speech through awareness of a "kernel of truth" located even in *lashon ha-ra*.

As B. Sotah addresses the implicit question of why the Torah describes only Caleb (and not Joshua) as attempting to quiet the rebellious people (Numbers 13:30), it overlays the scene with the sotah ritual:

A. "And Caleb quieted the people before Moses" [Numbers 13:30].
B. Said Rabbah: [He quieted them] because he incited them with words [*she-hesitan bi-dvarim*].
C. Joshua began and as he was speaking, they [the people] said to him: Does this cut-off head speak?!
D. He [Caleb] said:[55] If I speak, they will say a matter about me and silence me.
E. He [Caleb] said to them [the people]: And this alone did the son of Amram do to us?!
F. They thought he was saying something to his disgrace. They were quiet.
G. He [Caleb] said to them: He took us out of Egypt and parted the sea for us and fed us manna.[56] If he were to say, "Make ladders and go up to the firmament, would we not listen to him?!" "We shall surely go up and gain possession of her [the land]" [Numbers 13:30], etc.

In B. Sotah's retelling, Caleb must quiet the people because he first incited them with words (*she-hesitan bi-dvarim*) that could be understood as derogatory to Moses (A–B, D–F). In turn, Joshua cannot speak because the people interrupt him (C). Although the grammatical root of the word "incite" differs from that of "sotah" (*s.w.t.* vs. *s.t.y.*), Rabbah's explanation of why Caleb had to quiet the people would nevertheless have been heard as overlapping with and signaling the sotah (*hesitan* and *sotah*). Two eleventh-century medieval interpretations of the people's scornful and singular remark[57] to Joshua—"Does this cut-off head speak?!"—further point us toward the sotah ritual and the guilty sotah's punishment. For Natan ben Yehiel, "cut-off head" describes the spelling of Joshua's name: the first letter, *yod*, is a letter whose tail is cut off (shorter than that of the letter *vav*).[58] For Rashi, "cut-off head" indicates Joshua's childlessness: he does not have offspring who will inherit the land of Israel.[59] Natan ben Yehiel's interpretation (a cut-off letter) intertwines Joshua with the erasure of the sotah excerpt; Rashi's interpretation (childlessness) intertwines Joshua with the guilty sotah's miscarriage.

As B. Sotah continues on its exegetical way, it underscores the ways in which the spies' words ultimately lead the people to communal catastrophe. The spies pronounce that God lacks the power to eject his "possessions" from the land of Canaan;[60] witnessing the death of an important person in each place they arrive, the spies—unable or unwilling to notice that God has caused those deaths in order to ease their travel—declare the land a deadly place that consumes its inhabitants.[61] As a measure-for-measure response to the spies' collective distortions of language, God ordains the future destructions of the Jerusalem Temple on the ninth of Av, the same day on which the spies brought back their report of Canaan:

A. "And the whole community broke into loud cries, and they wept [that night]" [Numbers 14:1].
B. Said Rabbah in the name of R. Yohanan: That day was the [eve] of the ninth of Av.[62] Said the Holy Blessed One: "They wept for no purpose, so I will establish weeping for them for the generations."

Heightening the drama, when Joshua and Caleb try, yet again, to convince the people to ignore the other spies and the people exclaim that they should stone Caleb and Joshua (Numbers 14:10), B. Sotah depicts the people as throwing stones toward heaven. In contrast to M. Sotah's directive to inscribe stones with the words of Torah in multiple languages (7:7), these stones symbolize the ways in which *lashon ha-ra* results in the radical failure of covenant.

Connecting the transgression of *lashon ha-ra* directly to the sotah's transgression, the Bavli now depicts the spies dying by the medium through which they sinned. Much as M. Sotah describes the sotah's punishment as manifesting in the limbs with which she sinned (her belly distends, her thigh falls, and she eventually dies), so too, the spies die by the medium with which they sinned—their mouths:

A. "The men died in a plague, those who brought forth evil reports about the land" [Numbers 14:37].
B. Said Rabbi Shimon ben Lakish:[63] That they died a strange death.
C. Said R. Hanina bar Pappa:[64] Expounded R. Shila a man from the village of Temarta: This teaches that their tongues were prolonged so as to reach down to their navels. And worms would come out of their tongues and enter their navels. And from their navels they would enter their tongues.

D. And Rav Nahman bar Yitzhak[65] said: They died of croup/ choking.

In these three amoraic traditions, the spies suffer either an unusual death (B), a gruesome death in which their tongues extend and worms travel from tongue to navel and then back again (C), or a death from choking (D). The punishment—and even eventual death—of the woman guilty of sexual transgression against her husband becomes the particular punishment of the spies for their transgressions against God. Indeed, as we have seen, the Bavli subjects the entire nation to punishment with the ninth of Av.

Yerushalmi Taʿanit and Bavli Sotah's Project

B. Sotah's positioning of this section of the sugya as a response to language gone wrong contrasts with its appearance in Y. Taʿanit 4:6 (8), 68d. Y. Taʿanit does overlap with B. Sotah in its citation of Numbers 14:1 and in God's promise of punishment through the future destruction of the Temple. Yet the differences between the two tractates are instructive. Y. Taʿanit cites the passage in a mathematical context, calculating how the ninth of Av was, in fact, the date on which the spies returned from their mission. The spies return to find Moses and Aaron occupied with the laws of *hallah* (the portion to be separated from dough) and *ʿorlah* (fruits in their first four years), both of which would take effect only upon entry to Canaan.[66] Much as in B. Sotah, the community[67] responds by weeping, and God responds by punishing them with the destruction of the Temples. However, the precise wording of God's chastisement in Y. Taʿanit differs from that found in B. Sotah: "He [God] said to them: You have wept before me a licentious weeping [*bekhiyah she-le-tiflut*]. By my life, in the future you will weep a weeping of substance [*bekhiyah she-le-mamash*]." The word *tiflut* echoes M. Sotah 3:4 and R. Eliezer's prohibition against a father teaching his daughter Torah.[68] B. Sotah 35a does not utilize the word *tiflut*, signaling once again its retreat from female sexual sin and its shift to a nation gone wrong for other reasons. Although images of the sotah do shape B. Sotah's retelling of the spies narrative, the sotah and her sexual sin are not responsible for Israel's punishment. One may even read Y. Taʿanit as mapping the sin of human adultery onto Israel's rejection of God through the spies. The absence of the word *tiflut* from B. Sotah's account thus dovetails with the way in which B. Sotah does not think together with the golden calf episode and the sotah. The sotah's adultery as paralleling Israel's apostasy with the golden calf is remarkably absent from B. Sotah.

Further highlighting B. Sotah's particular intertwining of the spies story, language gone wrong, national catastrophe, and the sotah ritual, Y. Taʿanit 4:6 (8), 68d—as well as the similar sugyot found on B. Taʿanit 29a and B. Sanhedrin 104b—do not narrate the spies' gruesome deaths. And although Y. Sotah 7:5, 21d, does abstract from the weight of the covenantal stones to the weight of the grape cluster as well as interrogate how the spies carried that cluster, it does not turn to speech gone wrong or to the resistance of Joshua and Caleb to that speech. Even the extended passage on *lashon ha-ra* in B. Arakhin 15a–17a, while it begins with the spies, soon turns to exhortations cautioning the individual—rather than the nation—against the dire sinfulness of *lashon ha-ra*.[69] The translation of the sotah ritual into the communal catastrophe caused by the sin of *lashon ha-ra*—uttered by the spies and accepted by the nation—thus should best be viewed as a particular project of B. Sotah.

JOSEPH, THE PARTIAL SOTAH AND *LESHON HA-KODESH*: BAVLI SOTAH 36B

B. Sotah envisions names as language that signals attunement to speech gone wrong and hope for the ability to resist that speech. In the case of Caleb and Joshua, their names signal their willingness to obey God's command to invade and conquer Canaan. The extended exegetical passage that explicates the story of the spies and includes an explanation for Joshua's name also explicates part of the story of the biblical Joseph. As it does so, this passage includes three different explanations for Joseph's name. Like Joshua, B. Sotah 36b reads God's name into Joseph's name.[70] Yet unlike Joshua, B. Sotah positions Joseph as a partial sotah, intertwining his name with the sotah ritual through sexual sin and the erasure and writing of Torah. Simultaneously, Joseph's ability to resist sexual temptation and to learn *leshon ha-kodesh*, Hebrew as the holy tongue, will result in an imagining of communal power rather than the communal catastrophe caused by *lashon ha-ra*. Instead of signaling transmission of content knowledge, as does "their tongues" in the inscription of Torah and in the priest's explanation of the sotah ritual, mastery of *leshon ha-kodesh* signals the hierarchical status of Israel above other nations. When taken together, the different explanations for Joseph's name suggest the possibility of the colonized to resist foreign cultures and empire through *leshon ha-kodesh*.[71]

B. Sotah's mention of Joseph grows out of M. Sotah 7:4–7's description of the deuteronomic ritual of reciting blessings and curses on Mount Gerizim and Mount Ebal (Deuteronomy 27). The ritual requires six tribes to stand on Mount Gerizim—Joseph among them—and six on Mount Ebal (Deuteronomy 27:12–13). While M. Sotah lists the blessings and curses as one of the rituals that must be recited in *leshon ha-kodesh*, it does not provide a biblical proof text for why the blessings and curses must be recited in *leshon ha-kodesh*.[72] Instead of focusing on *leshon ha-kodesh*, M. Sotah portrays seventy languages as a key to understanding God's Torah: "And afterwards they brought the stones and they built the altar and they coated them with plaster and they wrote upon them all the words of this Torah in seventy languages. As it is said, 'very clearly [*ba'eir heiteiv*]' [Deuteronomy 27:8]" (M. Sotah 7:7).

The shift from the scriptural writing in one language to the mishnaic seventy stems from M. Sotah's understanding of the words *ba'eir heiteiv* in their post-biblical sense of "to interpret" or "to expound" rather than their biblical meaning of clear physical writing.[73] This mishnaic pericope constructs language's function as transmitting information about the revelation of God and Israel's Torah to all humanity, a process that requires seventy languages rather than just one, *leshon ha-kodesh*. In Steven Fraade's words, "To fully comprehend the written record of revelation, in a sense to penetrate its seemingly monolingual writing, requires retroverting it to the fullness of the seventy languages in which it was originally heard by Israel, that is, to the totality of human language."[74] The stories of Joseph's name, though, will retreat from these seventy languages. They will turn us back to one language, exalting *leshon ha-kodesh* above all other tongues.

Joseph's Name Part 1: Maternal Displacement and the Priestly Garments (Bavli Sotah 36b)

Most commonly in the Hebrew Bible, Joseph's name is spelled *yoseif*. However, Psalms 81:6 also records a spelling of his name as *yehoseif*, that is with the addition of the letter *heh* after the initial letter *yod* ("He appointed it as testimony upon *yehoseif* when He went forth against the land of Egypt; I heard a language that I knew not.") B. Sotah explicates this unique spelling of Joseph's name in four different amoraic traditions. Three of these are found on B. Sotah 36b.[75] The first tradition accounts for the addition of the extra letter as a way of arriving at a total of fifty letters engraved on the shoulder epaulets of the high priest's mantle (*ʾeifod*); the second tradition accounts for the extra letter by referencing Joseph's near miss with sexual sin; the third does so by narrating Joseph's learning of *leshon ha-kodesh*.[76] The location of these three traditions within proximity to one another and as part of a longer passage that also discusses *lashon ha-ra* signals B. Sotah's interest in language as a device through which Israel may "go right" or "go wrong." The use of Joseph as a model for learning *leshon ha-kodesh* is particularly ironic and, in a tractate full of mirroring, also appropriate. Joseph —similar to the spies with the land of Canaan—brings evil reports of his brothers (*dibatam raʿah*) to his father Jacob (Genesis 37:2).[77]

A baraita on B. Sotah 36a–36b depicts the two precious stones worn on the shoulder piece of the high priest's mantle, each engraved with the names of six of the Israelite tribes, with twenty-five letters on each stone for a total of fifty letters. The Bavli's anonymous voice questions the number fifty, remarking that the letters in fact total forty-nine (A):

A. These fifty letters [on the *ʾeifod*]—they are fifty deducting one!
B. Said R. Yitzhak: Joseph, they added one letter [to his name], as it says: "He appointed it as testimony upon *yehoseif* when He went forth against the land of Egypt; [I heard a language that I knew not]" [Psalms 81:6].
C. Rav Nahman bar Yitzhak attacked it: We require [names to be written] "according to their birth" [*ke-toledotam*; Exodus 28:10]. Rather, in the entire Torah *BNYMN* is written, and here *BNYMYN* in its complete form [with the letter *yod* after the letter *mem*]. As it is written, "And his father called him *binyamin*" [Genesis 35:18].

R. Yitzhak proposes solving the problematic calculation through Joseph's rewritten name, with the addition of the letter *heh* (B). Rav Nahman bar Yitzhak rejects this suggestion, instead contending that Benjamin's name solves the numerical conundrum. Rather than following a later change of name through an act of God, as is the case with Joseph, we should utilize names as they were given at the time of a person's birth (*ke-toledotam*). When Jacob named Benjamin, he called him *binyamin*, with the addition of the letter *yod* (C).

The two biblical proof texts for these competing positions (Psalms 81:6 and Genesis 35:18) subtly participate in an easily overlooked act of maternal effacement. Rachel, mother of both Joseph and Benjamin, is the original name-giver for her sons: respectively, *yoseif* (Genesis 30:24) and *ben ʾoni* (Genesis 35:18).[78] The name *binyamin* thus results from a name change much as does *yehoseif*, although here enacted as a paternal displacement done by the father rather than by the male God. Erasure of Torah as a response to sexual sin in the priestly sotah ritual mirrors the erasure of Rachel's two acts of maternal naming in an effort to properly create the masculine priestly garments.

Joseph's Name Part 2: Resisting Sexual Sin and Cultural Domination (Bavli Sotah 36b)

The second explanation for Joseph's name alludes to the biblical encounter between Joseph and Potiphar's wife (Genesis 39:7–20), a tale that, in its rabbinic expansions, has received considerable scholarly attention.[79] In brief, the biblical tale depicts Potiphar's wife as repeatedly asking Joseph, a servant to her husband, to lie with her. On a certain day, with no one else of the household present, she grabs Joseph by his garment and again makes her request. Joseph flees outside, leaving his garment in her hand. Potiphar's wife shows the garment to her servants, declaring that Joseph came to lie with her and that she screamed. The episode results in Potiphar's imprisonment of Joseph. Situating B. Sotah's expansion of the tale within the context of Greek romances and the adultery mime, Joshua Levinson demonstrates that these Greco-Roman intertexts contribute to the positioning of Potiphar's foreign wife "as wanton and wild" and "as a synecdoche for the seductive and dangerous character of foreign culture as a whole."[80]

Levinson's analysis of the seduction scene begins, as do those of other scholars,[81] with B. Sotah's exegesis of Genesis 39:11 ("One such day, he came into the house to do his work"). Shifting focus from the Greco-Roman literary context to the context of the tractate and beginning analysis a step earlier—with the second explanation for the name *yehoseif*—enables us to highlight the ways in which motifs of name changes and the sotah intertwine with one another in B. Sotah's retelling of the Joseph story. This intertwining of names with the sotah ritual renders *leshon ha-kodesh* a potent form of cultural resistance.

B. Sotah explains the addition of the letter *heh* from God's name to Joseph's name as a response to a private act of divine sanctification (A–B). It also compares Joseph's actions to those of Yehudah's public confession to Tamar's pregnancy (Genesis 38:6) (C). In so doing, B. Sotah positions Joseph—although unmarried—as a potential sotah vulnerable to sexual sin:

A. Said Rav Hanna bar Bizna in the name of R. Shimon Hasida:
B. Joseph who sanctified the name of heaven in private [*ba-seiter*], they added to his [name] one letter from the name of the Holy Blessed One.[82]
C. Yehudah, who sanctified the name of heaven in public, his whole [name] is called by the name of the Holy Blessed One.

This pericope's use of the root *s.t.r.* to depict where Joseph sanctifies God's name—in Potiphar's home—echoes the sotah's forbidden act of seclusion and the husband's required warning against this seclusion (*setirah*).[83] Here, though, rather than the female sotah going to seclude herself with the male, the male Joseph enters the female's home. Unlike pre-rabbinic, as well as certain rabbinic, traditions that portray Joseph as a paragon of virtue,[84] B. Sotah 36a—even before it begins explicating the biblical verses of the seduction scene—positions Joseph's new name as a marker of vulnerability to sexual sin.

As B. Sotah continues, it explicates Genesis 39:11. Now it toggles between Joseph as sinner and Joseph as virtuous.[85] A tradition in the name of R. Yohanan characterizes both Joseph and Potiphar's wife as intending to sin; two other traditions, one in the name of Rav and another in the name of Shmuel, depict Joseph as arriving at Potiphar's house either to perform his actual work (virtue) or to fulfill his sexual needs (sin). Yet Joseph symbolizes a struggle with not only sexual temptation but, as Levinson has pointed out, cultural temptation as well. Positioning Potiphar's wife as "the sexually voracious female,"[86] Joseph's "unruly body becomes a symptom of a threatened national culture."[87] Thus B. Sotah credits the seemingly strange phenomenon of the absence of people in Potiphar's house (Genesis 39:11) to that day being an idolatrous festival; Potiphar's wife is at home only because she feigns illness and does not attend the festival celebrations.

As Potiphar's wife moves into the position of a foreign sotah through her attempted seduction of Joseph, B. Sotah threatens Joseph with an erasure akin to that of the sotah ritual:

A. "And she seized him by his garment saying, ['Lie with me!' But he left his garment in her hand and got away and fled outside]" [Genesis 39:12].[88]
B. At that moment, the image of his father came and appeared to him in a window. He said to him, "Joseph, in the future your brothers will be written on the stones of the *ʾeifod* and you among them. Is it your will that your name be erased from among them and you be called a shepherd of prostitutes?!"
C. As it is written, "[A man who loves wisdom brings joy to his father,] but he who is a shepherd of prostitutes will lose his wealth" [Proverbs 29:3].
D. Immediately, "And his bow stayed taut" [Genesis 49:24].
E. Said R. Yohanan in the name of R. Meir: That his bow returned to its natural strength.[89]

This section of the narrative expansion returns us to the first explanation for the unique spelling of Joseph's name as *yehoseif*, that is as necessary to account for the fifty letters engraved on the precious stones of the *ʾeifod*. Here, echoing the writing and erasure of the sotah portion, Jacob threatens his son with the erasure of his name from the priestly garment and its replacement with a new name should he have sexual intercourse with Potiphar's wife. Rather than Joseph's name being inscribed on the stone of the *ʾeifod*, it will be erased, and he will be called a shepherd of prostitutes (*roʿeh zonot*) (A–C). Thus, the anonymous father in M. Sotah 3:4 who teaches his daughter Torah in order that she know merit delays punishment has become Joseph's father, Jacob, who teaches his son the consequences of forbidden sex.

Joseph may choose Potiphar's wife and idolatrous culture, erasing his name from the priestly garments much as Torah is erased in the sotah ritual. Alternatively, he may choose Israel and the priestly garments, inscribing his name into priestly ritual. B. Sotah's use of Jacob's image alone also hints at the erasure of Rachel. An earlier version of this tale found in Y. Horayot 2:4 (5), 46d, records a tradition that the image of Joseph's mother Rachel also appeared to confront him.[90]

As B. Sotah portrays the difficulty of Joseph's choice between cultural resistance and illicit sex, it further inscribes Jacob as a successful pedagogue:

> F. "And his arms were made firm" [Genesis 49:24]. He [Joseph] dug his hands into the ground and his sperm flowed out from between his fingernails.
> G. "By the hands of the mighty one of Jacob" [Genesis 49:24]. Who caused him to be engraved on the stones of the *ʾeifod*? Only the Mighty One of Jacob.
> H. "There, the Shepherd, the Rock of Israel" [Genesis 49:24]. From there he [Joseph] merited [*mi-sham zakhah*] to be called "shepherd" as it says, "Give ear, O shepherd of Israel who leads like the flock of Joseph" [Psalms 80:2].

Reading Genesis 49:24—Jacob's deathbed blessing of his son—as a reference to the engraving of Joseph's name on the stones of the *ʾeifod* and therefore to the success of Jacob's instruction (G), the passage again hints at M. Sotah 3:4 and B. Sotah's larger discussion of merit (*zekhut*). Joseph's ability to resist Potiphar's wife, a result of the appearance of and chastisement from his father, results in his meriting (*mi-sham zakhah*) to become a shepherd of Israel (H).[91]

While Joseph's name remains on the *ʾeifod*, B. Sotah goes on to imagine him as like and unlike the sotah. It also cites a baraita that depicts Joseph, similar to his father Jacob, as fitting to become the progenitor of the twelve tribes of Israel; the emission of sperm from between his fingernails, however, preempts that possibility. Finding a middle ground, these children instead descend from Joseph's brother Benjamin but are named after Joseph. Like the guilty sotah who miscarries, Joseph is punished by an inability to bear children.[92] Unlike the guilty sotah who causes the effacement of Torah and thus God's name, Benjamin's children carry Joseph's name. With the help of his father, Joseph chooses cultural resistance over sexual sin and so preserves his lineage. In the next section of the sugya, B. Sotah will move from Potiphar's house to Pharaoh's house and from father as teacher to angel as teacher. Providing yet another explanation for the unique spelling of *yehoseif*, this next passage marks Joseph as cultural resister through his ability to learn *leshon ha-kodesh*.

Joseph's Name Part 3: Learning Leshon Ha-Kodesh and Resisting Empire (Bavli Sotah 36b)

Now positioned as the powerful second-in-command within Pharaoh's house (Genesis 41:40) rather than the powerless slave in Potiphar's house, when B. Sotah imagines Joseph learning language for political power, it will elevate *leshon ha-kodesh* above all other languages. In this next section of the sugya, Pharaoh's astrologers protest his appointment of Joseph, a slave bought for only twenty pieces of silver,[93] to this high rank of second-in-command (A):

A. Said R. Hiyya bar Abba in the name of Rabbi Yohanan: At the time when Pharaoh said to Joseph, "Yet without you, no one shall lift up hand [or foot in all the land of Egypt]" [Genesis 41:44], Pharaoh's astrologers said: Shall a slave whose master purchased him for twenty silver pieces rule over us?!
B. He said to them: Royal manners I see in him.
C. They said to him: If so, let him have knowledge[94] of [all] seventy languages![95]

When Pharaoh replies to his astrologers that he appointed Joseph because of his royal manners (B), the astrologers reply that, if so, Joseph should know the totality of human languages (C). The astrologers connect linguistic abilities with political power. Regardless of Joseph's original status as a slave, if Joseph can demonstrate this particular form of knowledge, then he indeed merits political authority over an empire.

One manuscript prefaces this unit with the question, "What [is the meaning of the word] 'merit' [*zakhah*]?"and answers, "He merited [*zakhah*] and they added one letter from the name of the Holy Blessed One."[96] Echoing the sotah once again, this manuscript signals that it imagines Joseph's linguistic abilities—bestowed, as we will see, by the angel Gabriel—as resulting from his merit, that is Joseph's ability to withstand sexual and cultural temptation.

Much as Joseph requires his father's intervention to resist Potiphar's wife, Joseph similarly cannot learn seventy languages without heavenly pedagogical intervention from the angel Gabriel (D).[97] Even Gabriel is unsuccessful in his pedagogical task (E) until he adds the letter *heh* from God's name to Joseph's name (F):

D. Came Gabriel and taught him [Joseph] seventy languages.
E. He [Joseph] could not learn [them].
F. He [Gabriel] added one letter from the name of the Holy Blessed One [to his name], and he learned. As it is said, "He imposed it as a decree upon Joseph [*bi-yhoseif*] when he went forth from the land of Egypt; [I heard a language that I knew not]" [Psalms 81:6].
G. The next day, every language that Pharaoh spoke with him, he replied to him.

The addition of this one letter *heh* remakes Joseph as a master student of his master angelic teacher. It enables Joseph to learn a language, as read with Psalms 81:6, that he did not previously know. Through connecting language acquisition with the heavenly realm, B. Sotah implies that the ability of humans to learn languages has godly origins and that Israel's power, symbolized through language learning, has divine sanction.

Gabriel surfaces earlier in the seventh chapter of B. Sotah within a discussion about the permissibility of prayer (*tefilah*) in any language and the concomitant question of whether angels understand Aramaic (B. Sotah 33a). Explaining away the transmission in Aramaic by a heavenly voice (*bat kol*)[98] of news of two military victories,[99] B. Sotah suggests that the heavenly voice was Gabriel's. Referencing our Joseph story above ("Gabriel came and taught him seventy languages"), the passage proposes Gabriel's knowledge of Aramaic as unique within the heavenly realm. Generally, however, angels do not understand Aramaic.[100] Like the priest instructing the sotah in any language she understands, Gabriel's ability to speak and understand all languages (in this case, Aramaic in particular) represents the ability to transmit correct knowledge rather than lay a claim to national power.

By contrast, when B. Sotah elevates knowledge of *leshon ha-kodesh* above that of other languages, that elevation signals the eventual replacement of the powerful nation—Egypt—with the subjugated one—Israel:

H. He [Joseph] spoke in *leshon ha-kodesh.*
I. He [Pharaoh] did not know what he said.[101]
J. He [Pharaoh] said: Teach me!
K. He [Joseph] taught him but he [Pharaoh] did not learn.

L. He [Pharaoh] said to him [Joseph]: Take an oath to me that you will not reveal [that I could not learn *leshon ha-kodesh*].
M. He [Joseph] took an oath to him.
N. When he [Joseph] said to him: "My father made me take an oath, saying, ['I am about to die. Be sure to bury me in the grave which I made ready for myself in the land of Canaan']" [Genesis 50:5],
O. he [Pharaoh] said to him: Go and ask for absolution of your oath.
P. He [Joseph] said to him: And should I ask [for absolution] of yours?
Q. And even though it did not please him, he [Pharaoh] said to him: "Go up and bury your father as you took an oath" [Genesis 50:6].

In taking over Gabriel's role as a language teacher, B. Sotah positions Joseph as similar in status—but not identical—to the heavenly retinue. As was the case earlier with his teacher Joseph, Pharaoh is unable to learn a new language (H–K). However, Joseph does not, or cannot, add another letter to Pharaoh's name. Rather, Joseph successfully exploits his knowledge of Pharaoh's linguistic weakness. If Joseph must ask for absolution from his oath to bury his father Jacob in the land of Canaan, he will similarly dissolve the oath he took to hide Pharaoh's linguistic weakness (L–P). Pharaoh concedes to Joseph, allowing him to journey to Canaan to bury his father (Q).[102]

This section of the pericope establishes Pharaoh's inability to learn *leshon ha-kodesh* as a mark of shame that, if revealed, would reduce his authority in the eyes of his subjects. It is likely that the authors of this passage have in mind not only Joseph's status as a slave but also the soon-to-come enslavement of the entire nation of Israel. Indeed, the retelling of Israel's enslavement and Israel's subsequent rebellion against Egyptian subjugation play a prominent role in the first chapter of B. Sotah (B. Sotah 11a–13a).[103]

Pharaoh, ruler of Egypt, can learn *almost* the totality of spoken human languages; Joseph, former slave, can learn *every* spoken language. In imagining the inability to speak and understand *leshon ha-kodesh* as a source of shame, the Bavli elevates Joseph above even the empire that will soon enslave all of Israel. B. Sotah portrays *leshon ha-kodesh* as a language that only Israel, certain angels, and God can learn, speak, and understand. *Leshon ha-kodesh* thus becomes a tool for subverting the established political order of master and slave, Egyptian empire and soon-to-be subjugated Israel, and, one might conjecture, as a midrash attributed to a Palestinian amora, colonized Jews living in the Roman Empire.[104] The redaction of this passage in a tractate of the Babylonian Talmud also opens the possibility that it aimed to convince Jews in the Sassanian Empire of their unique status and their ability to resist cultural domination through their singular access to *leshon ha-kodesh*.[105] The extended aggadic passage found in B. Sotah's first chapter would reinforce this impression of Israel's ability to resist foreign powers.

While Joseph would not be misleading people in revealing Pharaoh's linguistic weakness, his threat against Pharaoh returns us again to the sotah and the necessity of her understanding the workings of the ritual—so that aspersions not be cast upon the bitter waters. The permission that M. Sotah and B. Sotah give the priest to explain and conduct the sotah ritual in a language other than *leshon ha-kodesh* (in order that the woman understand) implies that the language of resistance is unavailable to the accused woman. In contrast to Joseph, she does not have the tools to subvert the hierarchy of male over female, priest over accused.

CONCLUSION: LANGUAGE GONE WRONG YET AGAIN

This chapter has journeyed from the prominent role that language plays in the biblical sotah ritual (spoken, heard, written, erased), to the mishnaic delineation of ritual languages (*leshonam*, *leshon ha-kodesh*), and finally to the talmudic imaginary of language as constitutive of national status, whether destruction (*lashon ha-ra*) or restoration (*leshon ha-kodesh*). In B. Sotah, "their languages" become a mode through which to transmit correct knowledge and to redress gossip, that is language gone wrong on the individual level; *lashon ha-ra* becomes the constitutive factor in national subjugation; and *leshon ha-kodesh* a vehicle for envisioning national restoration. Throughout each of these models, the sotah threads her way, whether in the concern for correct understanding of the bitter waters and the procedure for the high priest's reading of the Torah, the brutal disfiguration of the spies' bodies, or the threatened erasure of Joseph's name. I also remind us at this point of the two women who open this book—their tale similarly found in the seventh chapter of B. Sotah—conversing and competing over Torah study. Their intimate speech, a marker of jealousy, is not, however, figured as a nation gone wrong.

The seventh chapter of B. Sotah leaves us with a warning about language's destructive powers. It concludes with an extended discussion of yet another type of improper language, flattery (*hanufah*), one that it will associate with *lashon ha-ra*. M. Sotah 7:11,[106] in describing the procedure for king's reading of the Torah scroll (*parashat ha-melekh*), includes an anecdote about King Agrippa, a king of questionable lineage.[107] M. Sotah 7:11 prescribes that a king stand, receive the Torah scroll, and then read the required portions while sitting; Agrippa, in contrast, reads the scroll while standing and is nevertheless praised by the sages. When Agrippa arrives at the words, "You must not set a foreigner over you" (Deuteronomy 18:15), he begins to weep. The sages comfort him with a twofold repetition of the words, "You are our brother." B. Sotah, however, does not use the Mishnah's version of this tale but rather the toseftan version of the story.[108] This version condemns Israel to destruction for flattering Agrippa (B. Sotah 41b). In other words, rather than valorizing the sages' speech as does M. Sotah, B. Sotah decries it. The sugya goes on to portray flattery as a type of speech that corrupts legal rulings, perverts people's actions, leaves them unable to state the truth, results in exile, and brings God's wrath upon the world.

In the last lines of the seventh chapter, B. Sotah 42a intertwines those who flatter with those who speak *lashon ha-ra*: "Said R. Yirmeyah bar Abba: Four groups do not greet the divine presence [*ʾein mekabelot penei shekhinah*]: scoffers [*kat leitzim*], and flatterers [*kat haneifim*], and liars [*kat shakarim*], and those who speak *lashon ha-ra* [*kat mesaperei lashon ha-ra*]." For B. Sotah, language gone wrong causes not only communal catastrophe but also a loss of God's presence. The misuses of language—whether the erasure of a portion of the Torah scroll through the preparation of the bitter of waters, the speaking of *lashon ha-ra*, or even the use of flattery—manifest themselves in the grotesque disfigurement of bodies, the destruction of all Israel, and the loss of God's presence. Mirroring the erasure and dissolution of the Torah scroll in the sotah ritual, a fear of the loss of Torah and the dissolution of society pervades B. Sotah. The next chapter, accordingly, will turn to the unraveling of rabbinic society and the ritual of the decapitated heifer (*ʿeglah ʿarufah*).

CHAPTER FIVE
FAILURES OF CARE

Although the Hebrew Bible does not discuss the sotah and *ʿeglah ʿarufah* rituals in conjunction with one another, they share a unique status within biblical literature: both are rituals carried out in response to a crisis of uncertainty in the judiciary. In the case of the sotah, that crisis is a lack of knowledge about *whether* a crime has been committed, although at least one of the potential "criminals" is known. In the case of the *ʿeglah ʿarufah,* the crime (murder) is known but the identity of the criminal(s) is not known. As neither of these crimes can be "solved" by the usual legal procedures and both are considered serious, biblical law mandates detailed ritual procedures to resolve, at least in theory, the crises of knowledge and the concomitant societal threats.[1] Fittingly, Mishnah Sotah—and Bavli Sotah following it—bring the sotah and *ʿeglah ʿarufah* rituals more directly into conversation with one another. Like the sotah, the *ʿeglah ʿarufah* becomes a significant site for detailing and prescribing rabbinic ethics.[2]

On the surface, B. Sotah's concern with the *ʿeglah ʿarufah* ritual manifests itself as yet another discussion of the moral male life, that is the behavior in which a rabbinic male must engage to maintain the stability of rabbinic society. Yet a deeper look under B. Sotah's behavioral demands reveals this tractate's concern for the ways in which the sages themselves may contribute to the unraveling of rabbinic society, an upside-down world in which even a sage may lead a student to become a heretic. Like the spies and like Joseph, male potential for sin contains national implications. On the one hand, this focus on sages almost (but not totally) disappears women. On the other hand, women—and the sotah in particular—are no longer the key to why society may unravel. On the contrary, as we will see, women, through the messianic line, become the hope for future salvation.

This chapter focuses on B. Sotah's interpretation of the words that the elders recite at the conclusion of the *ʿeglah ʿarufah* ritual (B. Sotah 38b) and then two aggadic passages that these interpretations generate (B. Sotah 46b–47a; B. Sotah 47a). The first aggadic passage weaves together the necessity for accompaniment on a journey, the story of the prophet Elisha and the bears, and the birth of Ruth. The second passage portrays sage-teaching gone wrong, the care of a female innkeeper, and Jesus's heresy. The beginning of the tractate cautioned men against drinking wine lest it lead them to sin with a potential sotah. These passages from the ninth and final chapter of the tractate warn not only about individual sin but even more broadly about the possible failure of rabbinic society itself. The *ʿeglah ʿarufah* ritual becomes a site through which B. Sotah implicitly reveals its fears about failures of care that contribute to the dissolution of rabbinic society.

"OUR HANDS HAVE NOT SHED THE BLOOD": BIBLICAL AND MISHNAIC FOUNDATIONS

Deuteronomy 21:1–9 prescribes an intricate ritual of purification for a case where a corpse is found and the identity of the killer is unknown. In the case of a known killer, pollution could be removed through the murderer's execution. Here, where the identity of the murderer is unknown and thus execution impossible, the *ʿeglah ʿarufah* ritual serves the same purpose as does execution: preventing God from punishing the nation Israel by removing it from its land as a result of pollution.[3] In this intricate ritual that involves elders, judges, and priests, the elders of the town nearest the corpse break the heifer's neck[4] in an uncultivated area near a wadi. The elders of this town then wash their hands and recite an exculpatory declaration: "Our hands did not shed this blood, nor did our eyes see. Absolve, O Lord, Your people Israel whom You redeemed, and do not let guilt for the blood of the innocent remain among Your people Israel" (Deuteronomy 21:7–8).[5] The passage concludes with a statement about the successful removal of innocent blood through conduct that God deems correct.

While biblical scholars have linked the sotah and *ʿeglah ʿarufah* rituals as responses to crises of judicial uncertainty, the Bible itself does not draw explicit connections between these rituals. M. Sotah's creation of a more textually direct connection between them is part of the Mishnah's larger project of the recomposition of Scripture, a process that involves the recategorization of biblical laws: the shifting of a law from one legal grouping to another.[6] Through literary, legal, and thematic contiguities, M. Sotah reveals that it understands the sotah and *ʿeglah ʿarufah* rituals to exist within overlapping but not identical legal webs. The ways in which these mishnaic rituals overlap *and* diverge from one another highlight the multiple pathways open to B. Sotah and its choice of particular interpretive directions.

M. Sotah indicates overlap between the sotah and *ʿeglah ʿarufah* rituals through literary conjunction and through ritual similarity. M. Sotah lists both rituals within its delineation of prescribed ritual languages (7:1–2); it follows mention of the cessation of the *ʿeglah ʿarufah* ritual with mention of the cessation of the sotah ritual (9:10–11). M. Sotah necessitates the involvement of priests (1:5–6 and more, 9:7), a two-tiered process of the local court (1:3, 9:5) followed by the High Court (1:4, 9:1–5), and a determination of what to do with consecrated materials and suspects if additional knowledge comes to light before or after a critical stage in the ritual (3:3, 9:8).[7] Both rituals also involve brutalized bodies: the accused sotah, the murdered corpse, and the slaughtered heifer.

Two of these bodies are gendered female—the sotah and the heifer. Deuteronomy and M. Sotah likely imagine the corpse to be male, evidenced by the use of grammatically male nouns to describe the corpse and by the lack of remarks about gender. Since female is commonly conceptualized as nonnormative (i.e., non-male) and thus with particular delineated rules, the lack of such rules reinforces the corpse's male identity. It is here, with the male corpse and the female heifer, that I want to highlight divergence. While M. Sotah amplifies the biblical sotah ritual, creating a brutal public performance to convince an accused woman to confess her guilt, it does not similarly amplify the biblical *ʿeglah ʿarufah* ritual. Rather, it excludes many instances of the murdered corpse from the necessity to conduct the *ʿeglah ʿarufah* ritual. If the corpse is found hidden in a heap of debris, hanging on a tree, or floating in water, the ritual is not performed; similarly, if the corpse is found close to the border, or close to a city where either the majority of its inhabitants are gentiles or it does not have a court, the ritual is not performed (9:2). In the case of the sotah, should the woman proclaim herself to be pure (*tehorah ʾani*; 1:5) rather than the ritual being suspended, she is led to the Nicanor gate where the priest rips her clothes and attaches a rope above her nipples (1:5–6). Her words—her declaration of innocence—result in her further degradation. In contrast, when M. Sotah turns to the elders' speech at the conclusion of the *ʿeglah ʿarufah* ritual, it emphasizes innocence and forgiveness.

Mishnah Sotah 9:6–7

M. Sotah 9:6–7[8] envisions Deuteronomy 21:7–8 as a tripartite conversation among elders, priests, and God:

A. The elders of that same city wash their hands in water at the place of decapitating the heifer. And they say: "Our hands did not shed this blood and our eyes did not see" [Deuteronomy 21:7].
B. How would it arise on our hearts that the elders of the court are blood-shedders?!
C. Rather, he did not come to our hands and we did not dismiss him [*u-ftarnuhu*]; and we did not see him and leave him [*ve-hinahnuhu*].[9]
D. The priests say, "Forgive Your people Israel whom You redeemed, Lord, and do not let guilt for the blood of the innocent remain among Your people Israel" [Deuteronomy 21:8].
E. It was not necessary to say, "And they will be absolved of bloodguilt" [Deuteronomy 21:8]. Rather, the Holy Spirit [*ruah ha-kodesh*] announces to them: When you do thus, the blood will atone for you.

These mishnayot solve one textual problem: although Deuteronomy 21:5 prescribes the priests' presence at the *ʿeglah ʿarufah* ritual ("The priests, sons of Levi, shall come forward, for the Lord you God has chosen them to serve Him and to bless in the name of the Lord, and every lawsuit and case of assault is subject to their ruling"), it does not prescribe any actions for them to perform. In the mishnaic version, the priests petition God for forgiveness (D). This task of the priests—forgiveness—contrasts with their role in the sotah ritual, where they coerce the woman to confess her guilt or to drink the bitter waters. Yet this mishnah does additional work besides solving a textual conundrum. It declares the elders of the court as innocent of sin[10] and God as affirming the efficacy of the *ʿeglah ʿarufah* ritual (A–C, E). In the case of the sotah, the bitter waters test the woman, possibly resulting in her gross bodily disfigurement. Here, God confirms the nation's innocence.

While the mishnah has "solved" one textual conundrum, it creates another. Relying on the assumption that the elders, as representatives of the court,[11] could not possibly be guilty of murder (B), the mishnah seeks out an alternative explanation for their declaration that their hands did not shed the dead person's blood and their eyes did not see: "Rather, he did not come to us and we did not dismiss him; and we did not see him and leave him" (C). Because the antecedent of the pronoun "he" is indeterminate, whether the elders' words refer to the murderer or to the murdered person is unclear. Do the elders declare their lack of culpability for dismissing the murderer or the victim? The Yerushalmi makes this question and its answer explicit by stating that Palestinian sages interpret the word "he" as referring to the murderer while Babylonian sages interpret "he" as referring to the murdered person.[12] Palestinian sages understand the elders to declare their innocence of judicial misconduct: they did not fail to execute the murderer or cover up his case. Babylonian sages understand the elders to declare their innocence of negligence in care: they did not fail to provide the murdered person with escort or provisions (*parnasah*) for a journey (Y. Sotah 9:6 [5], 23d).[13]

In contrast to the Yerushalmi, the Bavli does not present these two possibilities.[14] Rather than staging differences between Palestinian and Babylonian interpretations, B. Sotah ignores this interpretive ambiguity in the mishnah. It discards the possibility of the elders' judicial misconduct and emphasizes only the requirement that the elders provide food and escort. Failure to do so would potentially result in murder and thus the need for the *ʿeglah ʿarufah* ritual. In making this move, B. Sotah utilizes the *ʿeglah ʿarufah* as a pedagogical vehicle for declaring how to sustain rabbinic society and the converse, for declaring which actions may result in its dissolution. B. Sotah figures the elders as responsible for the care of strangers through food and accompaniment. This chapter of the tractate, though, gives us stories of men who are figured as mothers but nonetheless fail in their tasks of care. Yet again, women's sexual sins are not the culprit for societal failure.

SELFISHNESS AND SOCIETAL DESTRUCTION: BAVLI SOTAH 38B

This direct connection between the *ʿeglah ʿarufah* and the elders' culpability for care of the victim appears twice in B. Sotah, once in the tractate's seventh chapter (38b) and once in the ninth chapter (46b). In the former case, it appears as one in a series of statements quoted in the name of the Palestinian amora R. Yehoshua ben Levi that contrast the desired quality of generosity (*tov ʿayin*) with the undesired one of selfishness (*tzarei ʿayin*). According to R. Yehoshua ben Levi, the elders declare that they have not engaged in behavior characteristic of those who are *tzarei ha-ʿayin*, actions that would result in a person's murder by an unknown killer:

A. And said R. Yehoshua ben Levi: The *ʿeglah ʿarufah* only comes because of those who are selfish [*tzarei ha-ʿayin*]. As it is said, "And they answered and said, 'Our hands did not shed this blood [and our eyes did not see]'" [Deuteronomy 21:7].

B. And would it rise on our hearts that the elders of the court are bloodshedders?

C. Rather, he did not come to our hands and we dismissed him [*u-ftarnuhu*]; and we did not see him and leave him [*ve-hinahnuhu*].[15]

D. He did not come to our hands and we dismissed him without food [*u-ftarnuhu be-lo mezonot*]; we did not see him and leave him without escort [*ve-hinahnuhu be-lo levayah*].[16]

Paralleling M. Sotah 9:6 in sections B and C, section D adds details about which the elders proclaim their lack of culpability: they did not fail to provide the murdered person with food, and they did not leave him without escort on his journey.[17]

B. Sotah's unique emphasis on food and escort as measures that protect against the necessity for the *ʿeglah ʿarufah* ritual mirror the ways in which food and escort function in the sotah ritual. M. Sotah 1:3 rules that two sages (*talmidei hakhamim*) must accompany husband and accused wife to Jerusalem lest he have sexual intercourse with her, a prohibited act.[18] Were the two to engage in sexual intercourse, she would no longer drink the bitter waters (M. Sotah 4:2). B. Sotah 7a provides three different explanations for the requirement of two sages: to prevent the accused sotah from being alone with a man, to act as witnesses should husband and wife have sexual intercourse, or to correctly warn the husband about the prohibition of sexual intercourse. In both the case of the *ʿeglah ʿarufah* and the case of the sotah, accompaniment is a form of care, albeit with very different goals. In the case of the *ʿeglah ʿarufah,* care—through accompaniment—should be taken in order to prevent murder and the necessity of the ritual. In the case of the sotah, care—through accompaniment—should be taken in order to ensure the ritual's performance through the drinking of the bitter waters. In the case of the sotah, the bitter waters, the food of the ritual, may deform the woman's body. By contrast, the food the elders provide protects the traveler's body from murder.[19]

ACCOMPANIMENT, TORAH STUDY, AND FEMALE CARE: BAVLI SOTAH 46B–47A

When this tradition about the elders' lack of culpability appears later in B. Sotah (46b), it introduces an extended sugya that moves back and forth between law, exegesis of biblical narrative, and sage story (B. Sotah 46b–47a). Females appear in this sugya in prescriptive statements and stories, implicitly and explicitly. With one exception, they are depicted through familial relationships as mothers, sisters, daughters, and wives. Much as the *ʿeglah ʿarufah* is conducted in response to a death, these women's relationships are also intertwined with death, as well as its opposite, birth. And while the sugya in one instance describes mothers' sins as responsible for their children's deaths, the sugya's weight lies with male rabbinic responsibility for sin rather than female. The sugya found on B. Sotah 38b connects the *ʿeglah ʿarufah* with miserliness; this one utilizes it, at least initially, to focus on and explore the necessity for one person to escort or accompany another.

The sugya begins with a baraita that interrogates the elders' proclamation of innocence and, as before, interprets their words as a declaration they did not send the murder victim away without food or escort.[20] The baraita that follows contains the sugya's first mention of females, albeit implicitly. R. Meir declares that one must force a person to accompany another because the reward for accompaniment is immeasurable. As proof, he cites a story from Judges 1:22–26 in which a Canaanite man from the town of Bethel shows men from the house of Joseph how to enter Bethel in order to conquer it. The men from the house of Joseph reward this man by saving him and his family, despite slaughtering the rest of the city's inhabitants. The Bavli cites yet another baraita that interprets this Canaanite man and his family being let free as a reward for his gesturing (verbally or with his hand) to the men from the house of Joseph, an action that it equates with accompaniment.[21] If the Canaanite man's gesture resulted in a reward (that according to this baraita continues for eternity for all his descendants), all the more so should accompaniment by foot result in a reward. Despite the fact that the man helps the men of Joseph, reward accrues to his entire family, which we may assume includes a wife and children.[22] B. Sotah's unit of analysis here is the household family—and a family of Canaanite outsiders. The outsider Canaanite and his family thus provide the behavioral model for the rabbinic ideal, a theme that we will see repeated throughout this passage.[23] This use of the Canaanite man and his family as models becomes even more striking as the sugya next turns to the power of Torah study to safeguard a person from harm.

Playing on the similarities between the words for escort (*levayah*) and wreath (*livyah*), B. Sotah declares that Torah study will protect a man journeying alone: "Said R. Yehoshua ben Levi: A man who is walking on the road and does not have escort [*levayah*] should occupy himself with Torah. As it is said, 'For they are a graceful wreath [*livyat hein*] upon your head, a necklace about your throat' [Proverbs 1:9]."[24] This passage, with its vision of Torah study as protective, echoes B. Sotah's earlier debate over whether the merit of Torah study or the performance of commandments delays the accused sotah's punishment (B. Sotah 21a). As I observed in chapter 3, the Bavli there too depicts Torah study through a relational lens, where the woman, as wife and mother, ensures that her sons and husband learn the rabbinic curriculum. In the case of the *ʿeglah ʿarufah*, while the main image is that of a man walking alone, a closer look at the context of the Proverbs verse ("My son, heed the discipline of your father, and do not forsake the instruction [*torah*] of your mother; for they are a graceful wreath upon your head, a necklace about your throat," Proverbs 1:8–9) demonstrates that this passage also imagines the sage as embedded within a familial relationship. He even receives the Torah that protects him from his mother, as B. Sotah 21a earlier imagined more clearly.[25]

The sugya thus engages in a dialectic in which males are its surface concern but females are utilized—even images from female bodies—to illustrate its point. A baraita that prescribes, through a hierarchy of master-disciple relationships, the distance one man must escort another utilizes the word *ʿibur* (pregnancy), in the sense of city outskirts: "Our rabbis taught: A master [*rav*] [accompanying] a disciple [*talmid*]—until the outskirts of the city [*ʿiburah shel ʿir*]. A *haver* [accompanying] a *haver*—until the sabbath boundary. A disciple [accompanying] a master—there is no measurement."[26] Sarit Kattan Gribetz has pointed out the ways in which female bodies are evoked in calendrical time, drawing "on the stages and processes of women's bodies and the terminology associated with female bodily practices."[27] The word *ʿibur* (or *meʿubar*) is "extended to include the moon, which is metaphorically pregnant with an extra day, or a leap year, which includes an intercalated month."[28] This baraita, rather than use the female body for calendrical time, utilizes it to describe a city's geography. The terminology of a master accompanying his disciple for a "pregnant distance" may have enabled the baraita's authors to map the sage/disciple relationship onto a parent/child one. Much as the stories in this sugya portray one male escorting another,[29] the master nevertheless becomes like a mother, instructing his "son" as they walk. Female bodies, reproduction, and instruction act as undercurrents of this sugya, yet again illustrating the ways in which B. Sotah simultaneously disappears and reveals women's presence.[30]

Elisha, Bears, and Ruth

As the sugya on B. Sotah 46b–47a continues, it frames the consequence of a failure to escort another person in procreative terms. One who does not accompany another, or allow himself to be accompanied, is considered "as if he spills blood." This principle, cited by the Palestinian amora R. Yohanan in the name of R. Meir, introduces an extended analysis of the story of the prophet Elisha in which he incites two female bears to attack and kill forty-two children (2 Kings 2:23–25):

A. Said R. Yohanan in the name of R. Meir: Anyone who does not escort [another] or who [does not permit himself] to be escorted is as if he spills blood.
B. For if indeed the men of Jericho had accompanied Elisha, he would not have incited the bears against the children. As it is said, "From there he went up to Bethel. As he was going up the road, some little boys [*neʿarim ketanim*] came out of the town and jeered at him, saying, 'Go away, baldhead! Go away, baldhead!'" [2 Kings 2:23].
C. They said to him: Go up for you have made the place bare for us.

While R. Yohanan attempts to exonerate Elisha for inciting the bears by laying blame on the men of Jericho for failing to escort the prophet (A–B), B. Sotah undercuts that exoneration by interpreting the boys' jeer as criticism of Elisha for not having provided them with the proper care. By sweetening the waters of the town (2 Kings 2:19–22) and rendering needless their drawing clean water and selling it, Elisha had taken away their livelihood (C).[31] The men of Jericho fail to escort Elisha; in turn, Elisha fails to ensure the children have food. Despite the Bavli's continued attempts to further exonerate Elisha (the children did not perform any commandments; they were lacking in faith), this passage nevertheless presents us with two striking inversions. In the case of the *ʿeglah ʿarufah*, the elders are not guilty of homicide and the heifer atones for death; here the prophet is not blameless in the children's murder and the bears are the murderers.[32] The prophet as wrongdoer also echoes David and Joseph as sotah and partial sotah.

Elisha's act of indirect homicide further inscribes the master-disciple relationship in terms of familial, and in this case paternal, loss. B. Sotah 49a records an aphorism in the name of R. Ileʿa bar Yeverekhyah: "Two students of the wise [*talmidei hakhamim*] who are walking on the way and do not have between them words of Torah are fitting to be burned in fire. As it says, 'As they [Elijah and Elisha] kept walking and talking, a fiery chariot [with fiery horses suddenly appeared and separated one from the other; and Elijah went up to heaven in a whirlwind]' [2 Kings 2:11]. The reason is that there was speech; without speech, they would have been fitting to be burned." The Bavli attributes master and disciple not being burned by the fire—Elijah ascends while Elisha remains unharmed—to their act of "talking" Torah together. This incident with the bears occurs after Elijah's ascension and thus may also be read as a result of the student's grief at the loss of his master/father.[33] As Elisha exclaims on seeing Elijah ascend heavenward, "Father, father! Israel's chariots and horsemen" (2 Kings 2:12).

As the sugya continues, familial relationships and Torah study remain a framework through which B. Sotah attempts to exonerate Elisha. In another act of this tractate's mirroring, B. Sotah inverts the elders' declaration of their lack of culpability for murder through what their "eyes did not see." Now, the sugya declares Elisha culpable for homicide through his eyes:[34]

A. "He turned around and saw them and cursed them in the name of the Lord" [2 Kings 2:24].
B. What did he [Elisha] see?
C. Said Rav: He actually saw. As it is taught [in a baraita]: Rabban Shimon ben Gamliel says: Any place that the sages set their eyes —either death or poverty.
D. And Shmuel said: He saw that their mothers became pregnant with all of them on Yom Kippur.
E. And R. Yitzhak Nafha said: He saw a *belorit* on them like Amorites.[35]
F. And R. Yohanan said: He saw that they did not have in them any sap of commandments.
G. But perhaps in their descendants there would be!
H. Said R. Elazar: Not in them or their descendants until the end of all generations.

In the first of its four interpretations of the verb "see" in 2 Kings 2:24, B. Sotah proposes that "see" refers to Elisha's killing the children through the power of his gaze. The baraita that acts as a proof text for Rav's claim also inverts the elders' responsibility for food, this time in regard to the sages: now the sages' vision causes death or poverty (A–C).[36] The next three amoraic traditions move away from Elisha's deadly gaze and interpret the word "see" as a reference to Elisha's prophetic vision, whether of these children's conception on Yom Kippur (a day on which rabbinic law forbids sexual intercourse),[37] their Amorite haircuts,[38] or their total failure to perform mitzvot (D–F). The mention of mothers becoming pregnant on Yom Kippur presents us with the sole mention of human female sin in this sugya. Even here men are not blameless, for mothers must violate this prohibition with fathers. And even these women's sin is not the decisive interpretation of Elisha's curse. It is one possibility in a list of alternatives that marks these children as foreigners to rabbinic practice.[39]

As the sugya continues, it attempts to shift blame from Elisha to the Moabite king Balak, suggesting that the forty-two children died as a result of his offering forty-two sacrifices (Numbers 23). B. Sotah's objection to this proposal figures Balak as righteous and, even more significantly, a Moabite woman as the ancestral mother of Solomon, and thus the messianic line. It intertwines mothers, foreigners, and the performance of commandments:

A. Didn't Rav Yehudah say in the name of Rav: A man should always occupy himself with Torah and commandments, even when not for their own sake. Because through [studying Torah and performing commandments] not for their own sake, he will come [to perform them] for their own sake.[40]

B. That for the reward of the forty-two sacrifices that Balak king of Moab offered, he merited and Ruth descended from him from whom descended Solomon, about whom it is written: "A thousand burnt offerings offered Solomon" [1 Kings 3:4].

C. And said R. Yosi b. Honi: Ruth was the daughter of ʿEglon, son of Balak.

D. His desire, nonetheless, was to curse.[41]

This section reframes Balak's behavior within rabbinic categories, here the enigmatic concept of Torah study and performance of commandments for their own sake rather than for another reason (A). The passage implies that while Balak did not offer sacrifices for their own sake, he was nevertheless rewarded by becoming the grandfather of Ruth from whom would descend King Solomon (B–C). The sugya thus performs inversions: the Moabite king Balak who intended to curse Israel instead becomes an exemplar of a principle about Torah study and the performance of commandments; the name *ʿEglon* references the *ʿeglah ʿarufah* and represents the successful atonement of yet another Moabite king; in contrast to those Jewish mothers mentioned in the previous section of the sugya who violate the prohibition of sexual intercourse on Yom Kippur, Ruth's descendant—Solomon—offers multiple Temple sacrifices in keeping with rabbinic law. Even though the anonymous voice of the sugya reinscribes Balak's guilt ("his desire, nonetheless, was to curse" [D]), this section of B. Sotah nevertheless leaves us with Ruth in place as a Moabite mother central to messianic redemption and the continued performance of Temple ritual. Unlike the accused sotah who, if guilty, will miscarry and whose bodily deterioration has the potential to defile the Temple, Ruth gives birth to Solomon, who will fulfill rabbinic law by offering sacrifices in that same Temple.

Further illustrating the ways in which this tractate functions as an integrated literary unit, this mention of Ruth the Moabite foreigner as savior overlaps with the aggadic traditions about Pharaoh's daughter in the first chapter of the tractate.[42] Those traditions depict Pharaoh's daughter, another foreigner, as rejecting her father's idolatry, as seeing the *shekhinah* (God's presence), and as prophesying the end of Pharaoh's decree to kill all male newborns (B. Sotah 12b).[43] Thus, although this section of B. Sotah returns to seemingly familiar ground of the necessity for Torah study and the importance of the master-disciple relationship, it also undercuts what we might perceive as the "normative" form of both, that is Jewish males who engage in Torah study and sage-student replacing father-son.[44]

WOMEN, HERESY, AND CARE: BAVLI SOTAH 47A

The two stories that follow the Balak pericope—the first about Elisha and his servant Gehazi and the second about R. Yehoshua ben Perahya and Jesus[45]—take an additional step and depict the total failure of the master-disciple relationship.[46] In both of these stories, B. Sotah portrays the apostasy of Gehazi and Jesus as responses to improper actions by their masters.[47] In Gehazi's case, Elisha curses his disciple with eternal leprosy that extends even to his descendants (2 Kings 5:27). In Jesus's case, R. Yehoshua ben Perahya, intending finally to accept his student's offer of repentance, gestures at him unclearly while reciting the shema prayer, a motion that his student interprets as yet another rejection. B. Sotah even depicts Gehazi and Jesus as refusing their masters' entreaties that they repent by turning their teachers' words against them, with both declaring: "Thus I received from you: Anyone who sins and causes the many to sin, they do not provide him with the opportunity to repent" (B. Sotah 47a).[48] Not only does Gehazi turn sages away from studying Torah with Elisha, but both Gehazi and Jesus entice Israel to idolatry. As I have remarked, B. Sotah does not link the sotah to the golden calf. Here, though, it names Gehazi's possible sin as hanging a magnetic stone on King Jeroboam's golden calves or engraving God's name on the calves' mouths (1 Kings 26–30). Again, the tractate shifts its focus to male sin, with the act of engraving God's name evoking the sotah ritual.

Jeffrey Rubenstein observes that the stories of Elisha-Gehazi and R. Yehoshua ben Perahya-Jesus are both tied to the redactional context of the mishnaic *ʿeglah ʿarufah*. Like the elders, Elisha and Yehoshua inappropriately dismiss individuals who subsequently come to harm. They leave Torah, become heretics, and lose their share in the world to come.[49] Opening our lens to the redactional context of B. Sotah as a whole, though, enables us to highlight the absence of females in the Elisha/Gehazi story and the presence of women in the R. Yehoshua ben Perahya/Jesus narrative. In the latter case, women—figured as sister, spouse, and caregiver—prove crucial to the plot's advancement. I turn now to this narrative in more detail.

Yehoshua ben Perahya, Jesus, and the Innkeeper

The R. Yehoshua ben Perahya/Jesus pericope begins with a statement about King Yannai's attempt to kill the sages and R. Yehoshua ben Perahya's subsequent flight to Alexandria. According to the Vilna printed edition, the editio princeps, and at least one manuscript witness,[50] the sister of Shimon ben Shetah hides R. Yehoshua ben Perahya. When the killing stops, Shimon ben Shetah sends a message from Jerusalem to R. Yehoshua ben Perahya, one that figures the two cities as sisters and the husband of one as present in the other: "From me, Jerusalem the holy city, to you, Alexandria of Egypt. My sister: My husband [R. Yehoshua ben Perahya] dwells within you and I sit desolate" (B. Sotah 47a). B. Sotah thus depicts a sister who hides the sage R. Yehoshua ben Perahya and a man who imagines himself as a sister longing after her exiled husband. In contrast to the townspeople of the *ʿeglah ʿarufah* ritual who fail to protect the stranger in their midst, in this case, a sister saves a sage. And in contrast to the sotah who is suspected of betraying her husband, a man imagines himself as a woman calling her husband to return to her. In this upside-down world, a sage will even mislead his male student by using a word of multiple meanings (*ʾakhsanya*) and by assuming the inappropriateness of his student's reply.

When R. Yehoshua ben Perahya leaves Alexandria, he stops at an inn along the way:

A. When he [R. Yehoshua ben Perahya] came back [to the land of Israel] he came to a certain inn [*ʾushpiza*]. He [R. Yehoshua ben Perahya] rose before them with proper honor.
B. They accorded him much honor.
C. He [R. Yehoshua ben Perahya] sat and praised: "How nice is this inn/innkeeper [*ʾakhsanya*; feminine]."

D. One of his students [Jesus] said to him:[51] "My master, her eyes are bleary/dripping/slanted."

E. He [R. Yehoshua ben Perahya] said to him [his student]: "Evil one. With this you occupy [yourself]?!"

F. He [R. Yehoshua ben Perahya] took out four hundred shofars and excommunicated him.

The misunderstanding between R. Yehoshua ben Perahya and his student turns on one word with multiple meanings: *ʾakhsanya* (C). While the translation of *ʾakhsanya* as "inn" is the more straightforward reading of R. Yehoshua ben Perahya's comment (he compliments the lodging rather than the person), it is also possible that R. Yehoshua ben Perahya uses *ʾakhsanya* to mean "innkeeper," in this case a woman. In the more straightforward reading, R. Yehoshua ben Perahya excommunicates his student for looking at a woman and for falsely assuming that he, the master, was complimenting her appearance rather than the lodging. In the second reading, R. Yehoshua ben Perahua excommunicates his student for revealing his own transgression in complimenting a woman, the innkeeper. Note, too, that R. Yehoshua rises before those gathered in the inn, recalling the behavior of R. Abbahu's speaker mentioned in the introduction to this book (B. Sotah 40a), and yet another inversion of status.

In contrast to R. Yehoshua's ben Perahya's inability to speak clearly and his rage at his student's response, we may conceptualize the innkeeper's role as parallel to that of the elders in the case of the *ʿeglah ʿarufah*: She cares for the strangers in her midst, one of them returning after a war, by providing them with food and shelter. It is not simply that the innkeeper is blameless for Jesus's apostasy. Indeed, the pericope concludes with R. Yehoshua ben Perahya's refusal of his student/Jesus's attempts at repentance and the student/Jesus's setting up a brick and worshipping it. Rather, the innkeeper exemplifies the behavior that B. Sotah idealizes.[52]

Although we might be tempted to see the mention of women in this sugya as tangential, attention to the longer sugya's redactional context in B. Sotah (and not only the relationship of the different stories in the sugya to one another) highlights the women who appear in this sugya as integral to its cultural work.[53] The laws of accompaniment and the stories analyzed in this chapter not only enhance mishnaic ideas but transform them. While the *ʿeglah ʿarufah* ritual deems men responsible for taking proper care of strangers, these passages demonstrate the ways in which men may be figured as mothers but nevertheless commonly fail in the endeavor of care. The sage becomes like a mother when he escorts his student; the prophet Elisha is guilty of homicide; the master's failure to attend to his student results in the latter's apostasy. In contrast, the female innkeeper cares for her guests and Ruth mothers the messianic line. B. Sotah casts the greatest danger to rabbinic society as male action; it portrays females as both stabilizing and ensuring the long-term continuity of rabbinic society.

CONCLUSION

As we near the end of B. Sotah, male failures of care result in the murder of children, apostasy, a turning away from Torah study, and the departure of God's presence. In contrast, B. Sotah figures the successful male disciple as a mother teaching her child and names a foreign woman, Ruth, as the mother of Solomon and thus the messianic line. The female innkeeper is blameless while the sage leads his student to heresy. These moves do not mean that B. Sotah views women as free of sin. This passage does depict women as engaging in sexual intercourse with their husbands on Yom Kippur and as committing adultery. Yet B. Sotah also implicates men in these actions. The *ʿeglah ʿarufah*, read as a response to society's lack of care, becomes a location through which B. Sotah reveals its anxiety about the instability of the master-disciple relationship and thus the possible failure of rabbinic society. Female sexual sin does not lie at the center of that worry. Rather, B. Sotah embeds images of familial learning and female care in these sugyot as a bulwark against society's dissolution and as an implicit rebuke to male and rabbinic failures of learning and of care.

CHAPTER SIX

FROM WAR TO WOMEN

This book aims to make women visible. Through assuming and noticing female presence in Bavli Sotah as well as exposing the myriad of ways in which the tractate makes females disappear, I deny a myth of female absence. This process of making women visible does not require us to idealize women or to ignore patriarchal structures. But it does aim to denaturalize patriarchy and to center women as crucial to cultural formation. I do not want to excuse the deeply troubling sotah ritual—and the brutal mishnaic version in particular—but rather, through reading the tractate as a whole, to simultaneously engage in the constructive work of restoring female voice and presence.

Reading B. Sotah through a feminist lens of presence (rather than absence) enables us to see the many ways in which the sotah and the sotah ritual thread their way through this tractate, shaping concepts of knowledge, teachers, gender, empire, and cultural stability. This mode of reading also exposes the artful literary work involved in B. Sotah's redaction. It enables us to see how the tractate's redactors shift from the sinning sotah to orchestrate a new set of perceptions about gender and rabbinic society. In turn, this focus on the tractate enables us, as contemporary readers, to utilize the content of B. Sotah for the constructive act of restoring female voice and presence.

In this final section of the book, I move backward in B. Sotah from its eighth chapter to its first through close study of three passages, all of which relate to war. The first discusses laws of exemption from the battlefield (B. Sotah 44b); the second, Goliath, David, and Orpah (B. Sotah 42b); and the third, the righteous women for whose sake Israel was redeemed from slavery in Egypt (B. Sotah 11b). Together, these three passages enable me to highlight and reinforce a central theme of this book: the subtle ways in which this tractate hides the sotah's presence and the ways in which she nevertheless threads herself throughout the tractate. B. Sotah 44b intertwines the male battlefield with female sexual transgression and reveals the possibility of female Torah study. B. Sotah 42a–b intertwines the biblical story of David and Goliath's battle (1 Samuel 17) with Torah study and commandment performance. It also tells a brutal tale of the rape of Orpah, figured as Goliath's mother. Orpah becomes a tragic figure upon whom the tractate projects the ritual violation of the sotah's body. B. Sotah 11b mirrors the sotah ritual through a story of female rebellion against Pharaoh. In its depiction of sex simultaneously licit and illicit, dangerous childbirth, and divine and human care, it will point us toward the redemptive power of female sexuality and care amid devastation.

Julia Watts Belser observes that B. Gittin's tales of Roman conquest and destruction "suggest that masculine virtue might persevere in the face of disaster."[1] B. Sotah suggests an opposite occurrence: the loss of masculine virtue and communication with God. In contrast to this fear of masculine sin, in B. Sotah female virtue acts as a mirror to the sotah ritual, inverting both the performative details of the sotah ritual and, crucially, the notion of the destructive woman herself. Orpah and the righteous women will function as countertraditions to the sotah ritual, giving voice to the ritual's brutality while simultaneously subverting it.[2]

EXEMPTION FROM BATTLE AND SUSPENDED PUNISHMENT: MISHNAH SOTAH 8:9

The eighth chapter of M. Sotah interrogates two linked speeches concerning preparation for war, the first by a priest (*ha-kohen*; Deuteronomy 20:2–4) and the second by officials (*ha-shoterim*; Deuteronomy 20:5–8).[3] In the former, the priest—known in the Mishnah as *meshuah milhamah*—exhorts the soldiers not to fear because God is with them; in the latter, the officials provide a list of grounds for exemption from battle. These include building a new house and not dedicating it, planting a vineyard but not harvesting it, betrothing a woman but not yet marrying her, and being afraid and soft of heart (*ha-yarei ve-rakh ha-leivav*).[4]

M. Sotah 8:9[5] provides three different interpretations for the phrase *ha-yarei ve-rakh ha-leivav*:

A. "The officials shall go on addressing the troops and say: Who is the man afraid and soft of heart? Let him go and return to his home" [Deuteronomy 20:8].
B. R. Akiva says: "Afraid and soft of heart"—according to its meaning, that he cannot bear the battle ranks, seeing a drawn sword.
C. R. Yosi ha-Galili says: "Afraid and soft of heart"—that he is afraid of the transgressions in his hand [*ha-ʿaveirot she-beyado*]. Therefore the Torah enabled him to assign [*talat lo ha-torah ʾet kol ʾeilu*] the cause of returning to all of these [other reasons]."
D. R. Yosi says: A widow to a high priest; a divorcée and a woman released from levirate marriage to a regular priest; a female *mamzer* or *netin* to a male Jew, a female Jew to a male *mamzer* or *netin*—this is one who is "afraid and soft of heart."

For R. Akiva, the phrase "afraid and soft of heart" refers to an inability to withstand the terror of battle (B); for R. Yosi ha-Galili, it refers to a man's fear of unspecified sins he has committed (C); for R. Yosi, the phrase indicates a more specific list of sins, those of a man marrying a woman forbidden to him by rabbinic law (D). R. Yosi ha-Galili adds yet another line of explanation to his interpretation: the permission given to avoid battle because of building a new home, planting a vineyard, or betrothing a woman acts as a cover for this man's sins. Rather than expose his sins, whatever they may be, the Torah provides this man with the ability to attribute his return from battle to one of these other factors (*talat lo ha-torah ʾet kol ʾeilu*).

R. Yosi ha-Galili's use of the word *talat*—translated as "assign"—links this passage with M. Sotah 3:4–6, the discussion of whether merit suspends the accused sotah's punishment and the permissibility of female Torah study. Within M. Sotah, the verbal root *t.l.y.* appears only in these two locations. Both of these pericopes utilize *t.l.y.* in the sense of protection from sin, with one referring to sexual transgression (3:4–6) and the other leaving the type of sin unspecified (8:9). Both pericopes also refer to Torah, one linking suspension of punishment to Torah study (3:4) and the other to Torah's providing an alibi (8:9). Through these dual occurrences of the root *t.l.y.*, M. Sotah connects the male battlefield with the sotah, sexual transgression, and the possibility of female Torah study.

It should therefore not surprise that of the three different opinions provided by M. Sotah 8:9, B. Sotah evidences the most interest in that of R. Yosi ha-Galili, referencing his opinion a total of three times (43a–b, 44a, 44b). B. Sotah's lesser interests in R. Akiva and R. Yosi is in keeping with its turn to a wider field of correct moral behavior instead of a focus solely on battlefield behavior or sexual transgression. Rather than attribute B. Sotah's increased interest in R. Yosi ha-Galili to a compassionate desire to protect these men's reputations, its interest can more convincingly be accounted for by the root *t.l.y.* in R. Yosi ha-Galili's statement.[6] B. Sotah subtly amplifies these connections between the battlefield, the sotah, and Torah study.

EXEMPTION FROM BATTLE AND TORAH STUDY: BAVLI SOTAH 44B

B. Sotah 44b opens its commentary on M. Sotah 8:9 by interrogating the difference between the statements of R. Yosi ha-Galili and R. Yosi. It posits that R. Yosi ha-Galili would permit even those men who have committed sins that fall into the less severe category of violations of rabbinic law (*ʿaveirah de-rabanan*) to return from war; in contrast, R. Yosi would permit only those men who have violated biblical law to return from war. When it presents an example of a violation of rabbinic law, B. Sotah leaves behind R. Yosi in favor of R. Yosi ha-Galili:

A. According to whom does that which is taught [in a baraita] follow?
B. One who speaks between each tefillin capsule [*sah bein tefilah li-tfilah*]—this is a sin in his hand and he returns from the battle arrangements.
C. Like whom? Like R. Yosi ha-Galili.

Read straightforwardly, B. Sotah's example—a man who speaks between putting on the tefillin capsules of the arm and the head—aims only to provide an instance of the rabbinic commandments to which R. Yosi ha-Galili refers. However, the root of tefillin (*t.f.l.*) is the same as the root for lasciviousness (*t.f.l.*), that which R. Eliezer declares will be the consequence of a father teaching his daughter Torah (M. Sotah 3:4).[7] Indeed, as Elizabeth Shanks Alexander argues, the rabbis derive women's exemption from the commandment to wear tefillin from their exemption from Torah study: "Since tefillin are in their essence a form of Torah study, anyone who is exempt from Torah study is also exempt from tefillin."[8] Connecting R. Yosi ha-Galili's statement in the Mishnah with this baraita, B. Sotah links the necessity for a man to return from battle to his failure to properly fulfill part of a foundational commandment, one from which the rabbis exempt women.[9] B. Sotah's choice to leave behind R. Yosi (a more direct route to sexual transgression) and to emphasize R. Yosi ha-Galili (a more subtle route to sexual transgression) enables it to create a wider legal web of interconnected categories, in this case those of the battlefield, sexual transgression, and Torah study.[10]

In contrast to B. Sotah, when Y. Sotah examines the mishnaic phrase "that he is afraid of the transgressions in his hand," it discusses the importance of ensuring that a man's sins are not public knowledge (Y. Sotah 8:5 [9], 23a). Instead of connecting R. Yosi ha-Galili's words with a baraita about tefillin, it links them with a statement in the name of Reish Lakish about sacrificial law. According to Reish Lakish, the Torah rules that a sin offering is slaughtered in the same place as a burnt offering (Leviticus 6:18) in order to make it difficult to differentiate between the two sacrifices and so not publicize a person's sins. While we may contrast Y. Sotah's concern with hiding (male) sin to that of publicizing the sotah's sin, the Yerushalmi nevertheless does not intertwine M. Sotah 8:9 with the status of rabbinic commandments, tefillin, or Torah study.

In a talmudic chapter whose topic is the battlefield, one might argue that the move away from the sotah to the male Jew makes intuitive sense. However, M. Sotah's use of the root *t.l.y.* in connection with sin and B. Sotah's use of the root *t.f.l.* in connection with tefillin demonstrate that even in the context of the battlefield, this tractate is still thinking with and through the sotah. Its subtle allusions to the sotah ritual demonstrate that much as B. Sotah seeks to mute the horror of the mishnaic ritual its prescriptions for male life remain intertwined with the sotah.

ORPAH, DAVID, AND GOLIATH: BAVLI SOTAH 42B

B. Sotah's reimagining of the battle between David and Goliath blunts this tractate's attempt to soften the mishnaic sotah ritual. On the surface, its unique retelling of the biblical tale of David and Goliath (1 Samuel 17) presents us with a tale of Israel's victory over a foreign enemy through a model male warrior.[11] Yet a closer look reveals B. Sotah's suspicion of David's military prowess. David's victory over Goliath does not result from his skill as a warrior but rather from David's reliance on God's power, Goliath's misuse of language, and Goliath's attempt to prevent shema recitation and Torah study. This emphasis on language intersects with the oath of the sotah ritual (written, recited, and erased) and with the tractate's turn to *lashon ha-ra*. The turn to shema recitation and Torah study will once again bring us to the ways in which this tractate hides and surfaces women.

Words and War

M. Sotah 8:3[12] lays the groundwork for B. Sotah's retelling of the battle between David and Goliath. It exhorts the nation Israel not to fear in battle: unlike their enemies who rely on human strength, Israel relies on God's strength. As proof, M. Sotah 8:3 reminds its audience of how Philistine dependence on Goliath resulted in Goliath's death and subsequent Philistine defeat at Israel's hand. In its brief recapitulation of the battle, M. Sotah 8:3 does not mention David by name, a move that emphasizes the importance of Israel's reliance on God. B. Sotah, however, returns David to the center of this tale, even blurring the line between David and God.[13] The first half of the sugya is structured around four different statements attributed to the Palestinian sage R. Yohanan:[14]

A. Goliath—
B. Said R. Yohanan: That he [Goliath] stood audaciously [*be-gilui panim*] before the Holy Blessed One. As it is said: "Choose yourselves a man [*ʾish*] and let him come down against me" [1 Samuel 17:8]. And "man" [*ʾish*] refers only to the Holy Blessed One, as it is said, "God is a man of war [*ʾish milhamah*]" [Exodus 15:3].
C. Said the Holy Blessed One: Behold I will cause him [Goliath] to fall at the hands of a son of a man [*ben ʾish*].[15] As it is said, "And David was the son of this Ephrathite man [*ben ʾish ʾefrati*]" [1 Samuel 17:12].

Citing two verses from the David-Goliath story (1 Samuel 17:8, 12) and one verse from the Exodus narrative (Exodus 15:3) that use the word *ʾish*, R. Yohanan depicts God as a man (*ʾish*) and David as the son of that man (*ben ʾish*) (B–C). With its creation of a patrilineal ancestry for

David as the son of the warrior God and its blurring of the lines between David and God,[16] this passage appears to cast David as an ideal counterpart to the Torah-studying sage, one who battles through the sword rather than the word.[17] But B. Sotah undercuts that assumption by also attributing Goliath's defeat to his misuse of words rather than David's skill as a warrior. This occurs with Goliath's audacious demand that God descend to fight him and in R. Yohanan's (in the name of R. Meir) next explanation for Goliath's defeat, one that opens with yet another citation of 1 Samuel 17:8:

D. Said R. Yohanan[18] in the name of R. Meir: In three instances his [own] mouth caught that evil one [Goliath]:
E. First, "Choose yourselves a man [*ʾish*] and let him come down against me" [1 Samuel 17:8].
F. And another: "If he can best me in combat and kill me [we will become your slaves; but if I best him and kill him, you shall be our slaves and serve us]" [1 Samuel 17:9].
G. And another: That he said to David, "'Am I a dog that you come against me with sticks?' [The Philistine cursed David by his gods]" [1 Samuel 17:43].

Through three different verses (1 Samuel 17:8, 9, 43), B. Sotah posits that Goliath figuratively opened the door to his own defeat. He did so first in asking a man to come down to him—that is, to prevail over him—rather than fight with him (E);[19] second, in beginning with a statement presuming Philistine defeat and enslavement (F); and third, in positioning himself as a dog and cursing David (G).

The passage continues with two additional statements from B. Sotah's anonymous voice, the first implying that David acted in a similar way to Goliath, opening the door to his own defeat, and the second countering that proposition:

H. David also said to him: "You come against me with sword and spear and javelin" [1 Samuel 17:45].
I. Then he said to him: "But I come against you in the name of the Lord of Hosts, the God of the ranks of Israel, whom you have defied" [1 Samuel 17:45].

Although David initially names Goliath's weapons and thus his potential military prowess (H), he concludes by emphasizing his own reliance on God's power (I). Earlier in the tractate, B. Sotah positioned David as a male version of the sotah. Here, B. Sotah uses David to remind us of yet another key ingredient of its vision of rabbinic masculinity: that Israel's status depends on God's favor rather than male physical might.

Shema, Torah, and Goliath

The priest's address to the soldiers begins with the words "Hear, O Israel [*shema yisra'el*]" (Deuteronomy 20:3), identical to the opening words of the liturgical shema (Deuteronomy 6:4). Unsurprisingly, B. Sotah earlier connects the priest's words to the twice-daily recitation of shema: "Said R. Yohanan in the name of R. Shimon bar Yohai: Said the Holy Blessed One to Israel, 'Even if you have only fulfilled [the commandment of] reciting shema in the morning and evening, you will not be sent into their hands'" (B. Sotah 42a). Men's successful fulfillment of the commandment to recite shema twice a day results in God's protecting Israel from defeat at the hands of their enemies. In the next stage of B. Sotah's retelling of the story of David and Goliath, the attempt to prevent men from reciting shema becomes a mark of Israel's enemies. Goliath becomes the anti-Jew, a warrior who attempts—and fails—to prevent the male Israel from engaging in two central commandments, shema recitation and Torah study:

J. "And the Philistine stepped forward morning and night" [1 Samuel 17:16].
K. Said R. Yohanan: In order to prevent them from [reciting] shema morning and evening.
L. "And stood [*va-yityatzeiv*] for forty days" [1 Samuel 17:16].
M. Said R. Yohanan: This corresponds to the forty days during which Torah was given to them.

In the first of these next two statements attributed to R. Yohanan, the sage maps the twice-daily appearance of Goliath for battle (1 Samuel 17:16) onto the commandment to recite shema twice daily, morning and evening (J–K). In the second, he maps the forty-day period during which Goliath waited for a challenger onto the period of Moses's ascension of Mount Sinai to receive the stone tablets of God's covenant,[20] conflated with Torah itself (L–M). Since both shema recitation and Torah study are particularly male obligations—ones that become markers of male time[21]—this portion of the sugya engages the tractate's larger interest in gender, family, and Torah study. Indeed, it returns us to the sugya with which I opened this chapter, one that connects the exemption from battle to talking between putting on each of the tefillin capsules. In turn, that link brought us to the potential lasciviousness of female Torah study. When B. Sotah imagines Goliath as trying to prevent Israel from shema recitation and Torah study, it thus alludes to this interconnected and gendered web of tefillin, shema, Torah, sexual transgression, and fear. While females, and the sotah in particular, are not yet explicitly present in the Goliath and David story, close attention to textual clues enables us to surface them as visibly hidden.

Reading Orpah and the Sotah

R. Yohanan, in yet one more tradition, posits Goliath as the son of one hundred fathers and one mother, that is a man of uncertain patrilineage.[22] Although we might be tempted to read this tradition about Goliath's filiation, and the ones that will follow, as condemning women for sexual promiscuity, they may equally be read as condemning male sexuality. As B. Sotah continues to explore Goliath's parentage, it will bring Orpah into focus. Telling one story about Goliath's name and another about Orpah's, B. Sotah points us to male sexuality gone wrong and simultaneously maps the violence of the mishnaic sotah ritual onto Orpah's body. With its imagery of gang rape, this next section of the sugya returns us to M. Sotah's pornographic voyeurism and violence:

A. "And Goliath was his name, from Gat [*mi-gat*]" [1 Samuel 17:4].
B. Taught Rav Yosef: That everyone threshed [*dashin*] his mother like a vat [*ke-gat*] for wine-pressing.
C. It is written *ma'arot*, but we read *ma'arkhot* [In 1 Samuel 17:23: "While he was talking to them, the champion, whose name was Goliath, the Philistine of Gath, stepped forward from the Philistine ranks (*mi-ma'arot*) and spoke the same words as before; and David heard him"].
D. Taught Rav Yosef: That everyone had the initial stage of sexual intercourse [*he'eru*] with his mother.

Extrapolating from two different verses that give Goliath's name (1 Samuel 17:4, 23), the pericope presents two varying and yet overlapping traditions about the meaning of Goliath's name. In contrast to those characters in B. Sotah who receive their names as an indication of praiseworthy actions and even God's intervention (such as Joshua, Caleb, and Joseph),[23] each explanation of Goliath from Gat's name encodes his mother's sexual violation by the male everyone. The first (B) compares her rape and subsequent pregnancy with Goliath to the preparation of wine (Goliath is from *gat* and his mother was raped *ke-gat*), linking us back to the tractate's opening and its caution against men drinking wine.[24] The second (C) echoes the question of the time measurement sufficient for "hiding," also discussed in the tractate's first chapter (reading the word *ma'arot* as from the same root as *ha'ara'ah,* the initial insertion of the penis into the vagina).[25] Both of these portraits of Goliath's paternity thus remind us of larger themes within the tractate: of the need for men to take precautions against sexual sin and the sources of male knowledge (in B. Sotah 3b–4b, self-experience, teachers, or God). Crucially, though, rather than B. Sotah imagining brutality enacted upon the body of the sotah, it now transfers that brutality to his yet unnamed mother's body.

B. Sotah goes on to provide two names for Goliath's mother: Harafah and Orpah. 2 Samuel 21:15–17 describes an attack on King David and his army by the Philistines, led by a man descended from *ha-rafah,* a word that may refer to giants.[26] B. Sotah conflates this later attack by a descendant of *ha-rafah* with the earlier attack by Goliath. In the process, *harafah* becomes a name of Goliath's mother. Ruth 1:4 describes Orpah as the wife of one of Naomi's two sons. (Ruth is the wife of the other son.)

E. It is written *harafah* [2 Samuel 21:16] and it is written *'orpah* [Ruth 1:4].

F. Rav and Shmuel: One said, Harafah was her name. And why is her name [also] called Orpah? Because everyone covered [*'orfin*] her from behind.

G. And one said, Orpah is her name. And why is her name [also] called Harafah? Because everyone threshed [*dashin*] her like grits [*ke-harifot*]. And thus it says, "And the woman took and spread a cloth over the mouth of the well and spread over it grits [*harifot*]" [2 Samuel 17:19].

H. And if you want say [it is derived] from here: "Even if you pound

> the fool with a mortar with a pestle along with grits [*harifot*]" [Proverbs 27:22].

Like her son's name, Orpah-Harafah's name encodes sexual violence. In the one case, Harafah is the primary name; the secondary name Orpah depicts the way she was raped from behind (F). In the other case, Orpah is the primary name; the secondary Harafah depicts the relentless manner of her rape (G). Yet, even as B. Sotah names Orpah-Harafah for sexual violence, that naming is not without ambiguity. 2 Samuel 17:19 ("And the woman took and spread a cloth over the mouth of the well and spread over it grits")—one of the two proof texts for the name Harafah—depicts female heroism (G). When David's son Absalom attempts to overthrow him, this unnamed woman hides David's other son Jonathan and his loyal follower Ahimaaz in a well, enabling them to survive and to warn David of Absalom's plan. Goliath fails to defeat David and Israel in war; B. Sotah (in one tradition) derives his mother's name from the actions of an unnamed woman who proves crucial to David's victory. This woman's care for Jonathan and Ahimaaz should be conceptualized as a countervoice to the failures of care that result in homicide and the necessity for the *ʿeglah ʿarufah* ritual, that is the elders' failure to escort and provide food for a stranger in their midst. In contrast, the men's rape of Harafah-Orpah should be conceptualized as emblematizing a total failure of care, with Orpah's name echoing that of the *ʿeglah ʿarufah*.[27]

The sotah ritual requires that the sexual relationship be consensual and not one of rape. Regardless of her marital and national status, Orpah thus should not be imagined as a sotah. B. Sotah's refusal to position a named woman as a potential sotah contrasts with its rendering men sotah-like, as we saw earlier in the case of David and Joseph. Nevertheless, here in B. Sotah, the figure of Orpah, about whom the book of Ruth intimates no sexual violence, becomes a site for imagined violence. As Goliath's mother acquires a name, she becomes a tragic figure.[28]

WOMEN WHO CARE FOR A NATION: BAVLI SOTAH 11A–13B

The brutality that B. Sotah imagines for Orpah—rape and loss of her children—stands in stark contrast to B. Sotah's retelling of the story of the women from the Exodus narrative (Exodus 1:15–2:10).[29] While the biblical Exodus account surely imagines childbirth and care for those children—whether by mothers, midwives, sisters, or daughters—as core to Israel's liberation, the extensive aggadic sugya that retells the Exodus story (B. Sotah 11a–13b)[30] expands, enhances, and redraws this imaginary. Utilizing themes drawn from the sotah and *ʿeglah ʿarufah* rituals, B. Sotah depicts females—girls, women, spouses, sisters, daughters, mothers, and midwives—as engaged in personal and political rebellions that subvert patriarchal familial and political hierarchies.[31] M. Sotah 1:9's assertion that measure-for-measure applies as much to righteous as to wrongful acts[32] and its presentation of Miriam as an instantiation of this principle provide the impetus for B. Sotah's extended excursus on the females of the Exodus:[33] "And so too for matters of good. Miriam waited for her brother for one hour. As it says, 'And his sister stood at a distance [to learn what would befall him]' [Exodus 2:4]. Therefore, Israel waited for her for seven days in the wilderness. As it says, '[So Miriam was shut out of the camp for seven days;] and the people did not march on until Miriam was readmitted' [Numbers 12:15]." M. Sotah continues with a list of honorable burials that engage this principle of measure-for-measure: Joseph buried his father Jacob; as a result, Moses carried Joseph's bones out of Egypt; in turn, as a reward for carrying Joseph's bones, Moses merited burial by God. By including Miriam in a list along with Joseph and Moses, both of whom engage in the intimate act of burial and thus are themselves rewarded with honorable burials, M. Sotah intimates that her reward is also due to a comparable relational act. Miriam's behavior toward her brother (watching over him in the place meant to be his burial ground and witnessing his subsequent rescue) and Israel's behavior toward Miriam (waiting for her while she is exiled from the camp due to a skin disease that renders her comparable to a dead person) should be conceptualized as parallel to Joseph and Moses's care for the dead. Thus, while M. Sotah's brief portrayal of Miriam surely contains a literary kernel upon which B. Sotah builds, B. Sotah's transformation of Miriam into a rebellious prophet and national savior—and, crucially, the reading of all the women in the Exodus narrative in this light—reflects B. Sotah's particular ideological concern with the fate of the nation Israel and women's position as its saviors. As Adrienne Rich writes, "How have women given birth, who has helped them, and how, and why? These are not simply questions of the history of midwifery and obstetrics: they are political questions."[34]

THE RIGHTEOUS WOMEN: BAVLI SOTAH 11B

Ezekiel and the Righteous Women

Miriam traditions bookend B. Sotah's entire exegesis of the Exodus narrative;[35] the righteous women pericope introduces the section that centers on the females of the Exodus narrative. Each of the bookending Miriam pericopes explicates the same Exodus verse that appears in M. Sotah 1:9: "And his sister [Miriam] stood at a distance, to learn what would befall him [Moses]" (Exodus 2:4). The former pericope (B. Sotah 11a) reads each word of the verse as a reference to God's presence (*shekhinah*); the latter (B. Sotah 12b–13a) utilizes the same verse as evidence for Miriam's prophetic knowledge. In both cases, B. Sotah centers Miriam's unique partnership with God in delivering Israel from slavery, a theme that threads its way throughout the entirety of the pericope.[36] Indeed, the narrative of the righteous women engages in a similar centering. However, rather than being organized around verses from the biblical Exodus tale (including Exodus 2:4), the righteous women narrative centers around the book of Ezekiel. In light of Rosen-Zvi's argument for an intricate and profound connection between the book of Ezekiel and the mishnaic sotah ritual, where the details of M. Sotah's depiction of the sotah ritual closely echo those of Ezekiel's account of punishment for adulteresses,[37] the righteous women midrash should be read as an intentional continuation of B. Sotah's interrogation of the mishnaic ritual. The anchor of Ezekiel rather than Exodus 1:15–2:10 points to the larger context of the tractate as a driving force for the creation and inclusion of this midrash within B. Sotah. In addition, the righteous women midrash acts as a corrective to the disappearing female sotah. Much like the introductory sugya to the entire tractate, this midrash teaches us how to read the tales of women that follow. I present the midrashic pericope in full below:

A. Expounded Rav Avira:[38] For the reward of the righteous women who were in that generation was Israel redeemed from Egypt.
B. At the time when they went to draw water, the Holy Blessed One prepared for them small fish in their jars and they drew out half water and half fish. And they came and placed two pots, one for hot water and one for fish.
C. And they brought them to their husbands in the field and

washed them and anointed them with oil and fed them and gave them to drink and had sexual intercourse with them between the mounds in the field [*shefatayim*]. As it is said, "Even for those of you who lie among the sheepfolds [*shefatayim*] [there are wings of a dove sheathed in silver, its pinions in fine gold]" [Psalms 68:14].

D. For the reward of "you who lie among the sheepfolds" Israel merited the spoil of Egypt, as it is said, "there are wings of a dove sheathed in silver, its pinions in fine gold" [Psalms 68:14].

E. And when they became pregnant they went to their houses.

F. When the time of their giving birth arrived, they went and gave birth in the field under the apple tree. As it is said, "[Who is she that comes up from the desert, Leaning upon her beloved [*dodah*]?] Under the apple tree I roused you; [it was there your mother conceived you. There she who bore you conceived you]" [Song of Songs 8:5].

G. And the Holy Blessed One sent from heaven[39] one who cleansed and smoothed them like a midwife who smooths a newborn. As it is said, "As for your birth, when you were born and your navel cord was not cut, and you were not bathed in water to smooth you; [you were not rubbed with salt, nor were you swaddled]" [Ezekiel 16:4].

H. And He would gather for them two cakes, one of oil and one of honey. As it is said, "[He set him atop the highlands, to feast on the yield of the earth;] He fed him honey from the crag, and oil from the flinty rock" [Deuteronomy 32:13].

I. And when Egypt recognized them, they came to kill them and a miracle was done for them and they were swallowed by the earth. And they brought oxen and plowed over their backs. As it is said, "Plowmen plowed across my back; [they made long furrows]" [Psalms 129:3].

J. After they left, they broke through and came forth like the grass of the field, as it is said, "I let you grow like the plants of the field; [and you continued to grow up until you attained to womanhood, until your breasts became firm and your hair sprouted, you were still naked and bare]" [Ezekiel 16:7].

K. And when they had grown, they came in flocks to their houses, as it is written, "And you continued to grow up until you attained to womanhood [*va-tirbi va-tigdeli va-tavo'i ba'adi 'adayim*]" [Ezekiel 16:7]. Do not read, *ba'adi 'adayim* but rather, *be'edrei 'adarim*.

L. And when the Holy Blessed One was revealed at the Sea, they recognized Him first,[40] as it is written, "This is my God and I will glorify Him [Exodus 15:2]."

Although the righteous women midrash is structured around disparate verses from Psalms, Song of Songs, Ezekiel, Deuteronomy, and Exodus, the exegetical key to this narrative lies in an expanded exegetical reading of Ezekiel 16:3–13. Drawing on Ezekiel's tale of the birth and growth of Jerusalem—representative of the collective Israel—the midrash turns Jerusalem's "birth-day" (Ezekiel 16:4) into Israel's beginnings as a people in Egypt.[41] For example, when B. Sotah cites Song of Songs 8:5, it implicitly references Ezekiel 16:8 (F). That is, Song of Songs 8:5 is midrashically useful not only because of its mention of an apple tree or its description of birth but also because of the word *dodah* (beloved) in the verse's beginning. The word *dodah* links Song of Songs 8:5 to Ezekiel 16:8 and its mention of *'eit dodim*: "When I passed by you [again] and saw that your time for love [*'eit dodim*] had arrived. So I spread My robe over you and covered your nakedness, and I entered into a covenant with you by oath—declares the Lord God; thus you became Mine." In turn, when B. Sotah depicts God providing food for the infants and cites Deuteronomy 32:13 (H) it likely references Ezekiel 16:13: "Your food was choice flour, honey, and oil."[42] Thus, much as Ezekiel 16:3–13 casts the infant Jerusalem as an abandoned and naked female, without care until she enters puberty,[43] B. Sotah transforms this troubling imagery into a picture of female and divine care from the moment of birth. In the process, B. Sotah shifts attention from the graphic imagery of female sexual betrayal and subsequent punishment found later in Ezekiel 16—as well as in Ezekiel 23—to a historical tale of miraculous deliverance from death in a time of war. Indeed, B. Sotah does not cite verses from Ezekiel 16:15–63 or from Ezekiel 23.[44] In this midrashic pericope, rather than nakedness intimating abuse, it intimates an opportunity for care.

This process of transformation and shifting attention in regard to the book of Ezekiel is similar to the ways in which B. Sotah engages M. Sotah. As we have seen, B. Sotah does not erase the brutal mishnaic ritual but shifts our attention to male sin and even to men as potential sotahs. However, in this midrashic pericope, B. Sotah engages the mishnaic ritual in yet another way: it subverts the sotah ritual by disappearing men—rather than disappearing females—and, crucially, by mirroring the sotah ritual itself.

Mirroring and Subverting the Sotah Ritual

The midrash continues its interrogation of the sotah ritual not only through its use of the book of Ezekiel, but also through its mirroring of the sotah ritual. This mirroring of the sotah ritual extends beyond the book of Ezekiel, through the story's use of the motifs of seduction, pregnancy, birth, hiding, and home.[45] Yonah Fraenkel has pointed out the ways in which the themes of this story touch on the dictum of measure-for-measure (M. Sotah's 1:7): The field becomes a house, first by the women for their husbands (B–C) and then by God for the babies (G–I). The women cook two pots, one for hot water and one for fish; God, in return, gathers two cakes, one of oil and one of honey (B). The women wash and anoint their husbands; God cleans and smooths the newborn babies (C, G).[46] Yet, in ignoring the larger context of B. Sotah in which this midrash is embedded, Fraenkel fails to notice the ways in which these women, by doing in the field what is supposed to be "done" in the house, mirror the sotah herself.[47] In other words, the context of B. Sotah also drives the formulation of this midrashic pericope.

The sotah ritual legally enjoins a wife, through the process of warning, against secreting herself with another man for an amount of time long enough for them to potentially engage in sexual intercourse. In contrast, the righteous women defy Pharaoh's decree and go down to the field—an open space—to have sexual intercourse (C). The righteous women seek out their husbands (B, C); the sotah is accused of evading her husband. The righteous women bring water to the field to wash and feed their husbands (B, C); the sotah is forced to drink a water potion to test her innocence or guilt. As penalty for transgressing her husband's warning, the sotah will suffer some kind of injury to her reproductive organs; the righteous women, in transgressing Pharaoh and seducing their husbands, become pregnant (E).[48] In the one case God redeems the women and saves their children from death (I, J); in the other, God judges and punishes the woman, by miscarriage, infertility, or even death. God covers the babies with earth to protect them (I); a priest rips the sotah's clothing to reveal her breasts. The righteous women figure women's sexuality as redemptive; the sotah ritual figures women's sexuality as something that must be constrained and policed. Rather than the accused sotah being acted upon by those who presume her guilt and force her confession, B. Sotah positions women as subjects, signaling this move through the ongoing use of female-gendered active verbs. In B. Sotah, the field becomes a mirror of the home where what would be expected in the home (but is now forbidden by Egyptian decree) becomes a surprising and unexpected act of redemption where the righteous women, through their acts of seduction, are figured as saviors of a nation.

Later versions of the righteous women midrash crystallize the theme of mirroring.[49] The Tanhuma and Deuteronomy Rabbah both describe women bringing mirrors to the field and using them to arouse their husband's desire.[50] In the Tanhuma version, the mirrors are eventually donated by these women as freewill offerings to the tabernacle and then utilized to build the basin in which the priests wash their hands and feet to prepare for divine service.

The details of this B. Sotah midrash also reach beyond the sotah ritual to other passages within the tractate. The midrash on Goliath and David depicts God as "a man of war" (Exodus 15:3), saving David from defeat at the hands of Goliath; the righteous women passage cites "this is my God and I will glorify Him" (Exodus 15:2) as a proof text for the children's miraculous recognition of God at the Reed Sea. The children's ability to recognize God stems from God's care for them in the field. No longer a "man of war" (Exodus 15:3), God has become—in at least some versions of the text—a midwife who smooths the limbs of the newborn babies.[51]

This remaking of God into a midwife also previews the extensive discussion of midwives in this larger aggadic sugya about the Exodus. Not only does the passage provide names for the midwives—Shifrah, Puah, Yocheved, Miriam, and Elisheva—but it also imagines (in an otherwise unattested baraita) the human midwives acting much as the righteous women narrative imagines God acting. Like God, the midwives supply the newborn babies with water and food (B. Sotah 11b).[52] These acts of midwifery, by women and by God, are the inverse of one of the crimes that results in murder and the necessity for the *ʿeglah ʿarufah* ritual, that is neglecting to feed a stranger. So, too, the righteous women's accompaniment of their babies under the earth is the inverse of the neglect to accompany the stranger, another act that results in murder.

Later in this sugya, we find yet another inversion of the *ʿeglah ʿarufah* ritual in its representation of the daughter of Pharaoh. B. Sotah depicts her as intentionally walking to her death when she goes to rescue a baby (Moses) from the Nile. In another act of unnecessary care, she defies her attendants who remind her of her father's status and authority and miraculously extends her arm to save the baby.[53] We may add Pharaoh's daughter to our list of righteous women.

READING FORWARD

A reader of B. Sotah encounters models for male virtue and fears of male failure. These models draw on and reference the sotah ritual. In the context of the battlefield laws, not talking between putting on each of the tefillin capsules brings us to M. Sotah's debate about female Torah study and lascivious behavior. In turn, Goliath's defeat is partially attributable to his attempt to prevent men from shema recitation and Torah study. These claims require a particular form of careful reading, an attention to keywords that directs our attention to one pedagogical purpose of B. Sotah as a tractate: the induction of men into the rabbinic community.

Yet this tractate's method of induction into the male rabbinic community also utilizes the sotah. It is here that I would like us to move toward a more constructive stance, one that does not hide from the sotah ritual's brutality but does not conclude with that brutality. A reader of the entirety of B. Sotah will encounter the violent spectacle of the sotah ritual, the rape of Orpah-Harafah, and the grace and care of the righteous women for whose sake Israel was redeemed from slavery. We could choose to read all of these as policing women and women's sexuality, first through the ritual's coercion and second through the exemplar of what it means to be a "good" woman. If a woman leaves the home, she must do so in service of saving the people Israel. Indeed, we should not hide from the ways in which B. Sotah mutes the mishnaic ritual's horror and projects its violence onto Orpah-Harafah. Yet, we may remember this brutality and *also* choose another way to read B. Sotah.

When read outside of B. Sotah or even within the more local context of the tractate's midrash on Exodus 1:8–2:9, the homily of the righteous women can rightfully be conceptualized as a text of rebellion against Pharaoh and Egyptian domination and, as represented by the women's initiative, against male hierarchy more generally. When read within the context of B. Sotah, the righteous women midrash becomes not only rebellious but also subversive. This midrash admittedly does not portray the righteous women as rebelling against, that is trying to overturn, the sotah ritual. Nevertheless, its very placement in the first chapter of the tractate enables the midrash to act as a subversive countertradition, a voice antithetical to that of the sotah ritual and its attendant brutality. Within B. Sotah's literary structure, the illicit sexuality of the sotah flows into the licit sexuality of the righteous women, breaking down the dichotomy between the two and enabling the second to subvert the first. By locating and telling the story of these women as exemplars of rebellion and redemption in the midst of the sotah ritual, B. Sotah opens for its readers an imaginative gap toward alternative possibilities that run counter to those depicted through the ritual itself. The righteous women become political figures, subverting ideas of both who sins and who saves.

AFTERWORD

Reading Bavli Sotah as a tractate involves reckoning with the brutality of the sotah ritual as well as noticing the ways in which the tractate subverts this brutal ritual. It involves noticing the ways in which the sotah herself disappears and the ways in which she is replaced by moral men and sinning men alike. It involves noticing where and how females are present and the ways in which this tractate imagines females as vital to society's stability and its redemption. It involves noticing the ways in which the sotah and the sotah ritual overflow the boundaries of the ritual itself to inform and shape a range of topics within this talmudic tractate.

The methodological choice to analyze B. Sotah as a literary unit, a methodology that rests on the long-standing transmission of the two Talmuds through the smaller unit of the tractate as well as on the particular content of B. Sotah, has enabled these different acts of noticing. The intertwined nature of B. Sotah's literary composition indicates significant post-amoraic editorial activity, activity that we might consider as more akin to our modern concept of authorship. While M. Sotah is surely more literarily integrated than some previous scholars have contended, B. Sotah is literarily and topically integrated to a far greater extent. This integration includes the seventh through ninth chapters of the tractate, those about ritual language, the priest anointed for war, and the *ʿeglah ʿarufah*.

Late editorial hands have introduced B. Sotah with a pedagogical eye. By beginning with a pericope that emphasizes rabbinic learning and male potential for sin, the editors inform us that male learning and male sin—rather than female transgression—will be a main topic of this tractate. In other words, editorial hands have noticed and highlighted a particular thematic tendency throughout the tractate, pointed us toward it, and simultaneously intervened within the tractate to emphasize this theme. As we have seen, rabbinic learning and the disappearance of the rabbinic academy bookend this tractate.

Reading only the portions of B. Sotah that directly address the sotah ritual results in a misunderstanding of the tractate itself and of its approach to the ritual. B. Sotah does not depict the historical memory of an accused sotah, as do other mishnaic and talmudic tractates, or imagine a female sotah into presence. Remembering or reconstructing a historical sotah ritual and emphasizing female sin are not the tractate's main project. Neither is framing the sotah as an act of rebellion against God akin to the golden calf episode. Instead, B. Sotah constructs King David as the sotah whom Torah study protects from assassination. It mirrors the erasure of the Torah's text to create the bitter waters with the threatened erasure of Joseph's name from the priestly *ʾeifod* should he sin sexually with Potiphar's wife.

B. Sotah surely responds to M. Sotah's brutal reimagining of the sotah ritual by changing its—and our—focus to male responsibility for sin and to the creation of a moral rabbinic male. Yet, as I have observed, the sotah and the sotah ritual thread their way throughout entire tractate, becoming a vehicle through which this tractate interrogates and constructs its concerns with gender, authority, and national existence.

A crucial aspect of this book, then, lies in my desire to make evident the ways in which B. Sotah disappears women and, concomitantly, to search out and re-emphasize female presence throughout the tractate. In a tractate with a number of extended aggadic sections about women, it may seem paradoxical to emphasize the sotah's disappearance and female invisibility. Yet noticing the ways in which B. Sotah minimizes the sexual sin of the sotah and makes her relatively invisible also enables us to see the ways in which the tractate opens a space to imagine and name women as crucial to the creation, formation, and stabilization of rabbinic culture. Male sages, on the other hand, are imagined as responsible for the unraveling of rabbinic society. Women may teach their children Torah, as do the anonymous mothers; they may save a nation, as do the righteous women; they may talk with one another about the transmission of Torah, as do the wife of R. Abbahu and the wife of the speaker; or they may model care for travelers rather than instigate heresy, as does the female innkeeper. I recognize that I run the risk of oversimplification and falling into an all-too-familiar trap of idealizing women while leaving them powerless. Nevertheless, I contend that reading B. Sotah in such a way that recognizes both invisibility and presence enables us to posit a more complex picture of the Babylonian Talmud and of rabbinic culture where women are not simply enablers of male culture but vital creators. This wider picture involves the transmission and reception of Torah but is not limited to the text of the Torah, or even to talking about Torah. It includes familial learning and familial care; care for strangers and care for the nation; defiance of authority, whether foreign or within Israel itself.

Reading B. Sotah as a tractate enables us to think beyond a binary of the sexually sinning sotah and the perfectly righteous woman. B. Sotah does project the brutality of the ritual onto the figure of Orpah, depicting her as raped by numerous men and her children as killed in war. Yet the tractate also emblematizes her rape as a failure of care, with Orpah's name echoing the *ʿeglah ʿarufah*. The story of the righteous women for whose sake Israel is redeemed presents us with yet another voice, one antithetical to the ritual's brutality.

In reading B. Sotah as a tractate, I want us to acknowledge brutality yet not let it overwhelm us. Rather, I also want us to acknowledge the alternative possibilities held out by the women who are very much present in this tractate. The redactors of this tractate did not have to include these stories, including those of the righteous women, in this tractate. Yet, these stories made their way into the midst of B. Sotah. Rather than dismiss these stories, I hope that reading for female presence within the context of this entire tractate enables these women to subvert the ritual itself, opening possibilities for further knowledge of the past and a way forward of care.

ACKNOWLEDGMENTS

There are many friends, colleagues, family members, and institutions that played a role in the creation of this book. I want to begin by thanking my havruta Judith Kates. Over many years of studying different tractates together, Judith, a lover and teacher of midrash, kept insisting that we study Bavli Sotah. I resisted, scared of spending extended time with the sotah ritual's brutality. When I finally agreed, I found a complicated and complex combination of brutality and beauty. The idea to write a book about B. Sotah began in our havruta.

I thank a number of other friends and colleagues who helped in matters ranging from reading drafts, to consulting on translations, to finding articles, and much more: Mara Benjamin, Harvey Bock, Moriah Chriki, Sarah Fein, Alyssa Gray, Sarit Kattan Gribetz, Dan Judson, Michelle Kwitkin, Ebn Leader, Micha'el Rosenberg, Ishay Rosen-Zvi, Michael Satlow, Jordan Schuster, Devora Steinmetz, Harvey Sukenic, and Miriam-Simma Walfish. In particular, I want to thank Marjorie Lehman and Miryam Segal. Dialogues with Marjorie about B. Yoma and B. Sotah helped immeasurably to sharpen my ideas and push this book forward. I also thank Marjorie for her close and careful reading of earlier chapter drafts. Miryam invited me to write an article that eventually became chapter 1 of this book. I thank her for giving me the opportunity to try my ideas about the tractate in writing and for her sharp editorial eye.

I cannot thank Gillian Steinberg, my writing coach, enough. I would not have written this book without Gillian's sage support, encouragement, and advice. She helped me articulate what I wanted to say and then guided me to write those ideas. She reminded me that scholarship is always a work in process.

I also thank Tal Ilan for creating the Feminist Commentary on the Babylonian Talmud series. Tal's methodological approach, commenting on an entire tractate through a feminist interpretive lens, played a crucial role in shaping this book.

I thank Hebrew College for its support of this project, and in particular Sharon Cohen Anisfeld, president. I am grateful to work at an institution with deeply supportive colleagues and committed and creative rabbinical students. In two different seminars on B. Sotah, these students helped me shape the ideas in this book.

Feedback I received for papers at three conferences—Rabbinic Narratives (NYU, 2018); Association of Jewish Studies (2020); and TLC: Talmudic Literature Conference (Yale University, 2023)—helped invaluably to refine my ideas. I am also grateful to Jacob Cytryn and Camp Ramah in Wisconsin, where as scholar-in-residence I had the opportunity to write and workshop parts of this book over two summers. The wonderful group Jacob invited me to teach on Shabbat afternoons was one of the joys of this process.

Thank you to Brandeis University Press and to Sylvia Fuks Fried for shepherding this book. The two anonymous readers provided careful and insightful feedback that has helped improve this book immeasurably. Thank you.

An earlier version of parts of chapter 1 appeared as "The Moral Man and the Disappearing Sotah: The Bavli's Response to Mishnah Sotah," *Jewish Law Association Studies* 32. Anatomies of Home and Disruption (2023): 89–109. An earlier version of parts of chapter 6 appeared as "The Righteous Women of Bavli Sotah: On Reading Talmudic Narrative in the Context of a Tractate," in *Studies in Rabbinic Narrative*, vol. 1, edited by Jeffrey Rubenstein (Providence: Brown Judaic Studies, 2021), 79–91. I thank the Jewish Law Association and Brown Judaic Studies for permission to republish these articles.

Much of this book was written at home. I could not have begun or completed it without the help and support of Joyce Murray, our children's wonderful caregiver. Thank you also to my parents, Anna and David Kanarek, for their love and support. And most of all, thank you to Andy, my spouse and partner, and to our children, Lev, Tal, and Adin. In many different ways, big and small, Andy made sure that I had the time to write this book. He also did not hesitate to tell me when an idea was clear in my head but not on paper. Lev, Tal, and Adin never let this book interfere with their growing passion for all things football (soccer). Together, you bring wondrous chaos and care to my life. I am grateful.

NOTES

INTRODUCTION

1. MS Munich 95: "At first, I would say to them when I saw them . . ." The missing words, "that I was humble," appear to be a scribal omission.

2. MS Munich 95: "I am humble." This may be attributed to a scribal omission.

3. Respectively, *deveithu* and *deveiteih*. On these different forms, including the lack of explanation for the ending *hu* in place of *eih*, see Michael Sokoloff, *A Dictionary of Jewish Babylonian Aramaic of the Talmudic and Geonic Periods* (Ramat-Gan: Bar Ilan University Press, 2002), 312, s.v. *deveit-*. MS Vatican and MS Vatican 110: both mentions as *deveithu*.

4. MS Munich 95, MS Vatican 110, MS Cracow 2164 do not include: "His wife went and told R. Abbahu." Extant genizah fragments also do not appear to include the sentence, but these textual witnesses are more ambiguous. I discuss this inclusion/omission toward the end of the introduction.

5. MS Munich 95: She/he (?) said to her, "What do you derive? Through me [?], through you the Most High will be praised." MS Vatican 110: She/he (?) said to her, "What do you derive? From me and from her the Most High will be praised." I return to these differences toward the end of the introduction.

6. Richard Lewis theorizes that R. Abbahu's attribution of greater humility to R. Abba from Akko rests on a distinction between private and public reproof. Whereas R. Abbahu did not feel a need to correct his speaker when in private conversation with his wife, in public he might have done so; R. Abba from Akko, however, resisted making that correction even in public. One could also plausibly posit that the distinction between R. Abbahu and R. Abba rests on R. Abba's lack of anger. See Richard S. Lewis, *"And before Honor—Humility": The Ideal of Humility in the Moral Language of the Sages* (Jerusalem: Magnes Press, 2013), 174–75 [Hebrew].

7. On the social significance of standing within rabbinic culture, see Barry Scott Wimpfheimer, *Narrating the Law: A Poetics of Talmudic Legal Stories* (Philadelphia: University of Pennsylvania Press, 2011), 67–93.

8. On women as "failed males" who are nevertheless necessary to produce children, see Peter Brown, *The Body and Society: Men, Women, and Sexual*

Renunciation in Early Christianity, Twentieth Anniversary Edition with a New Introduction (New York: Columbia University Press, 2008), 10.

9. Melanie Johnson-DeBaufre, "'Gazing Upon the Invisible': Archaeology, Historiography, and the Elusive Wo/men of 1 Thessalonians," in *From Roman to Early Christian Thessalonike: Studies in Religion and Archaeology*, ed. Charalambos Bakirtzis, Laura Nasrallah, and Steven J. Friesen (Cambridge, MA: Harvard Theological Studies, 2010), 92. Johnson-DeBaufre uses the term "wo/men" to indicate that not all women are identical and that power relations are not solely dependent on gender. See Johnson-DeBaufre, "'Gazing Upon the Invisible,'" 73n2.

10. Tiya Miles, *All That She Carried: The Journey of Ashley's Sack, a Black Family Keepsake* (New York: Random House, 2021), 18. Miles writes to uncover the lives behind and history of a sack gifted from mother (Rose) to daughter (Ashley) when the daughter was sold away from her mother. The sack was eventually embroidered by Rose's great-granddaughter Ruth Middleton with the following words:

My great grandmother Rose
mother of Ashley gave her this sack when
she was sold at age 9 in South Carolina
it held a tattered dress 3 handfulls of
pecans a braid of Roses hair. Told her
It be filled with my Love always
she never saw her again
Ashley is my grandmother
Ruth Middleton
1921.
(Miles, *All That She Carried*, 5)

11. As Judith Plaskow wrote in her groundbreaking work of feminist theology: "The questions emerge out of a contradiction between the holes in the text and the felt experience of many Jewish women. For if Moses' words [addressing only the men at Mount Sinai; Exodus 19:15] come as a shock and affront, it is because women have always known or assumed our presence at Sinai; the passage is painful because it seems to deny what we have always taken for granted. Of course we were at Sinai; how is it then that the text could imply we were not there?" Judith Plaskow, *Standing Again at Sinai: Judaism from a Feminist Perspective* (San Francisco: Harper & Row, 1990), 27.

12. On "thinking with" women in the Talmud, see Marjorie Lehman, "Examining the Role of Gender Studies in the Teaching of Talmudic Literature," *Journal of Jewish Education* 72, no. 2 (2006): 109–21.

13. On this point, I am influenced by the work of Jocelyn Penny Small on digressions as culturally determined. That is, what may appear to a contem-

porary reader as a digression may not appear to an ancient reader as such; rather, an author may view a digression as an integral element of a particular rhetorical style (such is the case with Herodotus). See Jocelyn Penny Small, *Wax Tablets of the Mind: Cognitive Studies of Memory and Literacy in Classical Antiquity* (New York: Routledge, 1997), 214–17.

14. The scholarship here is too vast to list. On the voice of the redactor-authors, it is important to highlight the work of David Weiss Halivni and Shamma Friedman. Both Halivni and Friedman have emphasized the importance of distinguishing between earlier layers of the Bavli (tannaitic and amoraic) and the later anonymous dialectical layer. In Halivni's understanding, these later anonymous editors received earlier traditions without their justifications or reasons (apodictic teachings) and then engaged in a process of reconstructing these justifications. For Friedman, the anonymous editors engaged in a process of creatively reshaping earlier traditions rather than trying to reconstruct earlier opinions. Both scholars assume the possibility of reconstructing accurate versions of earlier statements. For an excellent explication of Halivni's methodology and conception of the Bavli's redaction, see Jeffrey Rubenstein's introduction to his translation of Halivni's *Mekorot u-Mesorot*. David Weiss Halivni, *The Formation of the Babylonian Talmud*, trans. Jeffrey L. Rubenstein (New York: Oxford University Press, 2013). The classic explication of Friedman's methodology is found in Shamma Friedman, "Perek ha-ʾishah rabbah ba-bavli," in *Mehkarim u-mekorot*, ed. H. Dimitorovsky (New York: Jewish Theological Seminary of America, 1977), 277–441.

15. On reading a sugya in its wider literary context, see Jeffrey L. Rubenstein, *Talmudic Stories: Narrative Art, Composition, and Culture* (Baltimore: Johns Hopkins University Press, 1999); and Jeffrey L. Rubenstein, *Stories of the Babylonian Talmud* (Baltimore: Johns Hopkins University Press, 2010). In the story of two women, the reader will notice that it is embedded in a larger chain of stories about Rabbi Abbahu and Rabbi Abba of Akko that concern correct ritual performance (the recitation of certain verses during the priestly blessing), political power (the appointment of the head of the academy in Caesarea), and scholarly expertise (the knowledge of authoritative tradition —commonly understood as halakhah—and of aggadah).

16. Marjorie Lehman, *Bringing Down the Temple House: Engendering Tractate Yoma* (Waltham, MA: Brandeis University Press, 2022); Mira Beth Wasserman, *Jews, Gentiles, and Other Animals: The Talmud After the Humanities* (Philadelphia: University of Pennsylvania Press, 2017). See also the monographs of Julia Watts Belser, *Power, Ethics, and Ecology in Jewish Late Antiquity: Rabbinic Responses to Drought and Disaster* (New York: Cambridge University Press, 2015); Charlotte Elisheva Fonrobert, *Menstrual Purity: Rabbinics and Christian Reconstructions of Biblical Gender* (Stanford:

Stanford University Press, 2000); Alyssa M. Gray, *A Talmud in Exile: The Influence of Yerushalmi Avodah Zarah on the Formation of Bavli Avodah Zarah* (Providence, RI: Brown Judaic Studies, 2005); and Christine Elizabeth Hayes, *Between the Babylonian and Palestinian Talmuds: Accounting for Halakhic Difference in Selected Sugyot from Tractate Avodah Zarah* (New York: Oxford University Press, 1997). See also the series founded and edited by Tal Ilan, *A Feminist Commentary on the Babylonian Talmud* (FCBT). Volumes in FCBT do, for the most part, take the tractate as the unit of analysis. Rather than tracing a particular theme through a tractate and positing a theory about redaction, volumes follow medieval Talmud commentary's more atomistic model. Volume introductions may, however, take a more thematic approach. See Ilan's observation about B. Hullin that when a beast or animal is gendered female, it is consistently presented positively: "Yet, in the animal kingdom, it is the female animals, who excel in this realm, to the detriment of their male counterparts. The rabbinic fantasy of the animal world is indeed a topsy-turvy world." Tal Ilan, *Massekhet Hullin: Text, Translation, and Commentary* (Tübingen: Mohr Siebeck, 2017), 24.

17. Lehman, *Bringing Down the Temple House*, 10. See also Moulie Vidas, *Tradition and the Formation of the Talmud* (Princeton, NJ: Princeton University Press, 2016) and, in particular, 45–80.

18. Jacob Neusner, *The Reader's Guide to the Talmud* (Leiden: Brill, 2001), 3–29. See also Zvi Septimus's work on trigger words and simultexts that similarly conceptualize the Bavli as a unified—but not uniform—work. In contrast to Neusner, Septimus emphasizes content over rhetorical forms. Zvi Septimus, "Trigger Words and Simultexts: The Experience of Reading the Bavli," in *Wisdom of Bat Sheva: The Dr. Beth Samuels Memorial Volume*, ed. Barry S. Wimpfheimer (Jersey City: Ktav, 2011), 163–85.

19. See also Abraham Cohen's dissertation where he argues, in regard to selected sugyot from the second and third chapter of B. Sotah, for a post-amoraic redaction, the process of which involves the generation of some completely original material. Abraham Cohen, "An Edition and Comprehensive Commentary on Chapters II & III of Tractate Sotah in the Babylonian Talmud" (PhD diss., Bar-Ilan University, 2013) [Hebrew].

20. J. N. Epstein, *Introduction to Amoraic Literature: Bavli and Yerushalmi* (Jerusalem: Magnes Press, 1962), 91 [Hebrew]. See also Epstein's fuller outline of B. Sotah on 84–94.

21. Lisa Grushcow, *Writing the Wayward Wife: Rabbinic Interpretations of Sotah* (Leiden: Brill, 2005), 269–70. See also Cohen where he argues for the lack of a connection between Bavli and Yerushalmi sugyot discussing the same mishnaic laws. He contends that amoraic statements were not trans-

mitted from Palestinian amoraim to Babylonian or vice versa. Cohen, "Edition and Comprehensive Commentary on Chapters II & III," 2.

22. As Lehman writes, "The tractate has been a defined unit of knowledge transmission for generations." Lehman, *Bringing Down the Temple House*, 8.

23. Scholars have variously identified these authors with, respectively, the last generation of amoraim, the stammaim, or the saboraim. For a summary of recent scholarship on each of these options, see Vidas, *Tradition and the Formation of the Talmud*, 3–4.

24. I intentionally use ambiguous language to describe B. Sotah's position in Nashim. B. Sotah 2a provides a partial list of the order of tractates as Ketubot, Nedarim, Nazir, and Sotah (our order). However, geonic and medieval traditions attest to three additional different orderings around tractate Sotah: 1. Gittin, Sotah, Nazir; 2. Gittin, Nazir, Sotah; 3. Nazir, Gittin, Sotah. See J. N. Epstein, *Introduction to the Mishnaic Text* (Jerusalem: Magnes Press, 2001), 983–86 [Hebrew].

25. Hanokh Albeck, following the tosafists (B. Sotah 31a; s.v. *mi she-kina lah*), contends that chapter 6 should more properly be placed as the third mishnah in chapter 1. Consequently, Albeck also theorizes that chapter 6 is a later addition to M. Sotah. In contrast, David Yechiel Ebner theorizes that the editor may have placed chapter 6 later in order not to disrupt the narrative sequence of the tractate. The separate placement of chapter 6 thus reflects a "finely-tuned pedagogical sense." I lean toward Ebner's hypothesis. See Hanoch Albeck, ed., *The Mishnah: Seder Nashim* (Jerusalem: Bialik Institute, 1988), 230 [Hebrew]; David Yechiel Ebner, "The Composition and Structure of Mishnah 'sotah'" (PhD diss., Yeshiva University, 1980), 45–47, in particular 46.

26. See, for example, Albeck, *Nashim*, 230–31; J. N. Epstein, *Introduction to Tannaitic Literature: Mishna, Tosephta and Halakhic Midrashim* (Jerusalem: Magnes, 1957), 399 [Hebrew].

27. See, for example, Avraham Walfish, who notes the repetition of the verb *m.d.d.* (measure) in the first (1:7), fifth (5:3), and ninth (9:4) chapters of the tractate, highlighting "measurement" as a redactional motif of M. Sotah. Avraham Walfish, "The Measure of Tractate Sotah: Justice beyond the Bounds of Human Jurisdiction," TheGemara, accessed May 7, 2025, https://thegemara.com/article/the-measure-of-tractate-sotah/. See also Gilad Landau, "An Edition and Comprehensive Commentary on Chapter IX of Tractate Sotah in the Babylonian Talmud" (PhD diss., Bar-Ilan University, 2016), 6–7 [Hebrew].

28. This is true even when taking into account the medieval commentaries on the printed page; the other chapters are significantly shorter (chapter 2: 5.5 folio pages; chapter 3: 5 folio pages; chapter 4: 4.5 folio pages; chapter 5: 4 folio pages; chapter 6: 1.5 folio pages; chapter 8: 3 folio pages; chapter 9:

5.5 folio pages). For Y. Sotah, the first and last chapters are the longest (8.5 columns in the Academy of Hebrew Language edition). While it is common for first chapters to be the longest in a tractate, it is less common for later chapters to be so.

29. It is impossible to precisely quantify the percentage of aggadah, since it hinges on one's definition of aggadah. With the scholarly recognition of the blurry line between halakhah and aggadah, this is an increasingly difficult delineation.

30. Cohen attributes the lack of medieval commentary to the fact that the tractate mostly concerns Temple matters. Cohen, "Edition and Comprehensive Commentary on Chapters II & III," ב. However, other tractates that similarly discuss Temple practices do have medieval commentary traditions. Therefore, it seems equally possible that B. Sotah lacks a commentary tradition because of its topic, the sotah ritual, rather than the lack of practical halakhah. In other words, I hypothesize that not studying B. Sotah became a way of retreating from the ritual in the medieval academies. I am, however, intrigued by Johann Christoph Wagenseil's annotated Latin translation of M. Sotah, published in 1674. Early modern Christian interest in the sotah ritual is certainly worthy of study. On Wagenseil's translation, see Piet van Boxel, "Johann Christoph Wagenseil: From Scholar to Missionary," in *The Mishnaic Moment: Jewish Law Among Jews and Christians in Early Modern Europe*, ed. Piet van Boxel, Kirsten Macfarlane, and Joanna Weinberg (Oxford: Oxford University Press, 2022).

31. Similar to Cohen, Landau assumes that B. Sotah was not studied in Babylonian yeshivot because, with the cessation of the sotah and *ʿeglah ʿarufah* rituals, the tractate lacked practical halakhah. He attributes the differences he finds in the literary composition of the ninth chapter to this lack of study in the academies and proposes that this may also explain the similarities Epstein noticed between B. and Y. Sotah. See Landau, "An Edition and Comprehensive Commentary on Chapter IX," 9. I am not convinced by this explanation. The amount of aggadah included in the tractate would seem to indicate that it was part of the (developing) rabbinic curriculum. Indeed, the composition of B. Sotah should challenge ideas of a halakhah-centric curriculum.

32. See, for example, Willem F. Smelik, *Rabbis, Language and Translation in Late Antiquity* (Cambridge: Cambridge University Press, 2013); Steven D. Fraade, "Before and After Babel: Linguistic Exceptionalism and Pluralism in Early Rabbinic Literature and Jewish Antiquity," *Diné Israel* 28 (2011): 31–68.

33. See, for example, Mika Ahuvia, *On My Right Michael, on My Left Gabriel: Angels in Ancient Jewish Culture* (Oakland: University of California Press, 2021), 150–51; Joseph Yahalom, "Angels Do Not Understand Aramaic:

On the Literary Use of Jewish Palestinian Aramaic in Late Antiquity," *Journal of Jewish Studies* 47 (1996): 33–44.

34. See, for example, the classic article by Ephraim E. Urbach, "When Did Prophecy Cease?," *Tarbiz* 17 (1946): 1–11 [Hebrew].

35. See, for example, Rubenstein, *Stories of the Babylonian Talmud*, 116–49; Peter Schäfer, *Jesus in the Talmud* (Princeton, NJ: Princeton University Press, 2007) and the literature review on pp. 3–6. I do wonder whether these sugyot were redacted in B. Sotah because the tractate became a (the?) textual locus for many of rabbinic culture's concerns or whether the scholarly attention devoted to these sugyot reflects our contemporary concerns rather than those of ancient rabbinic culture. Whichever the case, the appellations for B. Ketubot as *shas katan* (the miniature Talmud) or *mafteiah le-talmud* (the key to the Talmud), indicating that its content encompasses much of the Bavli, might equally be applied to B. Sotah.

36. See, for example, Steven D. Fraade, "Nomos and Narrative Before Nomos and Narrative," *Yale Journal of Law & the Humanities* 17, no. 1 (2005): 92; Jane L. Kanarek, *Biblical Narrative and the Formation of Rabbinic Law* (New York: Cambridge University Press, 2014), 14n40; Marjorie Lehman, *The En Yaaqov: Jacob Ibn Habib's Search for Faith in the Talmudic Corpus* (Detroit: Wayne State University Press, 2011), 56–58; Rubenstein, *Stories of the Babylonian Talmud*, 1–7. Law and narrative are the common and imprecise translations of halakhah and aggadah.

37. Ishay Rosen-Zvi, *The Mishnaic Sotah Ritual: Temple, Gender and Midrash* (Leiden: Brill, 2012); Grushcow, *Writing the Wayward Wife*. Other scholars who have written on the mishnaic and/or tannaitic ritual include Daniel Boyarin, "Women's Bodies and the Rise of the Rabbis: The Case of Sotah," in *Jews and Gender: The Challenge to Hierarchy*, ed. Jonathan Frankel (New York: Oxford University Press, 2000), 88–100; Adriana Destro, *The Law of Jealousy: Anthropology of Sotah* (Atlanta, GA: Scholars Press, 1989); Moshe Halbertal, *Interpretive Revolutions in the Making* (Jerusalem: Magnes Press, 1997), 94–112; Judith Hauptman, *Rereading the Rabbis: A Woman's Voice* (Boulder, CO: Westview Press, 1997), 15–25; Tal Ilan, *Jewish Women in Greco-Roman Palestine* (Peabody, MA: Hendrickson, 1996), 136–41; Sarra Lev, "Sotah: Rabbinic Pornography?," in *The Passionate Torah: Sex and Judaism*, ed. Danya Ruttenburg (New York: NYU Press, 2009), 7–22; Michael L. Satlow, "'Texts of Terror': Rabbinic Texts, Speech Acts, and the Control of Mores," *AJS Review* 21, no. 2 (1996): 273–97; Judith Romney Wegner, *Chattel or Person? The Status of Women in the Mishnah* (New York: Oxford University Press, 1988), 50–54. As Rosen-Zvi aptly notes, "Nearly any study of rabbinic relations to or attitude towards women, family and sexuality dedicates several paragraphs to the Mishnaic sotah ritual, in an attempt to settle it with the broader

picture that emerges from rabbinic literature." Rosen-Zvi, *Mishnaic Sotah Ritual*, 2n1.

38. See also Ebner's less appropriately titled dissertation, "The Composition and Structure of Mishnah 'Sotah.'" Ebner analyzes M. Sotah 1–4, 5:1, and 6, omitting the chapters of the tractate that are not directly concerned with the sotah ritual. Ebner intends his analysis of M. Sotah to elucidate scholarly debates about the composition of the Mishnah rather than a focus on the sotah ritual itself.

39. Ishay Rosen-Zvi, *Mishnaic Sotah Ritual*, 219. Like the sotah ritual, Ezekiel chapters 16 and 23 "depict a public and theatrical punishment, centered on a ritual of humiliation and degradation that takes place before an audience and ends with a torturous death combined with bodily mutilation." The details of the Mishnah's depiction of the sotah ritual closely echo those of Ezekiel's account of punishment for adulteresses: "humiliating gestures (M. Sotah 1:5–6); bodily mutilation and death following a forced drinking (M. Sotah 3:4); construing the various measures as part of a single punitive continuum of retribution 'measure for measure' (M. Sotah 1:7); and eliminating the presumption of innocence." Rosen-Zvi, *Mishnaic Sotah Ritual*, 184, 205. Rosen-Zvi also extends this connection to prophetic descriptions of adultery in Isaiah 47:2–23; 2 Samuel 12:11–12; and Nahum 3:5–6. Rosen-Zvi, *Mishnaic Sotah Ritual*, 206–7, 215n126.

40. Grushcow, *Writing the Wayward Wife*, 264.

41. Grushcow, 270. Grushcow also provides an excellent summary of previous scholarship on the sotah ritual on 19–31. Ariella Radwin's dissertation, completed after the publication of Grushcow's book, should also be added to this list of scholarship. Radwin argues that rabbinic interpretations of the sotah ritual are shaped by the metaphor of God and Israel as, respectively, husband and wife. I do not view the marital metaphor and the concomitant betrayal and link to the golden calf episode as central to the Bavli's understanding of the ritual. It is, however, certainly present in later interpretations of the sotah. See Ariella Michal Radwin, "Adultery and the Marriage Metaphor: Rabbinic Readings of Sotah" (PhD diss., University of California Los Angeles, 2007). Abraham Cohen and Gilad Landau's dissertations also provide textual resources for this book. As is common in Israeli scholarship, they center textual criticism rather than literary criticism. At the time of this writing, a dissertation by Moriah Chriki, a comprehensive commentary on chapter 7 of B. Sotah, similar in methodology to those of Cohen and Landau, is in progress.

42. The use of the word *shema'ta* rather than *halakhah* should be taken seriously with the two discourses not conflated. We might therefore reframe the tension as chronological rather than typological: that is, between newly

formulated traditions (*agadah*) and authoritative and received traditions (*shema'ta/halakhah*).

43. See n36 for bibliography.

44. On spinning women, see M. Sotah 6:1.

45. For a fuller explication of this point, see my more recent piece, Jane Kanarek, "A Tale of Two Women: Standing at the Center of the Talmud," *Sources: A Journal of Jewish Ideas* (Fall/Winter 2024): 141–51. This article does connect the halakhah and aggadah story with the tale of two women. Only once I began writing this book did I notice the connection between the two stories.

46. Evidence for the practice of the sotah ritual during the Second Temple period is inconclusive and scant. In addition, the depictions we possess do not resemble the ritual described in M. Sotah. The descriptions of the first-century Philo (*Special Laws* III.52–63) and Josephus (*Jewish Antiquities* III.270–73) do not contain the distinguishing elements that M. Sotah adds to the biblical ritual, such as warning, witnesses, humiliation, and audience. Philo and Josephus also do not appear to know of the actual performance of the sotah ritual toward the end of the Second Temple period. A fragment from the Damascus Document (4Q270 4:1–8) does contain traditions shared by the tannaitic sources (preliminary testimony and exemption for rape victims from the ritual). Yet, again, it also appears that the Qumranic version more resembles the biblical ritual than the mishnaic. Thus, if a version of the sotah ritual was practiced during the Second Temple period, it does not resemble the one described in M. Sotah. See the excellent summary of nonrabbinic material in Rosen-Zvi, *Mishnaic Sotah Ritual*, 154–56. See also the descriptions found throughout Grushcow, *Writing the Wayward Wife*.

47. Rosen-Zvi, *Mishnaic Sotah Ritual*, 153–81. On collective memory and the Mishnah's reshaping of Temple ritual, see also Naftali S. Cohn, *The Memory of the Temple and the Making of the Rabbis* (Philadelphia: University of Pennsylvania Press, 2012), 4.

48. On this passage and its appearance in B. Yoma 37b, see Lehman, *Bringing Down the Temple House*, 62–70. Lehman argues that B. Yoma depicts Helene as upstaging the priests with her knowledge of Torah, thus calling into question the authority of the priesthood and the necessity of blood kinship for transmitting Torah. See also Rosen-Zvi, *Mishnaic Sotah Ritual*, 158–61.

49. In Albeck, M. Sotah 9:9. These mishnaic passages have all been utilized as evidence for the practice of the sotah ritual during the Second Temple period.

50. T. Sotah 2:1 also mentions the golden tablet, however without a reference to Helene. Y. Sotah 2:2, 18a does not mention Helene by name but clearly references the tablet as her gift. It is also intriguing to note the presence of

the story of the nameless woman and the jealous husband on Y. Sotah 1:4, 16d. Toward the end of the story, after the woman spits into Rabbi Meir's eye seven times (at Rabbi's Meir's request), the sage assures his astonished students that he acted correctly by comparing his actions to the erasure of God's name in the sotah ritual. This story of a jealous husband and a wife who, as it were, cheats on him with the Torah of another man (R. Meir) does not appear in B. Sotah, perhaps again indicating that B. Sotah's redactors were less concerned with the possibility of actual women acting as a sotah. See also the version of this story in Leviticus Rabbah 9:9 (ed. Margulies 190–93) and its explication in Galit Hasan-Rokem, *Tales of the Neighborhood: Jewish Narrative Dialogues in Late Antiquity* (Berkeley: University of California Press, 2003), 55–74.

51. B. Sotah even omits mention of Karkemit in the parallel sugya found on B. Sotah 18b.

52. For a summary of scholarship on this point, see Grushcow, *Writing the Wayward Wife*, 234n6. The argument turns on the mishnah's citation of Hosea 4:14. In Grushcow's words: "Is the point that the women will not be punished, or is the point that the women will not be punished *because* the men turn aside to whores?" Grushcow, *Writing the Wayward Wife*, 234. Regardless of whether female sin alone or female and male sin are to blame, the mishnah does not criticize the sotah ritual when it describes its cessation. Much as in its description of the cessation of the *ʿeglah ʿarufah* ritual, it depicts its discontinuation as "*lament* of glories long gone," and part of "the demise of an entire institutional religion." Rosen-Zvi, *Mishnaic Sotah Ritual*, 180. See also T. Sotah 14:1–2, 9.

53. See Sifrei Bemidbar §21 (ed. Kahana, p. 56) for a similar baraita and see M. Sotah 5:1. This section of the sugya also includes a tannaitic tradition that requires a man to be free of sin in order for the ritual waters to effectively test his wife. See also the overlapping sugya on B. Sotah 27b–28a, which interrogates the ambiguity of the word *him* (*ʾoto*) in M. Sotah 5:1: "Just as the water checks her [*ʾotah*], so too the water checks him [*ʾoto*]."

54. Study of the rabbinic sotah ritual may even have functioned as a (re-imagined) substitute for the Temple ritual. On study as a substitute for Temple ritual, see Beth A. Berkowitz, *Execution and Invention: Death Penalty Discourse in Early Rabbinic and Christian Cultures* (New York: Oxford University Press, 2006), 18; Fraade, "Nomos and Narrative," 94; Rosen-Zvi, *Mishnaic Sotah Ritual*, 234–36.

55. Laura S. Lieber, "An Unholy Spectacle: The Ordeal of the Accused Adulteress in the Early Synagogue," *Jewish Studies Quarterly* 29, no. 2 (2022): 135–62.

56. For a summary of the ritual, see Michael D. Swartz, "Sacrificial Themes

in Jewish Magic," in *Magic and Ritual in the Ancient World*, ed. Paul Mirecki and Marvin Meyer (Leiden: Brill, 2001), 307–11. See also Peter Schäfer and Shaul Shaked, eds., *Magische Texte aus der Kairoer Geniza* (Tübingen: Mohr Siebeck, 1994), 17–44. For English translations of *ʿInyan Sotah*, see Grushcow, *Writing the Wayward Wife*, 297–99; Peter Schäfer, "Jewish Liturgy and Magic," in *Geschichte—Tradition—Reflexion: Festchrift für Martin Hengel zum 70 Geburtstag*, ed. Hubert Cancik, Hermann Lichtenberger, and Peter Schäfer (Tübingen: Mohr Siebeck, 1996), 1:541–44.

57. Gideon Bohak, "Jewish Magic in the Middle Ages," in *The Cambridge History of Magic and Witchcraft in the West*, ed. S. J. David J. Collins (Cambridge: Cambridge University Press, 2015), 273–74. For the relevant text of the *Chronicle*, see Robert Bonfil, *History and Folklore in a Medieval Jewish Chronicle: The Family Chronicle of Ahimaʿaz Ben Paltiel* (Leiden: Brill, 2009), 254–55. On the relationship between *ʿInyan Sotah* and the *Chronicle of Ahimaʿaz*, see Yuval Harari, "The Scroll of Ahimaʿaz and Jewish Magical Culture: A Note on the Ordeal of the Adulteress," *Tarbiz* 85, no. 1–2 (2006): 185–202 [Hebrew].

58. For a summary of the history of the Bavli's printing, see Barry Scott Wimpfheimer, *The Talmud: A Biography* (Princeton, NJ: Princeton University Press, 2018), 210–24.

59. Tal Ilan has explored the way in which rabbinic texts have been altered, or censored, in the process of their transmission—from the earliest redactional layers through manuscript copying and text printing—to exclude women. This censorship includes both the conscious erasure of women from variant traditions and from manuscripts and also the unconscious removal of women because the ideas recorded in a particular text did not accord with preconceived ideas about women and gender. Tal Ilan, *Mine and Yours Are Hers: Retrieving Women's History from Rabbinic Literature* (Leiden: Brill, 1997), 51–84.

CHAPTER 1: THE DISAPPEARING SOTAH AND THE MORAL MAN

1. B. M. Lewin, ed., *ʾIgeret rav sherira gaʾon* (Jerusalem: Makor, 1971), 71. For a summary of the arguments for and against whether or not these sugyot should better termed "late" rather than saboraic and an accompanying bibliography, see Richard Kalmin, "The Formation and Character of the Babylonian Talmud," in *The Cambridge History of Judaism*, vol. 4, *The Late Roman-Rabbinic Period*, ed. Steven T. Katz (New York: Cambridge University Press, 2006), 842–43. I choose the terminology "late" as indicating the chronology of these sugyot in regard to the Bavli as a whole but avoiding a definitive determination of whether or not the saboraim existed.

2. One exception to this trajectory is the nineteenth-century talmudic

scholar Nehemia Brüll. Brüll hazarded a guess that we consider the beginnings of seven tractates (B. Eruvin 2a, B. Yevamot 2b–3b, B. Kiddushin 2a–3b, B. Nedarim 2b–3a, B. Nazir 2a–3b, B. Sotah 2a, and B. Shevuot 2b–3a) to be introductory lectures to their respective tractates. Unfortunately, Brüll did not specify further what he meant by introductory lectures. N. Brüll, "Die Entstehungsgeschichte des babylonischen Talmuds als Schriftwerk," in *Jahrbücher für Jüdische Geschichte und Literatur II*, ed. N. Brüll (Frankfurt, 1876), 43–45. Avraham Weiss, writing in the twentieth century, understood Brüll to consider these sugyot to function as prologues to future lectures on the tractate. Avraham Weiss, *The Literary Activities of the Saboraim* (Jerusalem: Magnes Press, 1953), 9 [Hebrew]. I am not convinced of future lectures as the *sitz im leben* of these passages, but if Brüll and Weiss are correct, I would still assume that these sugyot have been literarily reworked.

3. Charlotte Elisheva Fonrobert, "The Place of Shabbat: On the Architecture of the Opening Sugya of Tractate Eruvin (2a–3a)," in *Strength to Strength: Essays in Appreciation of Shaye Cohen*, ed. Michael L. Satlow (Providence, RI: Brown Judaic Studies, 2018), 438–39, 454. Fonrobert considers the opening sugya of B. Eruvin to provide the tractate with "the veneer of an overarching intellectual project." Fonrobert, "Place of Shabbat," 439. I differ from Fonrobert in arguing that the thematic lines we can trace throughout B. Sotah reflect more than the veneer of an overarching intellectual project.

4. Weiss also categorizes the opening passages of B. Eruvin, B. Sukkah, B. Taʿanit, B. Moʿed Katan, B. Nazir, B. Shevuʿot, B. Makkot, B. Zevahim, B. Menahot, and B. Bekhorot as formalistic notes to their respective mishnah. Avraham Weiss, *The Literary Activities of the Saboraim* (Jerusalem: Magnes Press, 1953), 11 [Hebrew]. It seems that Weiss views these passages as commenting on the first mishnah of their respective tractates; however, that is not completely clear. Weiss follows Brüll in his categorization of B. Sotah as saboraic. Note that Weiss does not use the terminology *sugya* for the opening of B. Sotah. He reserves that terminology for longer opening passages. See Weiss, *Saboraim*, 12.

5. Weiss raises the possibility that in certain tractates the second sugya, although based on earlier amoraic material, demonstrates a late editorial hand. He does not include the second sugya of B. Sotah in his list. I consider the second sugya to be a late addition to the tractate. Weiss, *Saboraim*, 13.

6. Ishay Rosen-Zvi, "The Ritual of Suspected Adulteress (Sotah) in Tannaitic Literature: Textual and Theoretical Perspectives" (PhD diss., Tel Aviv University, 2004), 52–56 [Hebrew].

7. I make a similar argument about the opening sugya of B. Kiddushin in my article, "Thinking Gender through Grammar: B. Qiddushin 2a–3b," in

Jewish Culture and Creativity: Essays in Honor of Professor Michael Fishbane on the Occasion of His Eightieth Birthday, ed. Eitan P. Fishbane and Elisha Russ-Fishbane (Boston: Academic Studies Press, 2023), 123–36.

8. Judith Hauptman, for example, argues that the rabbis of the Talmud, while still operating within and maintaining a patriarchal framework, took steps to improve women's status and ameliorate their legal disadvantages. As she writes, "It seems to me that the major achievement of the rabbis of the Talmud with regard to women, in this tractate [Sotah] and also in general, was significantly to improve their status in a variety of important areas." Hauptman, *Rereading the Rabbis*, 28. Hauptman does not ignore the troubling material in M. Sotah or deny rabbinic patriarchy; she does, however, attempt to contain it. In contrast to Hauptman, my question is not whether or not the Bavli's approach to the sotah ritual represents an improvement in women's status. Instead, I investigate the Bavli's discourse as a multivalent response to the mishnaic sotah.

9. Hauptman makes a similar claim about M. Sotah as I do about the opening Bavli sugya. She observes that a standard editorial procedure in tannaitic literature is to bracket a chronologically earlier layer with a later one. With this in mind, Hauptman argues that the more troubling material in M. Sotah is earlier and bracketed by more reasonable later material, such as the judicial procedure requiring warning and witnesses. This approach is consonant with Hauptman's more general view of the ancient rabbis as generally trending toward ethical improvement. Hauptman, *Rereading the Rabbis*, 21–22.

10. For an argument for conscious change in the case of tannaitic midrash, see Halbertal, *Interpretive Revolutions*.

11. On this point see Rosen-Zvi, *Mishnaic Sotah Ritual*, 181. For other depictions of the tannaitic sotah ritual, see also T. Sotah 1–5 and Sifrei Bemidbar §7–21 (ed. Kahana 23–56).

12. The biblical Hebrew ש at times shifts in rabbinic Hebrew to ס.

13. Tikva Frymer-Kensky, "The Strange Case of the Suspected Sotah (Numbers V 11–31)," *Vetus Testamentum* 34 (1984): 11. See also Bonna Devora Haberman, "The Suspected Adulteress: A Study of Textual Embodiment," *Prooftexts* 20, 1–2 (2000): 15–16.

14. No comparable ritual exists for a man whose wife suspects him of adultery. With the exception of the list of prohibitions in Leviticus 18 and 20, biblical (and rabbinic law) does not prohibit a man from sexual intercourse with a woman other than his wife. In the case of the suspected wife, the lack of definitive proof about whether she engaged in consensual sexual intercourse with a man other than her husband legally differentiates this case from those of proven forbidden consensual sexual intercourse and rape. When there is

certainty about a married woman's sexual intercourse with another man, biblical law prescribes judicial execution for the woman and the man alike (Deuteronomy 22:22).

15. I have used the most common translation of *kin'ah* as jealousy. *Kin'ah* may, however, also be translated as "zeal," indicating, to use the words of Sarah Wolf, "a powerful force of violence and retribution, albeit one that is portrayed as legitimate and righteous." Sarah Wolf, "'Between Her and Others': The 'Spirit of Jealousy' in Numbers 5:14 and Its Ancient Jewish Reception," in *Making History: Studies in Rabbinic Literature, History, and Culture in Honor of Richard L. Kalmin*, ed. Carol Bakhos and Alyssa Gray (Providence, RI: Brown Judaic Studies, 2024), 467. See also Michael A. Fishbane, "Accusations of Adultery: A Study of Law and Scribal Practice in Numbers 5:11–31," *Hebrew Union College Annual* 45 (1974): 35–36.

16. Frymer-Kensky, "Strange Case," 13.

17. Frymer-Kensky, 11.

18. Haberman, "Suspected Adulteress," 9–20.

19. Biblical scholars largely divide into two camps about the composition of Numbers 5:11–31, one side emphasizing the composite nature of the passage and the other arguing for a unified composition. For a recent argument for the composite nature of Numbers 5:11–31, see Sarah Shectman, "Bearing Guilt in Numbers 5:12–31," in *Gazing on the Deep: Ancient Near Eastern, Biblical, and Jewish Studies in Honor of Tzvi Abusch*, ed. Jeffrey Stackart, Barbara Neverling Porter, and David P. Wright (Bethesda, MD: CDL Press, 2010), 479–93, and the scholars she cites therein. In the second camp, see Fishbane, "Accusations of Adultery"; Frymer-Kensky, "Strange Case"; Jacob Milgrom, "The Case of the Suspected Adulteress, Numbers 5:11–31: Redaction and Meaning," in *The Creation of Sacred Literature*, ed. Richard P. Friedman (Berkeley: University of California Press, 1981), 69–75.

20. My description draws on Frymer-Kensky's depiction of the ritual's order. Frymer-Kensky, "Strange Case," 14–18.

21. Fishbane, "Accusations of Adultery," 35; Frymer-Kensky, "Strange Case," 17. I follow Frymer-Kensky's division of verse 14 into two sections.

22. See Jacob Milgrom, *The JPS Torah Commentary: Numbers* (Philadelphia: Jewish Publication Society, 1990), 39, for possible orders of these actions.

23. The curse may indicate either eventual miscarriage or uterine prolapse. Baruch A. Levine, *Numbers 1–20: A New Translation with Introduction and Commentary* (New York: Doubleday, 1993), 182; Frymer-Kensky, "Strange Case," 18–19. For a survey of interpretations of the biblical punishment, see Grushcow, *Writing the Wayward Wife*, 161n6.

24. The passage ends with a statement that the husband will be clear of

guilt while the woman will bear her guilt (verse 31). Shectman, who divides the pericope into two earlier strands, one assuming the woman's guilt and the other her innocence, understands verse 31 as part of the strand assuming guilt. She argues, "The primary concern of this verse [Numbers 5:31] is not the husband's culpability but the woman's, and it is in this connection that the verse stipulates that the husband may not relent and attempt to absolve his wife of guilt, which has been proven by Yhwh through the ordeal." Shectman, "Bearing Guilt," 492.

25. See Frymer-Kensky, "Strange Case," 21–25. Frymer-Kensky makes two related points. First, if the verdict were immediate we would expect the woman, if guilty, to receive the punishment for adultery (execution). Second, that the ritual is best understood as a religious-legal procedure resembling a purgatory oath rather than a judicial ordeal. Judicial ordeals are distinguished by two characteristics: immediate manifestation of the god's decision and differentiation between verdict (given by the god) and punishment (carried out by the human court). In the case of the sotah, verdict and punishment are one and the same, and both are carried out by God.

26. On this point see Haberman, "Suspected Adulteress," 18. Haberman understands the ritual as a public mechanism to validate *and* domesticate the husband's jealousy. I differ from Haberman in viewing the biblical ritual as primarily a private rather than a public ritual.

27. On the repetition of jealousy as possibly hinting at male culpability, see Lev, "Rabbinic Pornography," 9–10.

28. While the shift from the biblical understanding of *kin'ah* (an emotion) to the rabbinic understanding of *kin'ah* (a legal requirement for warning and witnesses) may indeed render it more difficult for the husband to initiate the ritual, the process of warning and the presence of witnesses also lend a stronger basis to the husband's accusation. On the increased difficulty of performing the ritual, see Halbertal, *Interpretive Revolutions*, 110. For a convincing critique and summary of Halbertal's argument, see Grushcow, *Writing the Wayward Wife*, 30.

29. Lev, "Rabbinic Pornography," 10–19. Lev draws on the discourse of the gaze (film theory), scopophilia and voyeurism (psychology), pornography (feminist theory), as well as Foucault's analysis of the panopticon. Hauptman concurs that M. Sotah's description of the ritual can be called pornographic. However, in contrast to Lev, Hauptman argues that the pornographic elements of M. Sotah belong to the earlier core that the rabbis suppress by adding elements that step-by-step eliminate the ritual (witnesses and warning; punishment for the lover; a history of good deeds postponing the woman's punishment; the abolishment of the ordeal). Hauptman, *Rereading the Rabbis*, 27–28.

30. I intentionally use passive language as M. Sotah 1:1 presents two different opinions about the number of witnesses who must see the woman "secreting" herself with the forbidden man: R. Eliezer contends that one witness (who may even be the husband) is sufficient; R. Yehoshua requires two witnesses.

31. A minority opinion in the name of R. Yehudah does not require these two additional witnesses.

32. See M. Sanhedrin 1:6.

33. On the location and the name "Nicanor gate," see Joshua Schwartz, "Once More on the Nicanor Gate," *Hebrew Union College Annual* 62 (1991).

34. M. Sotah 1:5 includes a minority opinion in the name of R. Yehudah that prohibits the priest's uncovering the accused sotah's breasts and undoing her hair in the event that her breasts and hair are deemed "attractive" (*na'eh*). Attractiveness is, of course, a subjective opinion, one that in this case would be determined by the male priest's gaze. In any case, M. Sotah's majority opinion advocates for her physical exposure.

35. M. Sotah 1:6 does not specify who switches the woman's clothing or removes her jewelry but rather uses the impersonal plural.

36. See Marcus Jastrow, *A Dictionary of the Targumim, Talmud Bavli, Yerushalmi, and the Midrashic Literature* (New York: Judaica Press, 1996), 828 s.v. *mitzri*.

37. Here, too, the mishnaic ritual differs from the biblical one in the permission it gives the court to initiate the process of the sotah ritual if the husband proves unable to do so (M. Sotah 4:5).

38. Rosen-Zvi, *Mishnaic Sotah Ritual*, 184–87.

39. Rosen-Zvi, 3, 171.

40. Rosen-Zvi, 118–20.

41. Rosen-Zvi, 3, 49–61. See, for example, Sifrei Bemidbar §12 (ed. Kahana 40–41) and T. Sotah 1:6. On M. Sotah's omission of innocence, see also Lev, "Rabbinic Pornography," 12–13.

42. There is one exception to this statement: M. Sotah's description of the woman's bodily deterioration to the point of death if she is guilty (M. Sotah 3:4–5). On this, see Rosen-Zvi, *Mishnaic Sotah Ritual*, 112–14.

43. B. Sotah includes a toseftan baraita that depicts each individual reading from his own Torah scroll at the conclusion of the high priest's reading on Yom Kippur. In implicit contrast with the sotah's degradation, the baraita explains this practice as intended to demonstrate the beauty of each scroll. See T. Yoma 3:18 and B. Sotah 41a.

44. Although the root *s.m.kh.* used in section (C) denotes proximity and not necessarily order (*lamah nismekhah*), as section (E) of the sugya demonstrates, the Bavli's question is not only about adjacency but also about the order of the tractates.

45. MS Munich, MS Vatican 110–111: "What is the reason" (*mai shena* instead of *mai tena*).

46. MS Munich: omits *ve-khol*.

47. MS Vatican 110–11: *ʾin hakhi nami*.

48. M. Ketubot 7:1 (B. Ketubot 70a).

49. I borrow this term from Mira Balberg who uses it to describe the processes by which the ancient rabbis transform biblical law into rabbinic halakhah, "a discourse that is based on biblical law but is neither akin to it nor a commentary on it." Balberg, *Purity, Body, and Self in Early Rabbinic Literature* (Berkeley: University of California Press, 2014), 181.

50. In general, the order of tractates in each talmudic division (seder) follows the number of chapters in each tractate, from largest number to smallest. On this see Menahem Kahana who argues that a quantitative approach best explains the number of orders and tractates within them. Menahem Kahana, "The Arrangement of the Orders of the Mishnah," *Tarbiz* 86 (2007): 29–40 [Hebrew]. Kahana's observation does not preclude B. Sotah's ideological explanation of tractate order.

51. In contrast to Rosen-Zvi who reads *she-kol* here as nongendered, that is as referring to men and women, I understand it as referring only to men. This is consonant with B. Sotah's shift of emphasis from female to male sin. Rosen-Zvi, "Suspected Adulteress," 53–54.

52. Levine, *Numbers 1–20*, 215.

53. In general, tannaitic sources emphasize the ways in which the pedagogical message of the sotah is directed specifically toward women. Rosen-Zvi, "Suspected Adulteress," 54.

54. Rosen-Zvi, 54.

55. On "since with them she feels no shame," and the various readings of M. Sotah 1:6 see Rosen-Zvi, *Mishnaic Sotah Ritual*, 70, 89–100.

56. MS Kaufmann and MS Parma both include the word *rest* here ("and the rest of all the women"; *sheʾar kol ha-nashim*). The inclusion of *rest* makes clear that the previous clause refers only to female slaves who are not permitted to see the accused woman; in contrast, all other women are permitted to see her. Epstein proposes that this mishnah originally read, "and all other people [*ʾadam*] are permitted to see her." It was altered because of the citation of Ezekiel 23:48 and through the influence of M. Sotah 4:3. Epstein, *Introduction to the Mishnaic Text*, 725–26. See, though, Halivni who rejects Epstein's suggestion and instead proposes that M. Sotah 1:6 is a paraphrase of Sifrei Bemidbar §11. David Weiss Halivni, *Mekorot u-mesorot: nashim* (Tel Aviv: Devir, 1968), 440.

57. In this instance, I have translated according to the mishnah in the printed Vilna edition in order to facilitate B. Sotah's reading.

58. Rava rejects Abaye's proposed resolution to interpret both sentences as referring only to women. Rosen-Zvi understands Rava differently than I do: He understands Rava to read the first sentence as referring to men only and the second to women. Rosen-Zvi's reading is possible if we understand the words "la shena gavri ve-la shena nashi" to be a later editorial gloss. Rosen-Zvi, *Mishnaic Sotah Ritual*, 93.

59. As Daniel Boyarin argues in his reading of the Reish Lakish and Rabbi Yohanan tale (B. Bava Metzia 84a), a reconceptualization of male power does not in and of itself result in an end to patriarchy. Boyarin writes, "The fatal flaw, then, within the cultural system itself—represented almost allegorically within our story as a literally fatal flaw in its hero, Rabbi Yohanan—is in its nonrecognition of the fact that any resistance to power and masculinist constructions of the phallus must be accompanied by a revolution in the power relations between men and women as well, if it is to be material and critical." Daniel Boyarin, *Unheroic Conduct: The Rise of Heterosexuality and the Invention of the Jewish Man* (Berkeley: University of California Press, 1997), 150.

60. The first five mishnayot of chapter 7 of Mishnah Ketubot begin with the phrase, "A man who [makes] his wife vow." They continue with a series of different things or actions that if a husband were to prohibit to his wife, he must divorce her and give her the marriage contract (*ketubah*) payment that is her due.

61. The Bavli and Yerushalmi reinterpret certain of these mishnayot to mean that the wife takes the vow and the husband fulfills that vow. See also Mira Balberg's discussion of M. Ketubot 7:2–3. Mira Balberg, "'The Vows That He Annuls': The Definition and Classification of Annullable Vows in Rabbinic Literature" (master's thesis, Hebrew University, 2005), 96 [Hebrew].

62. Since Scripture includes males and females in general and nazirite vows, this emphasis on males is noteworthy.

63. On this passage and the ways in which the Bavli and Yerushalmi gender the gaze as masculine and the body as feminine, see Rachel Neis, *The Sense of Sight in Rabbinic Culture: Jewish Ways of Seeing in Late Antiquity* (New York: Cambridge University Press, 2013), 123. See also Ishay Rosen-Zvi, *Demonic Desires: "Yetzer Hara" and the Problem of Evil in Late Antiquity* (Philadelphia: University of Pennsylvania Press, 2011), 110.

64. See also B. Sotah 9b where Delilah believes Samson to tell the truth about the source of his strength (his uncut hair), because he does so through explaining that he is a nazirite to God (*nezir ʾelohim ʾani*) (quoting Judges 16:17).

65. I borrow this concept of hypersexualization from Rosen-Zvi. Rosen-Zvi argues for a larger Babylonian trend toward the hypersexualization of reality.

See Ishay Rosen-Zvi, "Hyper-Sexualization in the Bavli: An Initial Survey," in *Midrash and the Exegetical Mind*, ed. Lieve Teugels and Rivka Ulmer (Piscataway, NJ: Gorgias Press, 2010); Rosen-Zvi, *Demonic Desires*, 112–19.

66. This description of Philistine men bringing their wives to the imprisoned Samson so that he might impregnate them may also be understood as a narrative of male and female rape (of Samson and of the wives). This tradition overlaps with the description on B. Sotah 42b of the rape of Orpah, discussed later in chapter 6.

67. MS Oxford 2675: "Said Rav Pappa." This inclusion likely results from the mention of Rav Pappa at the end of the previous R. Yohanan tradition.

68. Although the first and second dicta overlap in their citation of Job 31:10, that overlap does not completely explain Samson's omission in this second dictum. The three final dicta mention Samson but not his sexual sins (or even sexual sin in general). The fourth dictum also connects to the sotah ritual: a discussion of the extent to which Samson's name echoes the name of God and thus whether or not his name may be erased.

69. Y. Sotah does declare that as a child Samson's abilities in sexual intercourse were equivalent to that of any man (*she-hayetah tashmisho shaveh le-khol ʾadam*). However, it does not, as does the Bavli, contain any equivalent comment about the power of Samson's sperm.

70. This particular section of the Y. Sotah explicates Judges 14:5 ("Samson and his father and mother went down to Timnah. And they came to the vineyards of Timnah, and a full-grown lion came roaring at him").

71. Grushcow, *Writing the Wayward Wife*, 264–71.

72. On warning as either permissible or obligatory, see also Sifrei Zuta Bemidbar 5:12 (ed. Horovitz 232) and Y. Sotah 1:1, 16b. For a discussion of these texts and the ways in which values rather than purely exegesis drive the different opinions, see Halbertal, *Interpretive Revolutions*, 100–104.

73. The Yerushalmi records the debate in the names of R. Eliezer (required) and R. Yehoshua (permissible).

74. MS Vatican 110–11: Missing "Reish Lakish." This appears to be a scribal omission.

75. MS Vatican 110–11: "A mnemonic: *bat kol, bei rav, zakhar, ʾahot, hatan, ʿeved, ve-ha-banot*."

76. I discuss the *bat kol* further in chapter 4.

77. *Ploni/t* is the Bavli's way of saying an anonymous person, equivalent to our "John Doe" and "Jane Doe."

78. On the ways in which these opening sugyot move between topics, see Rosen-Zvi, "Suspected Adulteress," 52. I will discuss topic-switching further in chapter 2.

79. Rosen-Zvi argues that M. Sotah and T. Sotah use the hermeneutic tool

of measure-for-measure in a unique manner. Tannaitic literature generally utilizes measure-for-measure to connect and explicate biblical texts; M. and T. Sotah do so in order to explain and justify the sotah ritual. Ishay Rosen-Zvi, "Measure for Measure as a Hermeneutical Tool in Early Rabbinic Literature: The Case of Tosefta Sotah," *Journal of Jewish Studies* 57, no. 2 (2006): 269–86.

80. For a similar point, see Rosen-Zvi, "Suspected Adulteress," 54.

81. On this, see Rosen-Zvi, "Suspected Adulteress," 54n153.

82. I discuss this Exodus narrative sugya in more detail in chapter 6. See chapter 4 for discussion of the spies narrative.

83. The first explication (in the name of R. Ami or R. Asi) declares that a man who does not perform the ritual of hand-washing before eating bread is comparable to a man who has sexual intercourse with a prostitute (*ʾishah zonah*); the second (in the name of Rav), that a man who has sex with a prostitute will eventually beg for bread; and the third, on the latter half of the verse (in the name of R. Yohanan), that an arrogant man will eventually transgress with a married woman.

84. See the discussion of this sugya in Lewis, *"And before Honor,"* 103–13.

85. Anonymous giving becomes the defining element of post-tannaitic approaches to charity. Gregg E. Gardner, *The Origins of Organized Charity in Rabbinic Judaism* (New York: Cambridge University Press, 2015), 153.

86. On *gehenna/gehinnom* as referring to two ideas of divine retribution within classical rabbinic literature, see Chaim Milikowsky, "Which Gehenna? Retribution and Eschatology in the Synoptic Gospels and in Early Jewish Texts," *New Testament Studies* 34, no. 2 (1988): 239–40; Chaim Milikowsky, "Gehenna and 'Sinners of Israel' in the Light of Seder ʿOlam," *Tarbiz* 55 (1986): 318–20 [Hebrew]. The first is eschatological and corporeal: After this world ends and the dead are resurrected, the wicked will be judged on the great day of judgment and sent to *gehenna* for their sins; the second is immediately post-death and incorporeal: After an individual's death, the individual's soul comes to the spiritual realm of *gehenna* where it receives its punishment. On the vocalization *gehinnam*, see Milikowsky, "Which Gehenna," 245n2. For clarity, I have used the more conventional vocalization.

87. For a summary of scholarship that depicts rabbinic Judaism as replacing sacrifices, see Mira Balberg, *Blood for Thought: The Reinvention of Sacrifice in Early Rabbinic Literature* (Oakland: University of California Press, 2017), 3–4. Balberg critiques this depiction for its focus on a small number of late sources instead of the extensive rabbinic literature that *does* discuss sacrifices.

88. Lewis, *"And before Honor,"* 97. Lewis does not specify whether or not his interpretation of *gas ruah* applies only to males or also includes females. Given the gendered nature of rabbinic Judaism, I think we may assume that

rabbinic literature likely applies the category of arrogance differently to females than it does to males.

89. On rabbinic anthropology as locating God and humans in two distinct realms, see Lewis, *"And before Honor,"* 96.

90. See my analysis of this material in chapter 3. Note, too, that the sugya on B. Sotah 4b–5b limits Torah study's protective power over a sage. Torah study does not protect a man who has sexual intercourse with a married woman or who is arrogant. Yet again, the Bavli shifts its eyes from female sin to male.

91. I follow Daniel Boyarin's translation of *tiflut* as lasciviousness. See his extensive footnote on the more literal translation of *tiflut* as "childish things" or "foolishness" and as a euphemism for lasciviousness. Daniel Boyarin, *Carnal Israel: Reading Sex in Talmudic Culture* (Berkeley: University of California Press, 1993), 171n3. See also Epstein, *Introduction to the Mishnaic Text,* 536–37, 670.

92. B. Sotah's discussion turns on exegesis of Proverbs 8:12 ("I, Wisdom [*hokhmah*], live with Prudence [*ʿormah*]") and Job 28:12 ("But where can wisdom be found [*ve-ha-hokhmah mei-ʾayin timatzei*]"). Reading "wisdom" as referring to Torah, B. Sotah cites two traditions, the first in the name of R. Yosi the son of R. Hanina and the second in the name of R. Yohanan. The former explicates Prov. 8:12 to indicate that Torah only endures in a man who makes himself "naked" (*ʿarum*) for its words. The latter plays on the word *ʾayin* (nothingness) in Job 28:12 to indicate the Torah only endures through a man who makes himself as if he does not exist.

93. For a summary of these seven different amoraic traditions about the behavior of an evil and cunning person, see Vidas, *Tradition and the Formation of the Talmud,* 136–37.

94. Vidas, *Tradition and the Formation of the Talmud,* 137.

95. On the centrality of discipleship to rabbinic ideology, see Martin S. Jaffee, *Torah in the Mouth: Writing and Oral Tradition in Palestinian Judaism, 200 BCE–400 CE* (New York: Oxford University Press, 2001), 126–52.

96. MS Munich 95, MS Oxford-Bodl. heb.d. 20 (2675), Venice Print (1520): R. Eliezer.

97. Here I draw on Moulie Vidas's definition of the *ʿam ha-ʾaretz* as "among those parts of Israel different from the rabbis." Vidas, *Tradition and the Formation of the Talmud,* 140.

98. On this observation and on the use of the term *ʿam ha-ʾaretz* in the Bavli more generally, see Jonathan Aaron Pomeranz, "Ordinary Jews in the Babylonian Talmud: Rabbinic Representations and Historical Interpretation" (PhD diss., Yale University, 2016). See also the baraita on B. Sotah 22a and its parallel on B. Berakhot 47b that convey a list of practices — or better

yet, not-practiced practices—that define a man as an *ʿam ha-ʾaretz*. These include the failure to recite the shema and its accompanying blessings in the morning and evening, don phylacteries, put fringes (*tzitzit*) on one's clothing, raise one's sons to learn Torah, and serve the sages.

99. Tannaim, or repeaters, are yet another category that this section of the Bavli names as not fully inside the community of sages. As Vidas argues, "What the composers of our *sugyot* insist on is the separation of scholars from transmitters and scholarship from transmission." Vidas, *Tradition and the Formation of the Talmud*, 147. For a discussion of the boundary between tannaim and sages, see Vidas, 139–49.

100. T. Sotah 7:20–21.

101. See Schremer's suggestion that this aphorism that recommends first establishing economic security is suggestive of a later age of marriage for men (twenties or perhaps thirties) in the land of Israel. Adiel Schremer, *Male and Female He Created Them: Jewish Marriage in the Late Second Temple, Mishnah and Talmud Periods* (Jerusalem: Zalman Shazar Center, 2003), 89 [Hebrew].

102. MS Munich 95; MS Vatican 110–111; Venice Printing: *talmud*. The intervention of the censor has resulted in the replacement of *talmud* with *gemara* since the Basel printing (1578–80). Hanoch Albeck, *Introduction to the Talmud Bavli and Yerushalmi* (Tel Aviv: Devir, 1987), 3 [Hebrew]; Hermann Leberecht Strack and Gunter Stemberger, *Introduction to the Talmud and Midrash* (Minneapolis: Fortress Press, 1996), 164–65.

103. MS Munich 95; MS Vatican 110–11; Venice Printing: *talmud*.

104. MS Munich 95; MS Vatican 110–11; Venice Printing: *talmud*.

105. Beginning in the third chapter of T. Sotah, the differences between the Vienna and Erfurt manuscripts lead Lieberman to present both manuscript traditions synoptically in the main body of the text rather than including Erfurt only in the critical apparatus. On this decision, see Saul Lieberman, ed., *The Tosefta: According to Codex Vienna, with Variants from Codices Erfurt, Geniza Mss. And Editio Princeps*, Vol. Nashim *(Venice 1521)* (New York: Jewish Theological Seminary, 1973), ה. See, however, Brody who critiques this decision arguing that the two traditions are more similar than Lieberman supposes. Differences reflect common scribal practices: greater liberty with aggadic material and with the extent of biblical citations. Robert Brody, *Mishnah and Tosefta Studies* (Jerusalem: Magnes Press, 2014), 79–89. The Vienna manuscript of T. Sotah 7:21 presents five different curricular possibilities. They include three categories that do not appear in the Bavli's version of the baraita: *midrash* (scriptural exegesis), *hagadot/agadot* (rabbinic narratives, maxims, and stories) and *halakhot* (laws). MS Vienna also includes *talmud* rather than *gemara*. The Erfurt manuscript presents only two curricular

possibilities. These curricula include *mikra, midrash,* and *halakhot* but not *gemara/talmud.* On the terminology *agadot/hagadot* as distinct from *midrash agadah,* see Marjorie Lehman, *The En Yaaqov: Jacob Ibn Habib's Search for Faith in the Talmudic Corpus* (Detroit: Wayne State University Press, 2011), 52–53. That T. Sotah 7:21 names *midrash* and *agadot/hagadot* as two separate categories provides additional evidence for Lehman's contention that these two modes of learning should not be conflated. Lieberman understands "interpret and receive a reward" as referring to learning simply for the sake of sharpening interpretation. Saul Lieberman, *Tosefta ki-fshutah: A Comprehensive Commentary on the Tosefta* (New York: Jewish Theological Seminary of America, 1962), 692 [Hebrew].

106. See Lehman, *Bringing Down the Temple House,* and her shorter articles on the same topics. Marjorie Lehman, "Imagining the Priesthood in Tractate Yoma: Mishnah Yoma 2: 1–2 and Bt Yoma 23a," *Nashim: A Journal of Jewish Women's Studies & Gender Issues* 28 (2015): 88–105; Marjorie Lehman, "Rabbinic Masculinities: Reading the *Ba'al Keri* in Tractate Yoma," *Jewish Studies Quarterly* 22, no. 2 (2015): 109–36.

107. See also B. Ta'anit 10b.

108. MS Vatican 110–11: missing "humility."

109. MS Munich 95; MS Vatican 110–11: Rav Nahman bar Yitzhak.

CHAPTER 2: CHANGING THE TOPIC

1. On this point, I am influenced by Boyarin's reading of the sotah ritual in Daniel Boyarin, "Women's Bodies and the Rise of the Rabbis: The Case of Sotah," in *Jews and Gender: The Challenge to Hierarchy,* ed. Jonathan Frankel (New York: Oxford University Press, 2000), 97; and Charlotte Fonrobert's reading of Yalta in Fonrobert, *Menstrual Purity,* 127.

2. See M. Sotah 6:2, 6:4.

3. The citation of M. Sotah 6:3 is consonant with Grushcow's point that B. Sotah further delineates the ritual through the examination of earlier traditions. B. Sotah ultimately redefines M. Sotah 6:3's citation of Deuteronomy 24:1 and Deuteronomy 19:15 to refer to a case where two witnesses see a man and woman having sexual intercourse where there has not been prior warning. Instead of the Deuteronomy verses being utilized to delineate the situation of the sotah, they now refer to any woman and any man. See also Shamma Friedman, who argues that the combination of divorce law (Deuteronomy 24:1) with the sotah is consonant with talmudic opinions that required divorce for inappropriate seclusion. Shamma Friedman, "Sorting Out the Wages of Adultery: Execution, Ordeal, or Divorce," in *Shoshannat Yaakov: Jewish and Iranian Studies in Honor of Yaakov Elman,* ed. Shai Secunda and Steven Fine (Leiden: Brill, 2012), 105–9.

4. The noun *setirah*—seclusion or hiding—draws on the verb *s.t.r.* in Numbers 5:13. In the biblical ritual, *s.t.r.* is used to describe the circumstances that might result in the husband's feeling of jealousy ("she keeps secret the fact that she has defiled herself"). In the rabbinic ritual, *setirah* becomes a legal requirement that follows the legal requirement of warning. *Setirah* moves from unfounded suspicion to required rule of evidence. On this point and its Second Temple antecedents, see Rosen-Zvi, *Mishnaic Sotah Ritual*, 22–23. See also Friedman, "Wages of Adultery," 107; Halbertal, *Interpretive Revolutions*, 95–97; Hauptman, *Rereading the Rabbis*, 17.

5. The full Bavli baraita is a composite of versions found in the Tosefta (T. Sotah 1:2) and Sifrei Bemidbar §7 (ed. Kahana 27). See also Y. Sotah 1:2, 16c whose version largely—but not entirely—corresponds to that of the Tosefta. I discuss the Yerushalmi passage further on in the main body of this chapter.

6. Satlow argues that the root *t.m.'.*, when used in reference to women who have engaged in nonmarital sexual intercourse, does not refer to ritual impurity but rather means "sin" (defilement rather than impurity). See Michael L. Satlow, *Tasting the Dish: Rabbinic Rhetorics of Sexuality* (Atlanta, GA: Scholars Press, 1995), 136–37.

7. The wording of sections A–G of the Bavli baraita is largely parallel to the opening of T. Sotah 1:2. Sections E–H parallel the Sifrei baraita in content but not in wording, with the Sifrei formulated as is characteristic of midrash halakhah.

8. The toseftan version of the baraita (T. Sotah 1:2) makes clear that each successive definition is meant to clarify the previous one.

9. See Satlow, *Tasting the Dish*, 42.

10. See Satlow who reads some of these images as sexually evocative. Satlow, *Tasting the Dish*, 127.

11. The Sifrei version of the baraita ends here. The rest of the baraita parallels the toseftan version.

12. On this phrase, see Assaf Rosen-Zvi, "'Even Though There Is No Proof to the Matter, There Is an Indication of the Matter': The Meaning, Character and Significance of the Phrase in the Tannaitic Literature," *Tarbiz* 78, no. 3 (2009): 323–44 [Hebrew].

13. On the different ways in which weaving is gendered as male or female, see Miriam B. Peskowitz, *Spinning Fantasies: Rabbis, Gender, and History* (Berkeley: University of California Press, 1997), 77–94. This section of the baraita calls to mind a passage found on B. Ketubot 39a–b in which male sages give voice to women's descriptions of their different experiences of first-time penetrative sex. The B. Sotah baraita does not give women a voice (even through men), yet it does use everyday experiences as a descriptive window for sex. On female pain, power, and agency in B. Ketubot 39a–b, see

Rebecca Kamholz, "Virginity in the Babylonian Talmud: Sex, Identity, and Epistemology" (PhD diss., Yale University, 2019), 175–76.

14. The attribution of actions differs in sections I–N of the first baraita. The Bavli does not cite the entirety of T. Sotah 1:2 but rather just the section that corresponds to I–N.

15. The Bavli does not decide between these alternatives.

16. MS Vatican 110–11: R. Yitzhak; Genizah fragment T-S F 8.1018: R. Yitzhak bar Rav Yosef.

17. Daniel Boyarin has convincingly argued that the solution of celibacy reflects Palestinian rabbinic culture, one that prioritized Torah study and then advocated later marriage. Babylonian rabbinic culture, on the other hand, solved the tension between marriage/procreation and Torah study through earlier marriage followed by husbands leaving their wives for extended periods of Torah study. On this point, see Boyarin, *Carnal Israel*, 134–66, and in particular 135, 154; Yishai Kiel, *Sexuality in the Babylonian Talmud: Christian and Sasanian Contexts in Late Antiquity* (New York: Cambridge University Press, 2016), 91–92. See also Jeremy Cohen, *Be Fertile and Increase, Fill the Earth and Master It: The Ancient and Medieval Career of a Biblical Text* (Ithaca, NY: Cornell University Press, 1989), 109–15; Eliezer Diamond, *Holy Men and Hunger Artists: Fasting and Asceticism in Rabbinic Culture* (New York: Oxford University Press, 2004), 35–54.

18. Epstein views this sugya as part of the phenomenon of doubled and transferred sugyot (*sugyot me-ʿuvarot u-kefulot*) particular to B. Sotah, with the original sugya the one on 4b. Epstein, *Introduction to Amoraic Literature*, 89–90.

19. In Albeck, M. Keritot 2:4.

20. Of course, Y. Sotah might have distinguished between the two cases by noting the gendered difference between the guilty parties.

21. On the phrase *leida milah* and this passage in particular, see Leib Moscovitz, *The Terminology of the Yerushalmi: The Principal Terms* (Jerusalem: Magnes Press, 2009), 345–46 [Hebrew].

22. The Yerushalmi baraita omits the measurement of the woman extending a finger into her mouth and includes that of the woman extending her hand to take bread from the basket. The latter is attributed to Minyamin rather than Peleimo, as in the Bavli.

23. See, for example, M. Shabbat 10:4; B. Bava Kamma 82a; Y. Megillah 4:1, 75a.

24. This is not the only example of discussions about sexual sin bookending a sugya in this tractate. See also B. Sotah 3b, which surrounds declarations about the significance of the performance or transgression of commandments with an amoraic statement that "whoring in the home is like

a pest to a sesame plant" and a discussion of Joseph's refusal of sexual contact with Potiphar's wife (Genesis 39:10). In its emphasis on Joseph and the consequences of his sin for his treatment in the world to come, this homily is also consistent with B. Sotah's increased emphasis on male responsibility for sexual sin. It is also consonant with the ways in which B. Sotah's discussion of sexual sin opens into a more generalized discussion of behavioral ethics, in this case the performance of commandments.

25. B. Sotah also utilizes the sotah to think about other ritual procedures, including purification after skin disease or childbirth, capital punishment, writing of Torah scrolls, death penalty procedure, and determination of the purity status of a person or object.

26. See Rashi s.v. *kefifah mitzrit*, and Jastrow following him: a basket made of palm twigs. Jastrow, *Dictionary*, 659, s.v. *kefifah*.

27. See also B. Sotah 8a, which adds that the accused sotah, similar to capital cases, would be brought up and down from the eastern gate in order to tire her, presumably so that she would confess her guilt.

28. Sifrei Bemidbar §11 (ed. Kahana 39).

29. Parenthetical phrase missing in: MS Vatican 110–11, MS Munich 95, MS Oxford 2675, *editio princeps* Venice (1520–1523). This portion of the sugya begins on 14a and concludes on 14b.

30. While the earliest stratum of the Tanhuma-Yelamdenu genre of literature likely stems from the fifth century CE, the majority appears to have been redacted in the sixth and seventh centuries, that is, toward the end of the Bavli's redaction. On the dating of the Tanhuma, see Marc Bregman, *The Tanhuma-Yelammedenu Literature: Studies in the Evolution of the Versions* (Piscataway, NJ: Gorgias Press, 2003), *5 [Hebrew]. The first part of Numbers Rabbah (chapters 1–14) was likely redacted in the twelfth century in Provence. See Marc Bregman, "Midrash Rabbah and the Medieval Collector Mentality," *Prooftexts* 17, no. 1 (1997): 64.

31. See, for example, Tanhuma 3:25–26 (ed. Buber); Numbers Rabbah 9:12. B. Sotah 14a briefly mentions the golden calf episode. The context, however, is a discussion of Moses's desire to enter the land of Israel at the end of his life rather than the sotah. Y. Sotah 3:4; 19a also mentions the golden calf episode, but the topic is not God's jealousy but male jealousy of women and Torah. References to God's jealousy in connection with the sotah in earlier rabbinic literature are also spare. On the Tanhuma, Numbers Rabbah, and Yerushalmi passages, see Grushcow, *Writing the Wayward Wife*, 69–74, 210–11. See also Destro, *Law of Jealousy*, 134–36; Radwin, "Adultery and the Marriage Metaphor," 271–304.

32. Of course, at this stage of the ritual she has already undergone public humiliation, so godly care is clearly limited.

33. In Albeck, M. Sotah 3:4–5.

34. B. Sotah's one clear mention of God's jealousy (to the best of my knowledge) also uses the sotah to extrapolate to a wider moral context (B. Sotah 3a). The baraita figures God as the jealous husband who publicly declares a person's sin: "R. Meir would say: a man [*ʾadam*] commits a transgression in private and the Holy Blessed One proclaims about him in public. As it is said, 'And a spirit of jealousy passes over him' [Numbers 5:14]. And [the word] 'transgression' refers only to the language of proclamation. As it is written, 'And Moses commanded and had this proclamation passed throughout the camp' [Exodus 36:6]." Rashi, intriguingly, and to my mind incorrectly, reads the word *ʾadam* as referring to the sotah and the proclamation as referring to God's causing the jealous husband to declare the sotah's sin (Rashi, s.v. *ʾadam ʿoveir ʿaveirah; ve-ha-kadosh barukh hu makhriz ʿalav be-galui*. Clearly, Rashi's gender-switching interpretation embeds this baraita in the larger context of the discussion of jealousy and the sotah ritual.

35. The version of the baraita in Sifrei Bemidbar includes the words *ve-ha-lo kal va-homer* (is it not a minor to major argument) before section (B) of the Bavli baraita. In the Sifrei, these words indicate an additional comment that is extrapolated from and added to a sage's original statement. B. Sotah has removed these words in formulating its version of the baraita, thus presenting (B) as a continuation of R. Eliezer's statement in (A). On this point and on the change as a conscious decision of the sugya's editor, see Cohen, "Edition and Comprehensive Commentary on Chapters II & III," 37, 40–41.

36. MS Oxford 2675: Torah.

37. MS Oxford 2675: This tanna.

38. See Numbers 5:26. The Bavli aligns R. Eliezer with the first anonymous opinion in M. Sotah 3:2 rather than that of R. Shimon, who proposes first offering the minhah sacrifice and then the woman drinking.

39. On this last point, see Rashi s.v. *mashkeh* along with Numbers 5:15.

40. The version of the baraita found in the Tosefta is similar, but not identical, to that found in B. Sotah. See Cohen, "Edition and Comprehensive Commentary on Chapters II & III," 50–57.

41. Temple service vessels (*kelei shareit*) refers to the implements used in the Temple sacrificial process, such as knives, vessels for blood and incense, and forks, as well as some of the Temple furnishings (the candelabra, altars, and show table).

42. From the Greek καλαθος, referring to baskets with a narrow base. Intriguingly, Jastrow states that this word refers particularly to a woman's work basket. Jastrow, *Dictionary*, 1383, s.v. *kalat*. See also Cohen, "Edition and Comprehensive Commentary on Chapters II & III," 48.

43. MS Oxford 2675: is not fitting as a service vessel.

44. See also B. Sukkah 50b and B. Menahot 28b. B. Menahot 28b cites the baraita as part of a discussion about the materials out of which the Temple candelabra might be fashioned. B. Sukkah 50b cites the baraita within a longer discussion about the Temple flute.

45. MS Oxford 2675: In a basket, no, as it is written, "Just offer it to your governor."

46. The referred-to material may be palm twigs. See Jastrow, *Dictionary*, s.v. *kefifah*, 659.

47. MS Munich 95 does not include the bracketed phrase.

48. In addition to proof-texts from Leviticus 2 (2:1, 2, 3, 8, 13, 16) the Bavli also cites Leviticus 6:8, 6:10, and Numbers 18:8. On the biblical minhah, see Baruch A. Levine, *The JPS Torah Commentary: Leviticus* (Philadelphia: Jewish Publication Society, 1989), 9–14. See also the textual analysis of this passage in Cohen, "Edition and Comprehensive Commentary on Chapters II & III," 50–76. Cohen's view of the sugya as a later editorial creation overlaps with my conclusions.

49. On the *minhat hotei* specifically, see Leviticus 5:11–13. On the trespasses for which a person is liable to bring a sin offering (*hatat*), see Leviticus 5:1–10. For the offerings of the *metzora*, see Leviticus 14:1–32 and specifically 14:21–30. On the nazir, see Numbers 6:14–15.

50. See, for example, T. Sotah 1:10, M. Menahot 1:1, 1:4, 5:3, 6:1; T. Menahot 5:8, 9.

51. See Cohen, "Edition and Comprehensive Commentary on Chapters II & III," 127–32 for an analysis of the phrase *ke-min homer* and its use in a variety of exegetical contexts.

52. This portion of the sugya is a composite, likely weaving together a passage from Sifrei Bemidbar §8 (ed. Kahana 31)—the words of Rabban Gamliel—and T. Sotah 3:4—the words of R. Meir. It is unlikely that Rabban Gamliel, a sage from the Yavneh generation (late first century to early second century CE) would have heard and responded to R. Meir's statement, a sage from the Usha generation (mid-second century CE). For more on the composition of the sugya, see Cohen, "Edition and Comprehensive Commentary on Chapters II & III," 123–126, 133. See also B. Sotah 9b.

CHAPTER 3: ERASED WOMEN AND TALMUDIC REDACTION

1. I rely here on Martin Jaffee's definition of discipleship as a hierarchical relationship that transmits cultural tradition. Discipleship is "a reconstruction of the parent-child relationship in a non-familial instructional setting analogous to the school. . . . Teachers are not biologically the mothers or fathers, the grandparents, uncles, or aunts of their pupils, and they do not normally relate to their pupils as kin. But in a system of discipleship the teachers

bear for each student a responsibility appropriate to that of kin—particularly the father or mother—or even replacing it." Martin S. Jaffee, "A Rabbinic Ontology of the Written and Spoken Word: On Discipleship, Transformative Knowledge, and the Living Texts of Oral Torah," *Journal of the American Academy of Religion* 65, no. 3 (1997): 530. On the privileging of study and teaching of Torah over other types of maternal work, see Mara H. Benjamin, *The Obligated Self: Maternal Subjectivity and Jewish Thought* (Bloomington: Indiana University Press, 2018). See also Mara H. Benjamin, "On Teachers, Rabbinic and Maternal," in *Mothers in the Jewish Cultural Imagination*, ed. Marjorie Lehman, Jane L. Kanarek, and Simon J. Bronner (Liverpool: Littman Library of Jewish Civilization, 2017), 359–76.

2. Sarit Kattan Gribetz makes the important point that transmission depends as much on the presence of a recipient as a transmitter. In other words, texts—whether oral or written—must be received in order to be transmitted; the work of the audience in responding to and shaping that text is as much a part of textual transmission as the work of the transmitter. The transmission of Torah should thus be understood as a relational process, one that is embedded within a network of social connections that includes the biological family. Sarit Kattan Gribetz, "Consuming Texts: Women as Recipients and Transmitters of Ancient Texts," in *Rethinking 'Authority' in Late Antiquity: Authorship, Law, and Transmission in Jewish and Christian Tradition*, ed. A. J. Berkovitz, and Mark Letteney (London: Routledge, 2018), 180.

3. Of course, this erasure has also taken place through scholarship. As Johnson-DeBaufre observes, "Predictably, what is true of ancient texts is also true of our scholarly texts: We make some people visible and hide others." Johnson-DeBaufre, "Gazing Upon the Invisible," 77.

4. In Albeck, M. Sotah 9:14.

5. Much as I focus here on the family of father, mother, son, and daughter, a rabbinic household might also include many other people who helped distribute familial labor, including slaves and wet nurses (Jewish and gentile). These nonbiological household members were also viewed as potential teachers.

6. Daniel Boyarin argues, "that for rabbinic patriarchy the central moment in the construction of gender and thus of the subjection of women is the exclusion of women from the study of Torah and that this exclusion fulfills the functions that in other patriarchies are fulfilled in the realm of economic activity (work) and sanctioned physical domination of women by men (*patria potestas* in its most extreme version)." Boyarin, *Unheroic Conduct*, 153. See also Boyarin, *Unheroic Conduct*, 167–96.

7. See, for example, Elizabeth Shanks Alexander, *Gender and Timebound Commandments in Judaism* (New York: Cambridge University Press, 2013),

200–205; Boyarin, *Carnal Israel*, 170–80; Ilan Fuchs, *Jewish Women's Torah Study: Orthodox Religious Education and Modernity* (London: Routledge, 2014), 9–30; Gribetz, "Consuming Texts," 182–85; Naomi Seidman, *Sarah Schenirer and the Bais Yaakov Movement: A Revolution in the Name of Tradition* (London: Liverpool University Press, 2019), 17–50. Works on the sotah ritual consistently discuss M. Sotah 3:4.

8. My use of the word *punishment* follows Rosen-Zvi's understanding of the mishnaic ritual as punishment rather than ordeal. That is, the woman's reaction to the waters is not meant as a test to reveal guilt or innocence but rather as a punishment for presumed guilt, with merit taking the place that innocence holds in the biblical ritual. Rosen-Zvi, *Mishnaic Sotah Ritual*, 118–20.

9. MS Munich 95, MS Oxford 2675, MS Regensburg: [1], [4], Genizah fragment, *editio princeps* Venice (1520–1523) and Vilna: *kol ha-melameid*.

10. Likely influenced by B. Sotah 21a, MS Munich 95 adds *keʾilu* (*keʾilu melamedah*). See Epstein, *Introduction to the Mishnaic Text*, 536–37; Rosen-Zvi, "Suspected Adulteress," 166n156.

11. On the words *mikan ʾameru* (in our mishnah *mikan ʾamar*) as indicating a citation from another source and the debate between Ben Azzai and R. Eliezer as originally from a context other than that of the sotah ritual, see Rosen-Zvi, *Mishnaic Sotah Ritual*, 167. See also the literature Rosen-Zvi cites there. The connection that M. Sotah 3:4 draws between the sotah ritual and Torah study is our redacted Mishnah's assumption and the assumption of the Bavli sugya.

12. While *ʾadam* can mean "person," the male pronoun used later in the sentence ("his daughter"; *bitto*), indicates that "man" is the better translation.

13. On merit referring to Torah study, see Boyarin, *Carnal Israel*, 170–80; Gribetz, "Consuming Texts," 182–83. On a more general understanding of merit, see Grushcow, *Writing the Wayward Wife*, 202. I lean toward Grushcow's understanding. See also Rosen-Zvi on M. Sotah as the sole instance in tannaitic literature that utilizes the concept of merit to mean suspending a person's own punishment. On merit more generally in rabbinic literature, see A. Marmorstein, *The Doctrine of Merits in Old Rabbinical Literature* (London: Oxford University Press, 1920).

14. The biblical text's lack of clarity about whether the punishment is immediate opens the textual door to this question of delay. On the ambiguity of the results' timing in the biblical ritual, see Frymer-Kensky, "Strange Case," 21–24.

15. On the possibility of an expansive reading of Torah to include the corpus of the rabbinic curriculum (Scripture, mishnah, midrash, halakhah, and aggadah), see Alexander, *Gender and Timebound Commandments*, 203–204

and her accompanying footnotes. See also MS Vatican 110–11, with the reading *talmud torah*, that is, the study of the full rabbinic corpus.

16. I hypothesize that Ben Azzai is thematized by B. Sotah to represent knowledge acquisition. See chapter 2, where I discuss how Ben Azzai comes to represent questions about male knowledge of bodily experience, sexual intercourse in particular.

17. Alexander, *Gender and Timebound Commandments*, 202.

18. Alexander, 202.

19. In Alexander's categories, the father teaches his daughter instrumental Torah (knowledge that serves a pragmatic and informational purpose) rather than ritual Torah (knowledge that inducts males into the rabbinic community and through which a father reproduces himself in the next generation). It is important to note that even if the goal of instrumental Torah study differed from that of ritual Torah study, the very fact (or possibility) of Torah study meant that females were engaging—in at least some way—in this central act of rabbinic culture. While Torah study may not embed the daughter within the sage fellowship, it does connect her to the ideological world of ancient rabbinic culture. The father does not simply inform his daughter that merit defers punishment but does so through the study of Torah, the particular cultural foundation of rabbinic Judaism. This observation need not end with describing females as engaged in a kind of second-class version of Torah study but, rather, in challenging us to expand our conceptions of where and how such study occurred and its role in shaping rabbinic culture.

20. Alexander, *Gender and Timebound Commandments*, 202.

21. This phrase "she is not in the category of one who is commanded and does" refers to the concept "greater is one who is commanded and does [the commandments] than one who is not commanded and [nevertheless] does [the commandments]." See B. Kiddushin 31a; B. Bava Kamma 38a, 87a; and B. Avodah Zarah 3a. For an examination of this principle through a philosophical lens, see David Benatar, "Obligation, Motivation and Reward: An Analysis of a Talmudic Principle," *Journal of Law and Religion* 17, no. 1/2 (2002): 1–17. See also Benjamin, *The Obligated Self*, 3; Robert M. Cover, "Obligation: A Jewish Jurisprudence of the Social Order," *Journal of Law and Religion* 5, no. 1 (1987): 65–74. See also Hauptman, who argues that the Yerushalmi and Bavli implicitly utilize the concept of women fulfilling commandments out of free will to explain leniencies in earlier rabbinic material; in so doing, the Talmuds pave the way for later halakhic adjudicators similarly to rule in a lenient matter, permitting women to perform commandments from which they are otherwise exempt. Judith Hauptman, "Women's Voluntary Performance of Mitzvot from Which They Are Exempt," *Proceedings of the World Congress of Jewish Studies* (1993): 161–68 [Hebrew].

22. Since the sugya has already signaled female exemption from Torah study, it is clear that males are the referent in this discussion.

23. The printed Vilna edition transmits the statements in the names, respectively, of R. Yosef, Rabbah, and Rava. MS Munich 95 and MS Oxford 2675 read Rava in both of the final instances. MS Vatican 110–11 omits the first occurrence of the name Rava/Rabbah. All also read Rav Yosef.

24. Rashi understands "protection" to refer to protection from suffering and "saving" to refer to saving a person from sin/the evil inclination. This interpretation is consonant with the statement's location in B. Sotah. Taken on its own, the statement does not necessitate this interpretation. It is clear that protecting and saving are hierarchical, with saving higher on the hierarchical ladder than protecting. Rashi s.v. *ʾamar rav yosef; mitzvah be-ʿidana de-ʿasik bah; be-ʿidana de-la ʿasik bah; ʾamai la magin ʿaleihen.*

25. MS Oxford 2675: who sinned.

26. M. Sanhedrin 10:2 mentions Gehazi and Balaam along with Doeg and Ahitofel as those who have no share in the world to come. Doeg, Ahitofel, Gehazi, and Bilaam are also listed in T. Sotah 4:19, and B. Sotah 9b following it, as among those who cast their eyes at things unfitting for them—in the case of Doeg and Ahitofel, David's kingdom. T. Sotah 4:19 concludes an extended series of examples that begins with the sotah as an example of a person who cast her eyes at someone who was not fitting for her (another man), turns to the primordial snake, and then finally to a list of men (T. Sotah 16–19; redacted in B. Sotah 9a-b). Gehazi also resurfaces toward the end of the tractate (B. Sotah 47a). See chapter 5 for more on Gehazi.

27. On Doeg and Ahitofel's excellence as Torah scholars, see, for example, B. Sanhedrin 106b.

28. The sugya shifts at this point to Ravina's discussion of mothers and Torah study, to be discussed later in this chapter. I thank my student Eliana Willis for the original insight on David as sotah.

29. This section of the sugya opens by citing the alternative opinion ("Another interpretation: A sin extinguishes a commandment, but a sin does not extinguish Torah") found at the conclusion of the baraita that depicts the superior protective powers of Torah study over commandments and a parable about a (male) traveler in the dark of night. The baraita attributes the homily to R. Menahem bar Yosi. Unlike the Bavli's anonymous voice which understands R. Menahem bar Yosi to interpret Deuteronomy 23:15, the baraita understands him to interpret Proverbs 6:23.

30. In naming sexual sin (*ʿervat davar*) as a reason for God's departure, B. Sotah also alludes to Deuteronomy 24:1, which gives *ʿervat davar* as reason for a husband to divorce his wife. Y. Sotah cites *ʿervat davar* toward the beginning of the tractate, establishing from the outset its greater interest in sex-

ual sin. See also Shamma Friedman on the conflation of divorce and sotah/adultery terminology in M. Sotah 6:3. Friedman, "Wages of Adultery," 105–9.

31. B. Sanhedrin 107a also understands David's initial sexual relationship with Batsheva as sinful, although there the Bavli portrays it as a response to a divine test.

32. B. Sotah portrays David both as a sotah who sins through sex and also as a person who sins through misinterpreting Torah. B. Sotah 35a attributes David's punishment—erring in a matter of law that even children know (carrying the ark of the covenant on a wagon rather than correctly on people's shoulders)—as a result of his calling the words of Torah songs (*zemirot*). This emphasis on mistaken language use is fitting for the larger context of the sugya, a section on *lashon ha-ra* (evil language). It is important to note that B. Sotah also imagines David as righteous. He is a model of humility (lowly and sincere to all; deferring to those with more knowledge of Torah in order to learn Torah), born circumcised and descended from the prophet Miriam (B. Sotah 10b, 11b). These varying portraits of David may coexist in the tractate without negating the portrayal of David as a sotah. See also Richard Kalmin, who hypothesizes differing Babylonian and Palestinian perspectives on David and Ahitofel based on the different social positions of Babylonian and Palestinian rabbis. While this historically oriented perspective is fascinating, one may also explain conflicting perspectives through attention to redactional context, as I have done. Richard Kalmin, *The Sage in Jewish Society of Late Antiquity* (London: Routledge, 1999), 83–93, 101–9.

33. For the biblical laws of levirate marriage, see Deuteronomy 25:5–10. On levirate marriage and the family in ancient Judaism, see Dvora E. Weisberg, *Levirate Marriage and the Family in Ancient Judaism* (Waltham, MA: Brandeis University Press, 2009). See also the absence of Karkemit and Queen Helene of Adiabene, discussed in the introduction.

34. I intentionally echo the title of Rachel Adelman, *The Female Ruse: Women's Deception and Divine Sanction in the Hebrew Bible* (Sheffield, UK: Phoenix Press, 2015). Adelman writes, "Through the female ruse, a 'method' she shares with the other matriarchs—Rebekah, Rachel, and Leah—Tamar inserts herself into the patriarchal history and, in effect, determines the heir for the chosen line." Adelman, *Female Ruse*, 69.

35. As a woman who awaits levirate marriage, Tamar could be considered guilty of adultery and thus subject to the death penalty for having sexual intercourse with a man other than her levir. See Nahum M. Sarna, *The JPS Torah Commentary: Genesis* (Philadelphia: Jewish Publication Society, 1989), 269–70.

36. Genesis 18.

37. The passage imagines Tamar acting with autonomy. Playing on the

biblical description of Tamar sitting at *petah ʿeinayim* (a place name that translates as "opening of the eyes"), the amora R. Shmuel bar Nahmani states that she "gave eyes to her words [*natenah ʿeinayim li-devareha*]." This phrase is used in M. Bava Metzia 5:10 to indicate intention in obtaining a loan. I thank my student Allan Lipson for this reference.

38. B. Sotah lists Isaiah and David. Since the Hebrew Bible explicitly supports only the first claim of royal lineage (1 Chronicles 2:4), the Bavli's extension of this claim to prophets and kings, and by implication the messianic line, is all the more striking. Y. Sotah 1:4, 16d similarly portrays Tamar as having knowledge of rabbinic law. However, the passage is significantly less intricate.

39. B. Sotah implies that Tamar sends Yehudah his signet, cord, and staff privately rather than publicly (see Genesis 38:18, 25).

40. "R. Shmuel bar Nahmani said: She gave eyes to her words. When he summoned her, he [Yehudah] said to her, 'Perhaps you are a gentile?' She said to him, 'I am a convert.' 'Perhaps you are married?' She said to him, 'I am unmarried/open.' 'Perhaps your father accepted betrothal for you?' She said to him, 'I am an orphan.' 'Perhaps you are impure?' She said to him, 'I am pure'" (B. Sotah 10a). Stepping outside of B. Sotah, the exchange between Tamar and Yehudah, with Yehudah figured as the sage with halakhic authority and Tamar as the petitioner of lesser legal authority, echoes the exchanges between R. Akiva and a nameless woman about her menstrual status (M. Niddah 8:3) and between Rav Nahman and Yalta about her desire to eat meat and milk together (B. Hullin 109b). In all of these cases, the Bavli depicts these women as using their legal knowledge to achieve their goals. On M. Niddah 8:3, see Fonrobert, *Menstrual Purity*, 112–15. The version found in the Vilna edition is closest to that found in MS Oxford 2675. MS Vatican 110–111, Munich 95, and *editio princeps* contain shorter versions in which Tamar testifies to her status without the prompting questions from Yehudah.

41. I have translated *beneihu* as "their sons," understanding the word *ben* as gendered exclusively male. It is worthwhile to consider whether we might understand the word inclusively here, that is, to also include daughters. I thank Mira Wasserman for raising this question when I presented a version of this paper at an Association for Jewish Studies conference (2020). By ignoring this possibility because of our assumptions about who learns Torah, have we contributed to the further erasure of females?

42. B. Sotah includes mention of grandfathers as teachers but not grandmothers (B. Sotah 49a, 49b). The place and image of grandfathers and grandmothers in rabbinic culture is a topic worthy of further attention. On old age in rabbinic literature, including mention of grandfathers, see Mira Balberg and Haim Weiss, *When Near Becomes Far: Old Age in Rabbinic Literature* (New York: Oxford University Press, 2021).

43. MS Munich 95: *zekhut de-mitzvah*. This version does not accord with the progression of the argument or with Ravina's following statement.

44. MS Munich 95: omits *beneihu* (sons).

45. Oral tradition here refers to tannaitic literature, that is mishnah, baraitot, etc. See Sokoloff, *Babylonian Aramaic*, 1221, *t.n.y.*

46. See, for example, Boyarin, *Carnal Israel*, 175. Boyarin also argues that the Bavli, by ignoring Ben Azzai and interpreting R. Eliezer's position, effectively suppresses "the possibility that women would be considered candidates for the study of Torah." Boyarin, *Carnal Israel*, 177.

47. Rashi s.v. *de-makreyan u-matneyan*.

48. For another earlier source that also holds out the possibility of women teaching Torah, see T. Ketubot 4:7 and Alexander's analysis of it. Alexander, *Gender and Timebound Commandments*, 194–96.

49. Raffaella Cribiore, *Gymnastics of the Mind: Greek Education in Hellenistic and Roman Egypt* (Princeton, NJ: Princeton University Press, 2001), 78–83.

50. The definitive explication of the intersection of the mimetic and textual transmission of rabbinic culture and its implications for twentieth-century North American Orthodoxy is Haym Soloveitchik, "Rupture and Reconstruction: The Transformation of Contemporary Orthodoxy," *Tradition: A Journal of Orthodox Jewish Thought* 28, no. 4 (1994): 64–130. See also the reassessments, including feminist, twenty-five years later, in "'Rupture and Reconstruction' Reconsidered: A Symposium," *Tradition: A Journal of Orthodox Jewish Thought* 51, no. 4 (2019).

51. On the oral nature of rabbinic culture and textual transmission, see Elizabeth Shanks Alexander, *Transmitting Mishnah: The Shaping Influence of Oral Tradition* (New York: Cambridge University Press, 2006); Talya Fishman, *Becoming the People of the Talmud: Oral Torah as Written Tradition in Medieval Jewish Cultures* (Philadelphia: University of Pennsylvania Press, 2013); Jaffee, *Torah in the Mouth*; Yaacov Sussmann, "'Torah she beʿal peh'—peshutah ke-mashmaʿah: koho shel kotzo shel yod," in *Mehqerei Talmud: Talmudic Studies Dedicated to the Memory of Professor Ephraim E. Urbach*, Vol. 3, ed. Yaacov Sussman and David Rosenthal (Jerusalem: Magnes Press, 2005), 209–384. In contrast, see Monika Amsler, who argues convincingly for a written model of transmission. Monika Amsler, *The Babylonian Talmud and Late Antique Book Culture* (Cambridge: Cambridge University Press, 2023). I lean to a model in which orality produces written texts, which in turn generate further oral transmission, which in turn generates written texts, and so on.

52. Judith Hauptman, "A New View of Women and Torah Study in the Talmudic Period," *Jewish Studies, an Internet Journal* 9 (2010): 249–92.

53. A similar tradition found on B. Berakhot 17b describes the sage Rav asking R. Hiyya why women merit a greater reward in the world to come than men. Rabbi Hiyya replies that they receive this reward for enabling their sons to learn Scripture in the synagogue and for waiting for their husbands until they return from the study house. Similar to the B. Sotah passage, R. Hiyya's answer uses the causative form of the verb. In contrast, it does *not* include the verb that refers to Oral Torah and *does* specify where that teaching will take place (the synagogue). In addition, the two tradents (Rav and R. Hiyya) are transitional figures between the tannaitic and amoraic periods while Ravina is a later sage. These two traditions, therefore, should not be conflated with one another, and the B. Sotah tradition should not be read as identical to that in B. Berakhot.

54. On this tradition and breastfeeding as a way of transmitting knowledge, see Jordan Rosenblum, "'Blessings of the Breasts': Breastfeeding in Rabbinic Literature," *Hebrew Union College Annual* 87 (2016): 172–76. See also B. Sotah 30b where breastfeeding children are able to see God.

55. Boyarin, *Carnal Israel*, 134–66.

56. Rashi understands this passage as consonant with husbands leaving their homes to study in other cities. Rashi s.v. *ve-natran le-gavreihu*.

57. In this vein, see the story on B. Ketubot 62b that depicts the absence of R. Hama bar Bisa for twelve years and his inability to recognize his son who has become a scholar. Read against the grain, this story credits the mother with inducting her son, in the absence of his father, into rabbinic culture. On the absent father in the B. Ketubot story cycle, see Haim Weiss and Shira Stav, *The Return of the Absent Father: A New Reading of a Chain of Stories from the Babylonian Talmud*, trans. Batya Stein (Philadelphia: University of Pennsylvania Press, 2022). On the depiction of the broken relationships between fathers and sons as opposed to the harmonious ones between mothers and daughters in this story cycle, see Moshe Lavee, "Like Mother Like Daughter: Mother-Daughter Relations in Babylonian Talmudic Stories," in *Mothers in the Jewish Cultural Imagination*, ed. Marjorie Lehman, Jane L. Kanarek, and Simon J. Bronner (Liverpool: Littman Library of Jewish Civilization, 2017), 105–28.

58. I draw here on Mara Benjamin's understanding of obligation to include the work of material care for a child, that is, "a self radically bound up with someone else. . . . To be an obligated self was to be subject to the law of another: the Law of the Baby. The law could not be fulfilled in the abstract but only in active, embodied, material actions: soothing, feeding, cleaning, comforting, distracting, smiling, and wiping." Benjamin, *The Obligated Self*, 8.

59. On female wool-work, see Peskowitz, *Spinning Fantasies*; Miriam Peskowitz, "Spinning Tales: On Reading Gender and Otherness in Tannaitic

Texts," in *The Other in Jewish Thought and History: Constructions of Jewish Culture and Identity*, ed. Laurence J. Silberstein and Robert L. Cohn (New York: NYU Press, 1994), 91–120. On male wool-work, see Gail Labovitz, "A Man Spinning on His Thigh: Gender, Positive Time-Bound Commandments and Ritual Fringes; Mishnah Moʿed Katan 3:4," *Nashim: A Journal of Jewish Women's Studies & Gender Issues* 28 (2015): 75–87.

60. For this list of work that a wife is obligated to do for her husband, see M. Ketubot 5:5. On the rabbinic obligation for mothers to breastfeed, see Gail Labovitz, "'These Are the Labors': Constructions of the Woman Nursing Her Child in the Mishnah and Tosefta," *Nashim: A Journal of Jewish Women's Studies & Gender Issues* 3 (2000): 15–42; Miriam-Simma Walfish, "Upending the Curse of Eve: A Reframing of Maternal Breastfeeding in BT Ketubot," in *Motherhood in the Jewish Cultural Imagination*, ed. Marjorie Lehman, Jane L. Kanarek, and Simon J. Bronner (Liverpool: Liverpool University Press, 2017), 307–25.

61. MS Parma 9:16; Albeck 9:14. MSS Kaufmann and Parma as well as Albeck divide this mishnah into two units, resulting in its appearing as the second-to-last mishnah in the tractate. MSS Kaufmann, Parma, and the printed Vilna differ from one another in content (i.e., what text makes up the mishnaic conclusion of M. Sotah) as well as the order in which the included text appears. Albeck understands the textual confusion as evidence for the late addition of the entire concluding mishnah to the tractate (in Albeck, M. Sotah 9:14–15). Albeck, *Nashim*, 394.

62. Jastrow, *Dictionary*, s.v. *ʾeirus*. See also B. Sotah 49b, which understands *ʾeirus* as a kind of drum.

63. MS Kaufmann and MS Cambridge: *kitom*. MS Parma and Albeck and Vilna (B. Sotah 49a): *titus*. Although scholars have identified Kitos with Lucius Quietus, the governor of Judea under Trajan, it nevertheless remains unclear which events this mishnah references. See Peter Schäfer, *The History of the Jews in the Greco-Roman World* (London: Routledge, 2003), 141–42; Moulie Vidas, "Greek Wisdom in Babylonia," in *Envisioning Judaism; Studies in Honor of Peter Schäfer on the Occasion of His Seventieth Birthday*, ed. Raʿanan S. Boustan et al. (Tübingen: Mohr Siebeck, 2013), 287n3. On the identity of Kitos with Lucius Quietus, see, for example, Lieberman, *Tosefta ki-fshutah*, Vol. 3, 767.

64. See also T. Sotah 15:8 and T. Avodah Zarah 1:20.

65. See also T. Sotah 15:8; Y. Sotah 9:14, 24c. On the practice of wearing marital crowns in ancient and medieval Judaism and the link between these practices and the mythical understanding of the sinaitic moment as a wedding between God and Israel where God crowns Israel as bride, see Arthur Green, *Keter: The Crown of God in Early Jewish Mysticism* (Princeton, NJ:

Princeton University Press, 2014), 78–87. B. Sotah 49b identifies the groom's crown as gold-embroidered silks used for wedding canopies and the bride's crown as the *'ir shel zahav* (city of gold). For a discussion of sabbath prohibitions associated with the *'ir shel zahav* and the gendering of rabbinic space, see Cynthia M. Baker, *Rebuilding the House of Israel: Architectures of Gender in Jewish Antiquity* (Stanford: Stanford University Press, 2002), 122–44.

66. This problematic is also reflected in M. Sotah 9:9 with its ascription of the cessation of the heifer ritual to the multiplication of murderers and the cessation of the sotah ritual to the multiplication of adulterers.

67. In addition to B. Sotah 49b, B. Bava Kamma 82b–83a and B. Menahot 64b, the term *hokhmat yevanit* also appears on B. Menachot 99b, the latter a passage similar to T. Avodah Zarah 1:20. Y. Sotah 9:15, 24c and the parallels in Y. Peah 1:1, 15c and Y. Shabbat 6:1, 7d report the ban as against Greek language. See also the earlier passages in T. Sotah 15:8 and T. Avodah Zarah 1:20. On the uniqueness of the term *hokhmat yevanit,* see E. E. Hallewy, "Concerning the Ban on Greek Wisdom," *Tarbiz* 41, no. 3 (1971): 272 [Hebrew]; Vidas, "Greek Wisdom," 290–91. The term "Greek wisdom" should be viewed as a later Babylonian interpolation into the baraita and thus representative of Babylonian ideology and not earlier Palestinian ideology. On this point, see Vidas, "Greek Wisdom," 290, 298. On the phenomenon of Babylonian literary reworkings of baraitot in accordance with Babylonian ideology, see Shamma Friedman, "Ha-baraitot ba-talmud ha-bavli ve-yahasan lemaqbilotehen she-ba-tosefta," in *Atara l'haim: mehkarim ba-sifrut ha-talmudit veha-rabanit li-khevod professor hayim zalman dimitrovsky,* ed. Daniel Boyarin et al. (Jerusalem: Magnes Press, 2000), 163–201.

68. For the opposite position, that this baraita represents a theoretical debate about the study and teaching of Greek wisdom, see for example E. E. Hallewy, "Concerning the Ban on Greek Wisdom," *Tarbiz* 41, no. 3 (1971): 273 [Hebrew]. I use the terminology *study* to indicate a person's self-acquisition of knowledge and *teaching* to indicate one person's transmission of knowledge to another. In this context, the distinction is important because of earlier scholarly attempts to identify the nature of the ban against Greek/Greek wisdom. Lieberman, for example, argues that the ban involved only the teaching of Greek language and wisdom to children but not the study of Greek wisdom and language by adults who were less susceptible to ideological corruption. Saul Lieberman, *Greek in Jewish Palestine/Hellenism in Jewish Palestine* (New York: Jewish Theological Seminary of America, 1994), 101–102. See also Hallewy, "Concerning the Ban on Greek Wisdom," 272. Neither address the gendered aspect of the prohibition.

69. For a summary of scholarship on the Christian context of the Babylonian Talmud, see Michal Bar-Asher Siegal, *Early Christian Monastic Liter-*

ature and the Babylonian Talmud (New York: Cambridge University Press, 2013), 1–34.

70. Vidas, "Greek Wisdom," 303.

71. Lieberman's work on this passage provides a classic example of understanding this baraita as a historical referent to Greek learning during the early second century CE. Lieberman, *Greek in Jewish Palestine*, 100–14.

72. See also Y. Ta'anit 4:6, 69a and B. Gittin 58a, which are clearly part of the same literary tradition as B. Sotah 49b. None, however, mention Greek or Greek wisdom. See also Lamentations Rabbah 3:51 (ed. Buber), which similarly does not mention Greek or Greek wisdom. Noah Hacham demonstrates that B. Sotah 49b, Y. Ta'anit 4:6, 69a, and B. Gittin 58a are reworkings of an earlier literary tradition. Noah Hacham, "Rabban Simeon Son of Gamaliel in Beitar," *Tarbiz* 74 (2005): 550–51 [Hebrew]. See also Landau's summary of the material. Landau, "An Edition and Comprehensive Commentary on Chapter IX," 350–56. On B. Gittin's narratives of destruction, but not this pericope in particular, see Julia Watts Belser, *Rabbinic Tales of Destruction: Gender, Sex, and Disability in the Ruins of Jerusalem* (New York: Oxford University Press, 2017).

73. On the destruction of Beitar, see Schäfer's chapter on the Bar Kokhba revolt in Schäfer, *History of the Jews*, 145–61 and specifically 154–58. Hacham hypothesizes that "beit 'abba" originally read "beitar" or "beitatar" and that the place name was switched in order to obscure a connection between Rabban Shimon ben Gamliel and the rebellion against Rome, consonant with Babylonian discomfort with rebellion against foreign rule. In contrast, the version of this passage found on Y. Ta'anit 4:6, 69a does not share a similar drive to hide such a link. Hacham, "Rabban Simeon Son of Gamaliel," 555–56.

74. On "the ways of the Amorites" as a method for the rabbis to prohibit practices for which they lack a clear justification to forbid but that they nevertheless do not condone, see Beth A. Berkowitz, *Defining Jewish Difference: From Antiquity to the Present* (New York: Cambridge University Press, 2012), 100.

75. Medieval to modern commentators have associated the prohibition against cutting one's hair in the style of *komi* with a particular hairstyle in which the front of the hair was cut and the back left long. Berkowitz raises another possibility: Cutting one's hair in the manner of *komi* refers to Roman hairstyles more generally and is associated "with efforts to blend into elite Roman society." Berkowitz argues for this more general understanding of *mesaper komi* concerning Mekhilta de-arayot on Leviticus 18:13, but it could also apply to this B. Sotah passage. On these points and for a summary of earlier scholarship on *mesaper komi*, see Berkowitz, *Defining Jewish Difference*, 100–106 and for the quotation, 103; Beth A. Berkowitz, "The Limits of

'Their Laws': Ancient Rabbinic Controversies about Jewishness (and Non-Jewishness)," *Jewish Quarterly Review* 99, no. 1 (2009): 145–51. See also the mention of the foreign hairstyle *belorit* on B. Sotah 46b and Berkowitz, *Defining Jewish Difference*, 118–22.

76. Vidas, "Greek Wisdom," 299–301.

77. In tannaitic literature, the most common term for the place in which rabbinic study occurred is *beit midrash*. However, the scope and details of the beit midrash are unclear. As *beit* can also mean "room," it is quite possible that the study house was either the master's own residence or a designated room in that house. The situation was largely the same in the amoraic period, with the Yerushalmi also referring to the *beit vaʿad* or *bei vaʿada* (assembly house) and the Bavli using *bei rav* (master's house) as the standard term for the place of study. The shift to larger academies (*yeshivah* [Hebrew] or *metivta* [Aramaic]) began in the later stammaitic period and was fully realized with the geonic academy. On this, see Jeffrey L. Rubenstein, "Social and Institutional Settings of Rabbinic Literature," in *The Cambridge Companion to the Talmud and Rabbinic Literature*, ed. Charlotte Elisheva Fonrobert and Martin S. Jaffee (New York: Cambridge University Press, 2007), 58–74. On the Bavli's anachronistic retrojection of the later stammaitic academy into earlier sources, see Jeffrey L. Rubenstein, *The Culture of the Babylonian Talmud* (Baltimore: Johns Hopkins University Press, 2003), 16–23. See also the detailed work of Catherine Hezser, *The Social Structure of the Rabbinic Movement in Roman Palestine* (Tübingen: Mohr Siebeck, 1997), 195–214, on amoraic period Palestine in particular.

78. Vidas, "Greek Wisdom," 300–301.

79. In MS Leiden 9:15. Transcription follows *Yerushalmi Leiden*, 950. The editors understand the word *la* (no/not) in the final line of the sugya to be an addition to the manuscript; I have translated according to that assumption. MS Vatican and the parallel text in Y. Peʾah 1:1, 15c do not include the word *la*. The similar version on Y. Shabbat 6:1, 7d does include the word *la* as well as a switch in speaker back to R. Abbahu. Although the evidence is inconclusive as to which is the correct translation, this one line is not central to my larger argument.

80. I want to remind us that R. Abbahu appears in the sugya I cite at the very beginning of this book (B. Sotah 40a) as an example of a humble Torah sage who chastises his wife for her attempt to protect his honor.

81. Vidas, "Greek Wisdom," 289. Ebner notes the overlap between the Yerushalmi's ban and the language of R. Eliezer in M. Sotah 3:4. However, Ebner conflates Greek wisdom with Greek language and does not recognize the position in the Yerushalmi permitting the teaching of Greek to daughters. Noting Lieberman's reading of the ban as focusing on the teaching of chil-

dren, he hypothesizes that a similar prohibition may be at work in M. Sotah 3:4. Like Lieberman, Ebner does not emphasize gender when it comes to the ban but age. Ebner, "Composition and Structure of Mishnah Sotah," 242n2; Lieberman, *Greek in Jewish Palestine*, 101–102.

82. *Yerushalmi Leiden*, 950.

83. On R. Akiva, his wife, and the *ʿir shel zahav*, see also Y. Shabbat 6:1, 7d; B. Shabbat 59a–b and B. Nedarim 50a. Y. Shabbat 6:1, 7d similarly redacts the story of the *ʿir shel zahav* near the passage about fathers teaching daughters Greek. Tal Ilan argues for the historicity of Rabbi Akiva's gift to his wife, but I do not find this to be necessary. Ilan, *Mine and Yours Are Hers*, 107–8; Tal Ilan, "'Yerushalayim shel zahav' ve-ha-garʿin ha-histori be-siporei eishet r. akiva," in *Woman in Jerusalem: Gender, Society, and Religion*, ed. Tova Cohen and Joshua Schwartz (Ramat-Gan: Bar-Ilan, 2002), 33–46. Susan Marks contextualizes these traditions about R. Akiva's wife and the *ʿir shel zahav* within the larger world of female patronage in the ancient Mediterranean. Susan Marks, "Follow That Crown: Or, Rhetoric, Rabbis, and Women Patrons," *Journal of Feminist Studies in Religion* 24, no. 2 (2008): 77–96. See also Krista Dalton, "Teaching for the Tithe: Donor Expectations and the Matrona's Tithe," *AJS Review* 44, no. 1 (2020): 49–73 and specifically 57–58. B. Nedarim 50a depicts a poverty-stricken R. Akiva desiring to give his wife a "Jerusalem of Gold" (*yerushalayim de-dahava*).

84. On female ornamentation in rabbinic culture and the Jerusalem of Gold, see Boyarin, *Carnal Israel*, 100–106. On women's headgear, including the *ʿir shel zahav* and the rabbinic courtyard and alleyway, see Baker, *Rebuilding the House of Israel*, 122–35.

85. Judith Hauptman's work has introduced important correctives to this approach. Hauptman argues that the fact that rabbinic study, at least in the tannaitic and amoraic periods, took place largely within the physical space of the household implies that females were likely to overhear conversations and even sometimes participate in them. Hauptman, "New View of Women and Torah Study," 250–51.

CHAPTER 4: LANGUAGE AND NATIONAL CATASTROPHE

1. The idea of Hebrew as *leshon ha-kodesh* (the holy tongue) dates to at least the late Second Temple period. Smelik, *Rabbis, Language, and Translation*, 42 and more generally on *leshon ha-kodesh*, 43–98. See, in contrast, the strain in early Hasidic thought that expands the notion of *leshon ha-kodesh* to the potential of any human language to become sacred. Ariel Evan Mayse, "Expanding the Boundaries of the Holy: Hasidic Devotion, Sacred Speech, and Early Modern Jewish Thought," *Jewish Social Studies* 25, no. 1 (2019): 47.

2. Both visual spectacle and language use combine to construct the ritual's efficacy and terror.

3. In the Hebrew Bible, the phrase "amen, amen" appears only here (Numbers 5:22) and in Nehemiah 8:6. It is also a phrase commonly written on incantation bowls, used as a formulaic conclusion to the incantation. See Ahuvia, *On My Right Michael*, 21–22 and n15.

4. I borrow this phrase from Kattan Gribetz, "Consuming Texts," 183.

5. I use the language of transmission in accordance with Kattan Gribetz's call to disturb "the binary of transmitter/recipient" and to "conceptualize the process of transmission as a process of continual or repeated reception." Kattan Gribetz, "Consuming Texts," 180.

6. The sotah portion refers to selections from Numbers 5:19–22. See M. Sotah 2:3–4 for different opinions on the precise verse selection.

7. As should be clear from the following examples, I do not believe the stylistic proclivities of the Mishnah sufficiently account for its use of *ʾ.m.r.* in M. Sotah.

8. Rosen-Zvi explains the mismatch between the husband's warning ("do not speak with a particular man") and the prohibition against the woman's seclusion with that man as engaging with underlying questions concerning freedom of movement and communication. Rosen-Zvi, *Mishnaic Sotah Ritual*, 21–48.

9. On the woman who refuses to drink or the woman who says she is impure, see also M. Sotah 1:5, 3:3, and 4:2.

10. On M. Sotah 6:1 and its use of the image of spinning to construct the sotah as Other among women, see Peskowitz, *Spinning Fantasies*, 133–39; Peskowitz, "Spinning Tales," 106–12. It is possible that B. Sotah 40a's story of two women talking with one another, discussed in the introduction, draws on this mishnaic portrayal of women in conversation with one another.

11. In Albeck, 6:4.

12. On lists as a fundamental mishnaic form, see Jaffee, *Torah in the Mouth*, 106–11; Martin Jaffee, "Writing and Rabbinic Oral Tradition: On Mishnaic Narrative, Lists and Mnemonics," *The Journal of Jewish Thought and Philosophy* 4 (1994): 135; Jacob Neusner, "The Mishnah's Generative Mode of Thought: Listenwissenschaft and Analogical-Contrastive Reasoning," *Journal of the American Oriental Society* 110, no. 2 (1990): 317–21; and Jacob Neusner, *A History of the Mishnaic Law of Purities* (Leiden: Brill, 1977), 191–96.

13. MS Munich 95, Venice, *editio princeps*, and Vilna: *be-khol lashon* (B. Sotah 32a). I will use both "their languages" and "any language" to refer to those rituals that may be recited in a language other than Hebrew.

14. M. Sotah does not offer any reason that these rituals in the first list may be recited in any language. Smelik hypothesizes the freedom of language

choice may be attributed to the fact that these rituals, with the exception of the sotah ritual, neither involve the recitation of biblical verses nor require priestly involvement. Of course, this points to the sotah ritual as "the odd one out" and may explain why B. Sotah emphasizes understanding. Smelik, *Rabbis, Language, and Translation*, 52.

15. See M. Sotah 7:9 for a description of the high priest's blessing as his public reading of the Torah on Yom Kippur, a reading followed by a series of blessings. On these mishnayot and the differing mishnaic and toseftan conceptions of the roles of priest and king, see David C. Flatto, *The Crown and the Courts: Separation of Powers in the Early Jewish Imagination* (Cambridge, MA: Harvard University Press, 2020), 119–22.

16. Similar to the high priest's blessing, M. Sotah 7:10 describes the king's reading of the Torah as followed by a series of blessings.

17. Although Deuteronomy 21:4 prescribes breaking the neck of the heifer, M. Sotah 9:5 prescribes the use of a hatchet. Since I trace the rabbinic *ʿeglah ʿarufah*, my translation reflects the mishnaic prescription.

18. The mishnah, as is characteristic of its terser literary form, does not articulate a connection beyond language requirements to explain the two groupings of rituals. Hauptman hypothesizes that the rituals in the second list were originally grouped together because all involve the recitation of biblical verses (a feature they share with the sotah ritual) and is an act that would, as a matter of course, have been done in Hebrew (a feature that differentiates them from the sotah ritual). In editing the collection, the mishnaic redactor later added the reference to Hebrew and made it the organizing principle of the second collection. Judith Hauptman, *Rereading the Mishnah: A New Approach to Ancient Jewish Texts* (Tübingen: Mohr Siebeck, 2005), 196–207.

19. On the control of speech as a scholastic interpersonal ideal of the rabbinic community, see Jonathan Wyn Schofer, *The Making of a Sage: A Study in Rabbinic Ethics* (Madison: University of Wisconsin Press, 2005), 137.

20. See also Sifrei Bemidbar §12 (ed. Kahana 40).

21. MS Munich 95: One makes her take an oath (*mashbiʿin ʾotah*).

22. Jastrow: waywardness.

23. T. Sotah 2:1 also contains the words "in order that she will know": "They announce to her in any language she understands in order that she will know why she drinks, how she drinks, why she is impure and how she became impure." These words make clear that the point of using any language is to ensure the accused's understanding of the ritual. On B. Sotah 32b, the first lines, which provide a biblical proof text for recitation in any language, utilize (at least in some manuscript versions) the phrase "in any language that she understands." In T. Sotah 2:1, the language section is preceded by a description of the gold tablet upon which the priest would write and then read

the portion of the sotah. This does not appear in B. Sotah, further evidence for the fact that B. Sotah's main concern does not lie with the actual performance of the sotah ritual.

24. On T. Sotah 2:1 presenting the ritual as an "instructive-educational event," see Rosen-Zvi, *Mishnaic Sotah Ritual*, 170 and also n71 there.

25. Since M. Sotah, and the Bavli following it, imagines a public ritual, it is possible that the priest's audience is wider than solely the accused woman.

26. Conversely, her failure to become pregnant after the ritual also may be ascribed to the waters' inapplicability, although this is not the emphasis of the passage.

27. See also the parallel in Sifrei Bemidbar §8 (ed. Kahana 33) and Rosen-Zvi, *Mishnaic Sotah Ritual*, 102–29.

28. The language of *motzi ʾatah sheim ra* also echoes Deuteronomy 22:13–19, the law concerning a husband who falsely accuses his wife of not being a virgin. This phrase is thus intertwined with a larger field of potential sexual transgressions.

29. See also B. Sotah 21b in MS Oxford 2675, which adds the phrase *le-hotzi laʿaz ʿal ha-mayim* in its recapitulation of M. Sotah 3:4: "From here said Ben Azzai: A man [*ʾadam*] is obligated to teach his daughter Torah so that if she drinks [the bitter waters] she will know that merit suspends. And all this why? So as not to cast aspersions on the waters."

30. On B. Sotah 9b and 28a, the phrase *le-hotzi laʿaz* is clearly used by the Bavli's anonymous voice, providing further evidence for the Bavli's reworking of the toseftan baraita. It is likely that the Bavli interpolates the phrase *le-hotzi laʿaz* into the baraita from the anonymous material.

31. Albeck: M. Sotah 7:7. See also M. Yoma 7:1.

32. This statement may introduce the next prescription in this mishnaic passage, the recitation from memory of Numbers 29:7–11.

33. See also B. Yoma 70a.

34. In order for the sotah pericope to be effective, it must be consumed by a woman who may be prohibited to study that passage! The sotah ritual's "successful" transmission thus depends as much on the female recipient as it does on the priestly transmitter. Kattan Gribetz, "Consuming Texts," 183. It may be this connection that leads MS Oxford 2675 to add the phrase *le-hotzi laʿaz ʿal ha-mayim* in its recapitulation of M. Sotah 3:4. On the ritual power of M. Sotah 3:4 as erased and consumed text, see Rebecca Scharbach Wollenberg, *The Closed Book: How the Rabbis Taught the Jews (Not) to Read the Bible* (Princeton, NJ: Princeton University Press, 2023), 202–5.

35. Although *laʿaz* is commonly understood as referring to Greek, it also denotes other languages. On *laʿaz* referring to languages other than Greek, see B. Megillah 18a; on *laʿaz* referring to Greek, see Y. Megillah 1.8 (11), 71b. As

Smelik notes, "It is more correct to say that it may refer to Greek in practice, but refers to any non-Hebrew vernacular in theory." Smelik, *Rabbis, Language, and Translation*, 34n77.

36. Y. Sotah 7:1, 21b neither broadens the priest's field of instruction nor mentions casting aspersions on the bitter waters. Rather, it explores whether God spoke with women other than the matriarch Sarah. Intriguingly, it does mention an interpreter, precluding his use. I am intrigued by this mention of an intermediary between priest and woman and its overlap with the mention of the speaker intermediary in the two women talking story on B. Sotah 40a.

37. According to M. Arakhin 3:6, God seals the punishment of the wilderness generation (death in the wilderness rather than completing the journey to Canaan) as a result of *lashon ha-ra*. M. Arakhin precedes the case of the wilderness generation and *lashon ha-ra* with that of the *motzi sheim ra*, another instance of thinking together with these two cases. See also T. Arakhin 2:6.

38. MS Kaufmann Arakhin 3:6 vocalizes the phrase as *leshon ha-ra*, that is in construct form, rather than the more common noun and adjective. See Nissan Berggrün, *Studies in the Hebrew Language* (Jerusalem: The Academy of the Hebrew Language, 1995), 178–79 [Hebrew]. Also available at https://hebrew-academy.org.il/wp-content/uploads/LashonHaRa.pdf.

39. Of course, *lashon ha-ra* may be said in *leshon ha-kodesh* much as in Greek or Aramaic.

40. In addition to the covenantal ceremony and the spies, the passage expounds and explicates David's return of the ark to Jerusalem and Uzzah's death (2 Samuel 6; 1 Chronicles 13); the Philistines' return of the ark to Jerusalem during the time of Samuel (1 Samuel 6); Joseph in Pharaoh's house (Genesis 39); and the crossing of the Reed Sea (Exodus 15).

41. The biblical version of this covenantal ceremony (Deuteronomy 27) includes the erection of large stones and their inscription with the words of the Torah (in Deuteronomy 27:3 likely a reference to some part of the book of Deuteronomy), the building of an unhewn stone altar and the offering of sacrifices, the recitation of blessings and curses on Mount Gerizim and Mount Ebal, and the levitical invocation and the people's affirmation of God's punishment of sins challenging for humans to prosecute. On the biblical version of the ritual, see Jeffrey H. Tigay, *The JPS Torah Commentary: Deuteronomy* (Philadelphia: Jewish Publication Society, 1996), 248–50, 486–89.

42. Although the blessings and curses are to be recited in *leshon ha-kodesh*, B. Sotah, like M. Sotah, does not provide the missing biblical proof text for the blessings and curses. It also does not engage in an extended legal analysis of the procedure for the blessings and curses.

43. See Tigay, *Deuteronomy,* 248. Whether the inscribed stones are identical to or different from those used to build the altar is a matter of controversy. For a summary of the arguments, see Tigay, *Deuteronomy,* 487–88. The Mishnah understands them as identical to the altar (M. Sotah 7:7).

44. Much like the mishnaic sotah ritual, the blessings and curses are depicted as a public ceremony. In addition, the recitation of amen and the writing of the Torah on another object both echo the sotah ritual, albeit with the sotah portion a smaller amount of writing.

45. Rabbinic traditions vary on the content of the ark, from one set of tablets from the sinaitic covenant, to two sets, to a Torah scroll. See, for example, T. Sotah 7:18, Y. Sotah 8:1 (2), 22b, B. Sotah 42b–43a, Y. Shekalim 6:1, 49c, and Wollenberg, *Closed Book,* 81–82.

46. The inclusion of males and females in this amoraic dictum is consonant with B. Sotah's expansion of sin to encompass males as well as females.

47. This toseftan baraita is one of a cluster of five baraitot that make up the beginning of the sugya: the first two from Sifrei Devarim §56 (ed. Finkelstein 123–24) and the last two from the Tosefta (T. Sotah 8:1; 8:2–4; 8:6).

48. Eight carry a grape cluster, one a pomegranate, and one a fig. See Numbers 13:23 for the list of fruits.

49. MS Vatican 110–11: Rabbah.

50. Genizah fragment T-S F 2(2).30: from his brothers (*mei-ʾehav*).

51. Genizah fragment T-S F 2(2).30: so you request mercy for me and I will be saved (*ve-ʾaf ʾatem bikshu ʿalai rahamim ve-ʾenatz*).

52. All extant textual witnesses include the adjective *ha-zonah.*

53. MS Munich 95 and MS Vatican 110–11: no mnemonic.

54. MS Munich 95 "will not have truth at its end" (*ʾein ʾemet be-sofo*).

55. MS Munich 95, MS Vatican 110–11: "I will open" (*ʾiftah ana*). The word *ʾiftah* (I will begin/open) is copied from the previous sentence.

56. MS Vatican 110–11: for forty years (*ʾarbaʿim shanah*).

57. To the best of my knowledge, this is the only occurrence of "cut-off head" (*rosh ketiʿah*) in the Bavli.

58. Arukh, *reish* 221.

59. Rashi, s.v. *de-hazyeih.*

60. Although B. Sotah 35a frames this statement in the context of *lashon ha-ra,* B. Arakhin 15a utilizes it to propose (unsuccessfully) the possibility that rather than being punished for *lashon ha-ra,* the spies were punished for blasphemy.

61. An alternative tradition in the same sugya posits that Job died and therefore the entire world was busy with his eulogy.

62. MS Munich 95, MS Vatican 110–11: without "Rabbah" or "That day was the [eve] of the ninth of Av." Like the Vilna print, MS New York—JTS Rab.

744.1–2 does include both of the above. However, like the *editio princeps*, it does not include the word *eve*. The addition of the clause specifying the ninth of Av is likely from the parallel versions found on B. Taʿanit 29a and B. Sanhedrin 104b.

63. Missing in MS Vatican 110–11.

64. MS Vatican 110–11: R. Hiyya bar Abba.

65. MS Munich 95: Rav Nahman.

66. See Numbers 15:18; Leviticus 19:23.

67. The language of Y. Taʿanit 4:6 (8), 68d is ambiguous as to whether "community" refers just to the spies or to the entire nation.

68. Since *tiflut* can also mean "childishness," it also overlaps with B. Sotah 32b and the use of the word "childishness" (*yaldut*) as part of the priest's speech to the accused sotah.

69. The condemnations of *lashon ha-ra* in B. Arakhin echo those against arrogance (*gasut ruah*) found in B. Sotah (4b–5a). They include the assertions that speaking *lashon ha-ra* is equivalent to rejecting God and to violating the prohibitions against idolatry, forbidden sexual liaisons, and murder. Both B. Sotah 5a and B. Arakhin 15b make this overlap explicit, proposing that Psalms 101:5 can be interpreted to refer either to *lashon ha-ra* or to arrogance.

70. Precedent for mention of Joseph's name is also found in M. Sotah 1:10 (Albeck 1:9): Joseph's burial of his father Jacob and Moshe's subsequent burial of Joseph's bones.

71. This shift from language and its connection with revelation to the consequences of language for human society is also part of B. Sotah's move away from Temple ritual to rabbinic ritual. As Seth Schwartz observes, *leshon hakodesh* likely originally meant "temple language." He hypothesizes that "the decision to compose the Mishnah . . . in Hebrew—and in a type of Hebrew that was especially associated with the temple, as the Rabbis themselves knew—constituted an act of appropriation, an assertion of rabbinic control over what was symbolically central in Judaism." Seth Schwartz, "Language, Power and Identity in Ancient Palestine," *Past & Present* 148 (1995): 34.

72. In this lack of a proof text, M. Sotah departs from the two previous cases of first fruits (*bikkurim*) and release from levirate marriage (*halitzah*).

73. Fraade, "Before and After Babel," 50.

74. Fraade, 50. See also Smelik, *Rabbis, Language, and Translation*, 29–30. And see T. Sotah 8:6–7; Sifrei Devarim §343 (ed. Finkelstein 395); B. Shabbat 88b.

75. The fourth occurrence is found much earlier in the tractate (B. Sotah 10b) and is parallel to the second explanation found on B. Sotah 36b. However, on 10b, the story of Joseph's name is part of a longer explication of the Yehudah and Tamar story (discussed in chapter 3).

76. Of these traditions, Y. Sotah alludes only to the necessity for fifty letters (Y. Sotah 7:5 [4]; 21d).

77. On Second Temple and rabbinic interpretations of these "evil reports," see James L. Kugel, *In Potiphar's House: The Interpretive Life of Biblical Texts* (Cambridge, MA: Harvard University Press, 1994), 79–84.

78. See NJPS on this as "son of my suffering [or, strength]." Note that Rachel and Leah name all twelve children, including those of Bilhah and Zilpah.

79. See, for example, Robert A. Harris, "Sexual Orientation in the Presentation of Joseph's Character in Biblical and Rabbinic Literature," *AJS Review* 43, no. 1 (2019): 67–104; Kugel, *In Potiphar's House*; Marjorie Lehman, "Searching for Redemptive Readings: Grappling with Homophobia," *Journal of Textual Reasoning* 10, no. 1 (2018): 53–71; and Joshua Levinson, "An-Other Woman: Joseph and Potiphar's Wife. Staging the Body Politic," *Jewish Quarterly Review* 87, no. 3/4 (1997): 269–301.

80. Levinson, "An-Other Woman," 292.

81. See also Kugel, *In Potiphar's House*, 95.

82. MS Oxford 2678: "Joseph who merited [*zakhah*] and sanctified the name of God in private, merited [*zakhah*] and they added one letter." Similarly, Genizah fragment T-S C 2.23: "merited [*zakhah*] and one letter was added." The word *zakhah* ties this clause to the sotah.

83. This passage on B. Sotah 10b cites Psalms 81:6, making clear the tie to the verse.

84. Kugel, *In Potiphar's House*, 21–26; Levinson, "An-Other Woman," 274.

85. For parallel traditions, see Genesis Rabbah 87:7 and Y. Horayot 2:4 (5), 46d. For a hypothesis of the ways in which B. Sotah 36b relies on these two traditions, see Levinson, "An-Other Woman," 279n34. For an analysis of the prehistory of this passage, see Kugel, *In Potiphar's House*, 94–124.

86. Levinson, "An-Other Woman," 282.

87. Levinson, 275.

88. MS Oxford 2675: "It teaches that both of them went up to the bed naked." Similarly, Genizah fragment T-S C 2.23.

89. Per Levinson's translation. Levinson, "An-Other Woman," 278 and n32.

90. See also Genesis Rabbah 86:6 on Joseph resembling Rachel in appearance. On this, see Neis, *Sense of Sight*, 149n153.

91. Psalms 80:2 can be understood to figure both God ("shepherd of Israel") and Joseph (shepherd of the "flock of Joseph") as shepherds.

92. Note that Joseph does later have two children: Manasseh and Ephraim (Genesis 41:50–52). Similarly, the sotah's punishment does not seem to be total childlessness.

93. Genesis 37:28.

94. MS Vatican 110–11: "Interpret" (*doreish*).

95. MS Oxford 2675: "Tomorrow let us test him."

96. MS Oxford 2675.

97. On angels as mediators between heaven and earth, see Ahuvia, *On My Right Michael*. See also B. Sotah 13b where Gabriel castrates Potiphar. On this, see Lehman, "Searching for Redemptive Readings."

98. On the *bat kol* as a reverberating sound or an echo, see Tal Ilan, *Massekhet Ta'anit: Text, Translation, and Commentary* (Tübingen: Mohr Siebeck, 2008), 259; Lieberman, *Greek in Jewish Palestine*, 194. I also want to note Tal Ilan's translation of *bat kol* as "a daughter's voice," that is, in Ilan's words, "a feminization and diminution of an object, in this case, a voice." Ilan, *Ta'anit*, 259. When God communicates through a female manifestation, the Bavli imagines that voice as diminished, a resonance of the original sound.

99. On this passage and a comparative analysis of the earlier toseftan and Josephan traditions, see Vered Noam, "Why Did the Heavenly Voice Speak Aramaic? Ancient Layers in Rabbinic Literature," in *The Face of Torah: Studies in the Texts and Contexts of Ancient Judaism in Honor of Steven Fraade*, ed. Michal Bar-Asher Siegel, Tzvi Novick, and Christine Hayes (Göttingen: V&R Academic, 2017), 157–68.

100. This mention of Gabriel occurs at the end of a discussion about the permissibility of reciting prayer (*tefilah*) in any language. B. Sotah problematizes the mishnaic permission by engaging a number of traditions that differ on the question of whether angels understand Aramaic.

101. MS Oxford 2675 and Genizah fragment T-S C 2.23 portray Pharaoh as not even knowing the name of the language Joseph speaks.

102. Joseph's oaths are yet another literary motif in B. Sotah's imaginary. B. Sotah 13a depicts Moses learning Joseph's burial place in the Nile River from Serah bat Asher and pleading with Joseph to reveal himself. Like Joseph with Pharaoh, Moses tells Joseph that the moment has arrived in which God swore to Israel that Moses would redeem them. If Joseph does not reveal himself, then Moses will be free of the oath he swore to bury Joseph.

103. Likely following the sequence of M. Sotah 1:9–10, B. Sotah 13a moves directly from exegesis of Miriam watching her brother at the Nile (Exodus 2:4) to exegesis of the story of Joseph. (Here B. Sotah begins with Genesis 50:7, Joseph's journey to bury his father, Jacob.)

104. Despite the Bavli's geographical distance from Rome, Babylonian rabbinic communities were not immune to Roman military and cultural influence. On this, see Belser, *Rabbinic Tales of Destruction*, 43.

105. See Leviticus Rabbah 32:5 (ed. Margulies 2:746) for the tradition that Israel retained its identity in Egypt because they did not change their names and language (*leshonam*), speak *lashon ha-ra*, or engage in forbidden

sexual activity. In this Leviticus Rabbah pericope, *leshonam* refers to *leshon ha-kodesh*.

106. In Albeck 7:8.

107. I am here deliberately eliding the question of Agrippa's identity. On this question, see Dalia Trifon, "A Mishnah Fragment as Evidence of the Status of King Agrippa," *Cathedra: For the History of Eretz Israel and Its Yishuv* 53 (1989): 27–48 [Hebrew].

108. See T. Sotah 7:16. See also Flatto, who argues that the differences between the mishnaic and toseftan versions preserve two different perspectives toward the monarchy, the former positive and the latter more ambivalent. Flatto, *Crown and the Courts*, 122. Flatto's position about differing attitudes to the monarchy in the Mishnah and Tosefta is another example, albeit from an earlier stratum of rabbinic literature and from a complete textual corpus rather than one tractate within a larger corpus, that argues for an overarching ideology of a document.

CHAPTER 5: FAILURES OF CARE

1. Frymer-Kensky, "Strange Case," 11.

2. My claim here is similar to that made by Mira Balberg in regard to tannaitic literature's treatment of sacrificial ritual. That is, rather than seeing sacrifices "as metaphors or placeholders of the forlorn past," they should instead be treated as windows into rabbinic intellectual history. Balberg, *Blood for Thought*, 4.

3. See, for example, Numbers 35:33–34 and Leviticus 18:25.

4. The Hebrew Bible prescribes this method of killing an animal in only one other instance, that of the firstling donkey (Exodus 13:13; 34:20). On *ʿ.r.f.* as breaking the neck, see Tigay, *Deuteronomy*, 381n18. Whether the killing of the heifer represents the symbolic or vicarious execution of the murderer, the penalty the elders will suffer if their declaration is untrue, or the reenactment of the murder is unclear. Tigay leans toward the killing of the heifer as a reenactment of the murder. Tigay, *Deuteronomy*, 473–74.

5. Tigay hypothesizes that, in an earlier stage, the elders' declaration may have been an exculpatory oath. If this is the case, then the killing of the heifer would have represented the fate of the elders if they were lying (explanation two above in note 4). Tigay, *Deuteronomy*, 474.

6. On this process of recategorization and a specific example of the recategorization of the biblical *ʿarakhin* (vows of valuation) from Temple ritual to vows, see Jane L. Kanarek, "Rewriting ʿArakhin: Women and Tannaitic Vows of Valuation," *AJS Review* 40, no. 2 (2016): 261–77.

7. See Avraham Walfish, https://thegemara.com/article/the-measure-of-tractate-sotah/ (January 16, 2022). Basing himself on the recurring use of

the root *m.d.d.* (measure), appearing in the beginning (1:7), middle (5:4), and end of the tractate (9:3), Avraham Walfish argues that we may also understand the project of M. Sotah as delineating, that is measuring, the boundaries of human civilization, justice, and jurisdiction. Walfish's argument about M. Sotah is useful because it highlights another interpretive possibility that was open to B. Sotah, a proverbial "road-not-taken." See also Landau, who argues that the *ʿeglah ʿarufah* ritual concludes the tractate because it functions as a parallel ritual to the sotah. Landau, "An Edition and Comprehensive Commentary on Chapter IX," 6n29.

8. MS Parma: M. Sotah 9:5–6; Albeck M. Sotah 9:6.

9. This is the text of MS Kaufmann and MS Parma. T. Sotah 9:2 similarly divides Deuteronomy 21:7–8 into a tripartite speech by, respectively, the elders, priests, and God but does not further elaborate on the elders' words. See also Sifrei Devarim §210 and the accompanying manuscript notes (ed. Finkelstein 243–44). The additions to the mishnah in the printed versions of B. Sotah and in some manuscripts ("we did not dismiss him *without food*, and we did not see him and leave him *without escort*") most likely stem from the amoraic statement and possible baraita found, respectively, on B. Sotah 38b and 46b. On this, see Albeck, *Nashim*, 392; Epstein, *Introduction to the Mishnaic Text*, 955–56; Landau, "An Edition and Comprehensive Commentary on Chapter IX," 123. On the verbs *p.t.r.* and *n.w.h.*, see Landau, "An Edition and Comprehensive Commentary on Chapter IX," 123n12.

10. While the mishnah here assumes that a court would be free of sin, such an assumption is problematic. When rabbinic sources (tannaitic and later) express resistance to a single judge, they recognize the possibility of a corrupt court. On resistance to a single judge, see Flatto, *Crown and the Courts*, 145–48.

11. On the *ziknei beit din* (the elders of the court) in B. Yoma, see Lehman, *Bringing Down the Temple House*, 47.

12. On the phrase "the sages of there/here" in the Yerushalmi, see Moscovitz, *Terminology of the Yerushalmi*, 549–52.

13. Intriguingly, Y. Sotah 9:6 (5), 23d continues with four examples of tripartite conversations: the first, between the elders, the priests, and the Holy Spirit (similar to M. Sotah 9:6–7); the second, between Tamar, Yehudah, and the Holy Spirit; the third, between Joshua, the spies, and Caleb; and the fourth, between Sisera's mother, her daughters-in-law, and the Holy Spirit. Of these four examples, only the last narrative (Sisera's mother) is not referenced in B. Sotah. The chain of references in this Y. Sotah passage is yet another indication of the ways in which the Talmuds associate these biblical narratives with one another. It may also represent an earlier kernel of B. Sotah's more extensive aggadic traditions.

14. For a summary of the different positions of Epstein and Moskovitz on whether or not B. Sotah knew Y. Sotah's version (Esptein: no) and the larger question of Yerushalmi awareness of Bavli sugyot, see Landau, "An Edition and Comprehensive Commentary on Chapter IX," 123–24n12. Although I lean toward B. Sotah's awareness of this Y. Sotah sugya, my argument does not require a definitive answer to the question of whether or not one Talmud knows the other. I am interested in the literary universes each Talmud constructs and the ways in which differences between the two Talmuds highlight the themes of B. Sotah.

15. MS Munich 95 adds: "without escort" (*be-lo levayah*). MS Vatican 110–11: "Rather, he did not come to our hands and we dismissed him without food [*u-ftarnuhu be-lo mezonot*]; we did not see him and leave him without escort [*ve-hinahnuhu be-lo levayah*]."

16. Not in MS Munich 95 or MS Vatican 110–11, likely because these manuscripts conflate lines C and D.

17. I am unsure whether lines B–D should be attributed to R. Yehoshua ben Levi or whether they are a later interpolation added to unit A that the Bavli attributes to him. Arguing for the former, B. Sotah does not use terminology that introduces lines B–D as a baraita. Arguing for the latter is the appearance of these sentences in a baraita on 46b. Of course, it is possible that the baraita is also a later construction of B. Sotah, influenced by R. Yehoshua ben Levi. Later in this chapter, R. Yehoshua ben Levi connects escorting a person to Torah study, evidence for escort as a significant aspect of rabbinic ethical behavior.

18. See M. Sotah 1:2. B. Sotah 25a also alludes to an incident in which ten men transport a woman outside of the city on a funeral bier, presumably to rape her. B. Sotah 7a (and the parallel on B. Kiddushin 80b) utilize this story as an illustration of male promiscuity and untrustworthiness. On B. Kiddushin 80b, see Israeli, Fisher, and Raveh, *Qiddushin*, 200–205. B. Sotah 25a discusses the requirement for two accompanying sages within a discussion about whether or not a husband may retract his initial warning of his wife. This move would halt the sotah procedure and enable the husband legally to engage in sexual intercourse with his wife.

19. Accompaniment as a method of protecting rabbinic society can also be seen elsewhere in B. Sotah in the story of R. Abbahu's unusual escort of R. Hiyya bar Abba in order to restore his sense of honor (B. Sotah 40a). The story of R. Abbahu's escorting R. Hiyya bar Abba concludes the chain of tales about R. Abbahu's humility, including the passages, respectively, about gossiping wives, aggadah, and authoritative tradition.

20. Landau theorizes that this sugya began as an independent collection of Palestinian amoraic traditions about accompaniment upon which were

layered Babylonian additions. Landau, "An Edition and Comprehensive Commentary on Chapter IX," 129–48.

21. According to the baraita, this man founds the miraculous city of Luz, a place where the angel of death has no power and which the elderly need to leave in order to die. The contrast between "legitimate" slaughter (of the men from the house of Joseph) with that of the murder victim is striking.

22. It is possible that the story of Lot, his unnamed wife, and children (Genesis 19) functions as the implicit intertext.

23. B. Sotah follows the story of the man from Bethel with a tradition cited in the name of R. Yehoshua b. Levi that Pharaoh's escort of the patriarch Abraham (Genesis 12:20) resulted in Israel's eventual four-hundred-year slavery in Egypt.

24. Missing in MS Munich 95. This is a scribal omission, likely resulting from the repetition of the name R. Yehoshua ben Levi.

25. See also B. Eruvin 53b–54a, where this tradition about escort is preceded by a series of traditions that portray, respectively, an anonymous woman (*ʾishah*), young girl (*tinoket*), young boy (*tinok*), and finally Beruriah as besting sages in Torah knowledge. B. Eruvin's portrayal of the anonymous woman as an innkeeper (*ʾakhsanya*) literarily intertwines this text with the story of Rabbi Yehoshua ben Perahya and the innkeeper (analyzed further on).

26. The sugya goes on to propose a measurement for the undefined and potentially limitless distance as well as to differentiate between various types of masters.

27. Sarit Kattan Gribetz, "Women's Bodies as Metaphors for Time in Biblical, Second Temple, and Rabbinic Literature," in *The Construction of Time in Antiquity: Ritual, Art and Identity*, ed. Jonathan Ben-Dov and Lutz Doering (New York: Cambridge University Press, 2017), 192.

28. Gribetz, "Women's Bodies as Metaphors for Time," 193–94.

29. Ravina and Rava bar Yitzhak; Rav Kahana and R. Shimi bar Yitzhak; Rav Mordechai and Rav Ashi. The former pair illustrates the principle that a person who accompanies another within a city is not harmed and the latter two are stories about sages who travel longer distances.

30. B. Sotah also evokes and disappears pregnant female animal bodies. Explaining why the Torah commands the killing of a year-old female heifer in an uncultivable wadi, B. Sotah 46a remakes the female heifer into a male: "Said R. Yohanan ben Shaul: Why does the Torah say bring a female heifer [*ʿeglah*] in a wadi? Said the Holy Blessed One: Let a thing come [*yavo davar*] that has not produced fruit [*she-lo ʿasah peirot*] and be killed [*ve-yeiʿarif*] in a place that has not produced fruit, and atone [*ve-yikhaper*] for a person who has not been left to produce fruit." The use of masculine nouns and verbs transforms the deuteronomic female heifer into a male.

31. See Rashi, s.v. *she-hikrahta ʿaleinu et ha-makom.*

32. Although B. Sotah does not remark on the bears as female, the bears' gender remains noteworthy. We may understand these female bears as counter-images to the mothers who teach Torah to their sons. Or we may understand them more chillingly as sustaining Torah by killing these boys who do not perform commandments.

33. Moses's striking of the rock after the death of Miriam may be read in a similar manner, a grieving brother's improper action.

34. This section is preceded by a baraita that figures the boys as older boys (*neʿarim*) rather than young children (*ketanim*) and thus as bearing greater responsibility for their actions. The amora Rav Yosef objects to this assertion by proposing that the word *neʿarim* refers to their town, *neʿoran.* As proof, he cites a verse from the book of Kings that depicts the Arameans kidnapping a young girl (*naʿarah ketanah*; 2 Kings 5:2). The Bavli's rejection of Rav Yosef's proposition reinstates the baraita (and thus Elishah's lack of culpability) but also demonstrates the ways in which violence against females has become a tool with which to think. Here the violence is committed against a girl who is an outsider.

35. MSS Munich 95, Vatican 110–11, Oxford 2675, *editio princeps*: "like gentiles" (*ka-goyim*).

36. On the motif of rabbis killing with their gaze, see Neis, *Sense of Sight,* 63–64; Sinai (Tamas) Turan, "'Wherever the Sages Set Their Eyes, There Is Either Death or Poverty'—on the History, Terminology and Imagery of the Talmudic Traditions about the Devastating Gaze of the Sages," *Sidra: A Journal for the Study of Rabbinic Literature* 23 (2008): 137–205 [Hebrew], and in particular 165–66.

37. See M. Yoma 8:1.

38. The criticism for Amorite haircuts also represents an inversion: the children taunt Elisha as bald, and B. Sotah portrays him as seeing the children violate rabbinic law through their haircuts. On the *belorit,* see Berkowitz, *Defining Jewish Difference,* 118–22. See also my discussion of B. Sotah 49b and another Amorite haircut (*komi*) in chapter 3.

39. This portion of the sugya concludes with a debate about the miraculous nature of the bears' appearance from a forest.

40. Sentence missing in MS Munich 95 and MS Vatican 110–11.

41. See the parallel passage on B. Nazir 23b. The Nazir passage merits further investigation, in particular the intersection of the concepts of *ʿaveirah lishmah* and *mitzvah she-lo lishmah* with the stories of Yael, Ruth, and Lot's two unnamed daughters.

42. It is also possible that Ruth's inclusion in this sugya stems from the bib-

lical depiction of her insistence on accompanying her mother-in-law Naomi after the death of their husband/son (Ruth 1:14–19).

43. The traditions about Pharaoh's daughter do not appear in Y. Sotah. In this context, I also remind us of Rahav's appearance on B. Sotah 34a (see chapter 4). As I noted there, the toseftan version of the baraita does not contain the epithet "the prostitute" although B. Sotah does. Reading the textual difference in the context of this chapter's argument points to the possibility of attributing the difference in wording to the ways in which the Bavli is thinking with the sotah and inverting the expected behavior of those who might otherwise be expected to sin.

44. When this sugya returns to discussing Elisha, it again inverts the sotah as wife gone astray with an amoraic aphorism that declares a wife's pleasantness (or perhaps her beauty) lying in the eyes of her husband. "Said R. Yohanan: There are three favors—the favor of a place to its inhabitants; the favor of a wife to her husband; the favor of a purchase to its purchaser." Yet again, B. Sotah does not delineate women's sexual sin as the primary reason for society's unraveling.

45. See also B. Sanhedrin 107b; Y. Sanhedrin 10:2, 29b (Elisha/Gehazi); and Y. Sanhedrin 6:8, 23c (R. Yehoshua ben Perahya/Jesus).

46. My summary draws on Jeffrey's Rubenstein's detailed analysis of these two stories in Rubenstein, *Stories of the Babylonian Talmud*, 116–49. See also Schäfer, *Jesus in the Talmud*, 34–40. Schäfer utilizes the version found on B. Sanhedrin 107b as his base text. The scholarly literature on this Jesus story is extensive. For a summary of scholarship, see Rubenstein, *Stories of the Babylonian Talmud*, 264–65nn1–3; Schäfer, *Jesus in the Talmud*, 2–4.

47. On the rabbinization of biblical characters in this passage, see Rubenstein, *Stories of the Babylonian Talmud*, 124.

48. See also M. Avot 5:18.

49. Rubenstein, *Stories of the Babylonian Talmud*, 143. See also the motif of hands, which additionally connects the stories of Elisha-Gehazi and R. Yehoshua ben Perahya-Jesus to M. Sotah. Rubenstein, *Stories of the Babylonian Talmud*, 143.

50. MS Oxford 2675.

51. MS Oxford 2675: "Said *yeishu ha-notzri* to him."

52. See also the description of Abraham on B. Sotah 10a as planting an orchard or establishing an inn at Be'er Sheva.

53. My claim that tangents are not really tangents overlaps with Rubenstein's observation that "It would behoove us, therefore, to consider the seemingly meandering traditions that precede stories as thoughtful compositions and deliberate segues, designed to integrate stories that enhance

Mishnaic ideas." Rubenstein, *Stories of the Babylonian Talmud*, 145. While Rubenstein does read the Jesus story in the context of its longer sugya, much as is the case for some of the other well-analyzed sugyot in this book, the story has been understudied in regard to its location in B. Sotah.

CHAPTER 6: FROM WAR TO WOMEN

1. Belser, *Rabbinic Tales of Destruction*, xxvi.

2. Here I extend Ilana Pardes's conception of the countertradtion in biblical texts to rabbinic texts. See Ilana Pardes, *Countertraditions in the Bible: A Feminist Approach* (Cambridge, MA: Harvard University Press, 1993), 144.

3. M. Sotah 7:1 lists the *'eglah 'arufah* before the *meshuah milhamah*. It is possible that M. Sotah reverses this order when it explicates the list of rituals that must be recited in *leshon ka-kodesh* (the *'eglah 'arufah* follows the *meshuah milhamah*) because of the mention of the foreign king Agrippa at the conclusion of chapter 7. See also Albeck who raises the possibility that the reversal of order may be attributed to the *'eglah 'arufah* section as a more fitting conclusion to the tractate. Albeck, *Nashim*, 231. The eighth chapter of M. Sotah is structured similarly to midrash halakhah, that is, explicating the legal details to be drawn from each verse of Deuteronomy 20:2–9 as well as Deuteronomy 24:5.

4. M. Sotah 8:7–8 expands (or further specifies) each of these categories of men to include, for example, a man who has built a storehouse for wood or a cattle stable, planted five fruit trees or grafted tree branches, and betrothed a widow or a woman awaiting levirate marriage. Note that M. Sotah differs from Deuteronomy 20:5–8 in distinguishing between those men who do not report to battle and those who leave for the battlefield and return home.

5. In Albeck 8:5. See also T. Sotah 7:22.

6. Sifrei Devarim §192 (ed. Finkelstein 232–33), at least in some manuscript versions, attributes the Torah's provision of additional reasons (e.g., engagement, building a house) as due to God's care for human dignity (*has ha-makom 'al kevod ha-beriyot*). Sifrei Devarim does not utilize the root *t.l.y.*, strengthening my claim that the use of *t.l.y.* is specific to M. Sotah. See also Finkelstein's notes on this pericope, where he observes that the section in which this comment is found was added to some manuscripts from a marginal note.

7. As the root *t.f.l.* also implicates slander (Jastrow, s.v. *t.f.l.*), this discussion overlaps with the tractate's theme of language gone wrong.

8. Alexander, *Gender and Timebound Commandments*, 176. See also Dvora E. Weisberg, *Massekhet Menahot: Text, Translation, and Commentary* (Tübingen: Mohr Siebeck, 2020), 90–93. For rabbinic sources, see Mekhilta de-Rabbi Ishmael *bo* 17 (ed. Horovitz-Rabin 68) and B. Kiddushin 34a.

9. The baraita also is cited on B. Menahot 36a as part of a larger discussion about the proper method for reciting the blessings over tefillin. B. Menahot does not connect the baraita with R. Yosi ha-Galili. The baraita does not appear in extant tannaitic sources, lending more strength to a hypothesis of its formation for the B. Sotah context.

10. On the Bavli's tendency to avoid the most direct route to a law and thereby link that law to a wider legal web, see Jane L. Kanarek, *Biblical Narrative and the Formation of Rabbinic Law* (New York: Cambridge University Press, 2014).

11. B. Sotah's midrashic expansion of the encounter draws from a combination of traditions found throughout the rabbinic corpus. For example, the phrase *gilui panim* appears in Y. Eruvin 6:2; 23b, Mekhilta de-Rabbi Ishmael *masekhta de-ʿamalek* 1 (ed. Horovitz-Rabin, 176), and B. Eruvin 69a. Its use here with Goliath is unique to B. Sotah. Similarly, the phrase *ʾein ʾish ʾela ha-kadosh barukh hu* appears three other times in the Bavli, and a similar phrase appears in Bereishit Rabbah, none of which mention Goliath. As does our Goliath text, B. Sanhedrin 93a cites *ʾein ʾish ʾela ha-kadosh barukh hu* in the name of R. Yohanan. In B. Sanhedrin 93a, R. Yohanan utilizes the phrase, unsurprisingly, in a context of war but there of complete divine destruction. Finally, the idea that Goliath's birth is the result of his mother's gang rape by one hundred Philistines is found in Y. Yevamot 4:2, 5c in the name of *rabanan de-ʾagadeta*.

12. In Albeck, M. Sotah 8:1.

13. Y. Sotah does not explicate this section of the mishnah. It focuses largely on the ark of the covenant, mentioned at the end of M. Sotah 8:3.

14. B. Sotah depicts R. Yohanan as having a particular interest in gentile hyper-sexuality/sexual sin. In addition to the already mentioned traditions, B. Sotah 10a cites R. Yohanan as interpreting Judges 16:21 to indicate that all the Philistine men brought their wives to the imprisoned Samson in order that he impregnate them.

15. MS Munich 95, MS Vatican 110–11: missing "son of" (*ben*). These versions would imply either that God took the form of David or that God utilized David as an instrument for God's own victory. In any case, the second verse (1 Samuel 17:12) still implies David as the son of God.

16. Given the reference to Jesus later in B. Sotah (47a), this passage may also constitute a polemic against Jesus as the son of God and his Davidic lineage. Intriguingly, Matthew 1:1–17, in its genealogy of Jesus, lists, among others, Tamar, Rahav, and Ruth, all three of whom are mentioned in B. Sotah.

17. I have in mind David Weiss Halivni's monograph *The Book and the Sword: A Life of Learning in the Shadow of Destruction* (Boulder, CO: Westview Press, 1998). See also Halivni's citation of Deuteronomy Rabbah 4:2

in the epigraph ("Said R. Elazar: The sword and the book came down from heaven bound together. He said to them: If you do what is written in this book, you will be saved from this sword. If you do not, you will be killed by this sword").

18. MS Vatican 110–11: Missing Yohanan.

19. See Rashi s.v. *ve-yeireid ʾeilai.*

20. See Exodus 24:18, 34:28; Deuteronomy 9:9, 11; 9:18, 10:10. The word *va-yityatzeiv* echoes the description of Israel's at the mountain: "And they stood [*va-yityatzevu*] at the foot of the mountain" (Exodus 19:17). While the seventh chapter of B. Sotah discusses the Torah's revelation, I do not think that the tradition about Goliath is driven by this thematic overlap.

21. On the rabbinic innovation of regular shema recitation and the exclusion of women, enslaved people, and children from this obligation, see Sarit Kattan Gribetz, *Time and Difference in Rabbinic Judaism* (Princeton, NJ: Princeton University Press, 2020), 135–87. Kattan Gribetz contrasts the male time-marker of shema with the female time-marker of the embodied practice of niddah.

22. This section of the sugya explicates 1 Samuel 17:4. It provides three different answers to the meaning of the word *beinayim,* the first of which is attributed to Rav. This stage of the sugya marks a turn to the inclusion of Babylonian sages into the midrash, producing a composite Palestinian-Babylonian exegetical narrative.

23. See chapter 4.

24. This again echoes the possible gang rape on B. Sotah 7a.

25. See chapter 2. See also a similar anonymous statement about Goliath's mother in Y. Yevamot 4:2, 5c that reads *mi-maʿarkhot pelishtim* (1 Samuel 17:23) as referring to either a hundred Philistine foreskins or to the hundred Philistine foreskins that engaged in the initial stage of sexual intercourse with her. Y. Yevamot 4:2, 5c does not contain the fuller midrashic tradition detailed in B. Sotah; in addition, the immediate context of Y. Yevamot is a discussion of whether a woman can become pregnant from two men simultaneously.

26. See NJPS.

27. The rape of Harafah-Orpah may also be read as an intertext with the story of the concubine on the hill (Judges 19–20) who is gang-raped and dismembered, another total failure of care. This, too, results in war and the slaughter of the tribe of Benjamin by the rest of Israel.

28. Orpah-Harafah differs from and overlaps with the sotah in her ability to bear children. 2 Samuel 21:22 refers to four descendants of "the Rafah at Gat." As it did earlier in this sugya, B. Sotah rereads the reference to giants as the name Harafah, positioning Harafah as the mother of four children — Goliath, Saf, Madon, and Yishbi. These four are killed by David and his men. Unlike the

sotah, Harafah does not miscarry a pregnancy. Similar to the sotah who loses a fetus through miscarriage, Harafah loses her grown children in war. Note also the connection to Ruth and the messianic line, a bit further on in the sugya: "Said R. Yitzhak: Said the Holy Blessed One, Let the children of the one who kissed [Orpah] fall by the hand of the children of the one who clung [Ruth]."

29. This biblical citation begins and ends with clear mentions of women, respectively midwives and Pharaoh's daughter.

30. Like the long aggadic sugya on B. Megillah 10b–16b, the B. Sotah sugya opens with a series of homilies by Rav and Shmuel built around five verses. However, in contrast to the B. Megillah sugya, which is built mainly from Babylonian homilies, the B. Sotah sugya contains homilies primarily from second- and third-generation Palestinian amoraim. On this, see Joshua Levinson, *A Twice Told Tale: A Poetics of the Exegetical Narrative in Rabbinic Midrash* (Jerusalem: Magnes Press, 2005), 292 [Hebrew]. David Rosenthal argues that this collection was redacted into B. Sotah as an already complete story-cycle. David Rosenthal, "ʿArichot kedumot ha-meshuqaʿot ba-talmud ha-bavli," in *Mehqerei Talmud: Talmudic Studies 1*, ed. David Rosenthal and Yaacov Sussman (Jerusalem: Magnes Press, 1990), 168–69n25. Since, as we will see, so many of the details of the narrative intertwine with themes of B. Sotah, I doubt the completeness of the cycle before its redaction into the tractate. If there was a skeleton, its order and literary details have been augmented and reorganized in accordance with its location in B. Sotah.

31. See Levinson, *Twice Told Tale*, 296–306.

32. In contrast to the examples of wrongful behavior, the reward for righteous behavior outmeasures the initial behavior. See also B. Sotah 11a, which recognizes this mismatch between righteous behavior and subsequent reward. The sage Abaye proposes to emend the mishnah to state, "and for the matter of good, it is *not* so." In contrast, Rava proposes a reinterpretation of the mishnah: A person is rewarded with the same *type* of righteous deed, but the reward is greater than the initial deed.

33. On a late antique or early medieval note, see Elisheva Baumgarten's discussion of the ninth-century midrash Tanna de-Vei Eliyahu and its citation of M. Sotah's principle of measure-for-measure to depict the biblical Deborah's leadership as judge and teacher of Torah. Elisheva Baumgarten, *Biblical Women and Jewish Daily Life in the Middle Ages* (Philadelphia: University of Pennsylvania Press, 2022), 95.

34. Adrienne Rich, *Of Woman Born: Motherhood as Experience and Institution* (New York: W. W. Norton, 1995), 184.

35. The B. Sotah passage begins with exegesis of Exodus 1:8, the rise of a new Egyptian ruler. For an analysis of the full passage, see Levinson, *Twice Told Tale*, 291–306.

36. These two Miriam traditions combine with a third tradition that depicts Miriam rebelling against her father Amram (B. Sotah 12b). In response to Pharaoh's genocidal decree that male babies be cast into the Nile to die, Amram divorces his wife; the other men follow in his footsteps. Miriam chastises her father for behavior that condemns males and females to death (through lack of conception of any children). Amram remarries his wife; once again, the other men follow in his footsteps. B. Sotah's version of this tale differs from earlier versions found in *Biblical Antiquities* 9 and in the Mekhilta de-Rabbi Shimon bar Yohai 6:2 (ed. Epstein-Melamed 2), both of which depict Amram—not Miriam—as the hero who challenges the other men's despair and insists on marrying his wife and conceiving a child. On this, see Levinson, *Twice Told Tale*, 302–3.

37. Rosen-Zvi extends this connection to additional prophetic descriptions of adultery in Isaiah 47:2–23, 2 Samuel 12:11–12, and Nahum 3:5–6. Rosen-Zvi, *Mishnaic Sotah Ritual*, 206–7 and 215n126.

38. MS Munich 95, MS Vatican 110–11, and MS Cambridge 2675: R. Akiva. *Editio princeps*: Rav Ezra. R. Akiva likely refers to a third- and fourth-generation Palestinian amora and not the tannaitic sage. On the Palestinian amora R. Akiva, see Albeck, *Introduction to the Talmud*, 346; Levinson, *Twice Told Tale*, 298.

39. MS Oxford 2675: "Descended from heaven" (*yoreid mishmei marom*), eliminating the intermediary, that is, with God acting directly as midwife.

40. MS Oxford 2675: "And every individual pointed with his finger" (*vekhol ʾehad ve-ʾehad moreh be-ʾetzbaʿo*).

41. On the Exodus narrative as the story of the birthing of a nation, see Ilana Pardes, *The Biography of Ancient Israel: National Narratives in the Bible* (Berkeley: University of California Press, 2000), 16–39.

42. I draw this description from Avigdor Shinan, "Aggadic Motifs between Midrash and Story," *Jerusalem Studies in Hebrew Literature* 5 (1984): 208–10 [Hebrew].

43. Pardes, *Biography of Ancient Israel*, 23–24; Mary E. Shields, "Multiple Exposures: Body Rhetoric and Gender Characterization in Ezekiel 16," *Journal of Feminist Studies in Religion* 14, no. 1 (1998): 7–9.

44. Overlapping with the sotah ritual, Ezekiel 23:30–34 includes a declaration that Oholibah will be made to drink the poisonous cup of her sister as judgment for her unfaithfulness (Ezekiel 23:30–34). Moshe Greenberg notes that in exposure stories, between the foundling's rescue and revelation, the foundling usually lives under the care of a guardian. In the Ezekiel passage, the foundling is abandoned until marriage, an adjustment of the narrative to fit the Exodus traditions of Israel's beginnings as a people. Moshe Greenberg,

Ezekiel 1–20 (New York: Doubleday, 1983), 301. In the rabbinic reading of the Ezekiel passage, the foundlings are under care from the moment of birth, a shift back to the more "usual" version of exposure stories and a rewriting of Israel's beginnings to include God's maternal care. On the shift from the father-son relationship depicted in the Exodus narratives to the marital bond of Ezekiel, see Pardes, *Countertraditions*, 23–25.

45. On the motifs of seduction, pregnancy, birth, hiding, and home in this story (but not the B. Sotah context), see Yonah Fraenkel, *Darkhe ha-ʾaggadah ve-ha-midrash* (Givʿatayim: Yad la-Talmud, 1991), 306.

46. Fraenkel, *Darkhe ha-ʾaggadah*, 306–7.

47. Fraenkel is not alone in overlooking the context of B. Sotah. Even Rosen-Zvi, who cites this story and the larger story-cycle in which it is embedded as an example of a Babylonian trend toward the hyper-sexualization of reality, does not expand his lens beyond that of the story-cycle to the tractate. To be fair, this is not the project of his book *Demonic Desires*. Rosen-Zvi, *Demonic Desires*, 114–16. Levinson, cited above in note 30, also does not expand his lens to the tractate as a whole. These scholars participate, even if inadvertently, in obscuring the sotah herself.

48. See also the versions in Deuteronomy Rabbah and the Tanhuma (cited in the next note) where each woman gives birth to multiple children.

49. See Deuteronomy Rabbah 15 (ed. Lieberman 14–15), Tanhuma, *Pekudei* 9, and Exodus Rabbah 1:12 (ed. Shinan 54–56). Based on Deuteronomy Rabbah, Fraenkel argues for the composition of the Bavli midrash from two originally disparate and independent blocs of material: the first an exegetical homily centered on Ezekiel 16 and the second a story without explicit exegetical content. B. Sotah connects these two traditions through the theme of the house. Fraenkel reads this story as similar to other rabbinic miracle stories where human actions are matched by divine intervention, marking the narrative of the righteous women as similarly religious in nature. On this, see also Levinson, *Twice Told Tale*, 299. Due to uncertainty around the dating of Deuteronomy Rabbah, it is not clear to me that the Deuteronomy Rabbah version of two stories need be the basis for B. Sotah's version. After being removed from its B. Sotah context, the one narrative could have subsequently been divided into two separate stories. On the dating of Deuteronomy Rabbah, see Bregman, "Midrash Rabbah," 64–67 and the relevant footnotes.

50. I thank Judith Kates for this insight. The imagery of the mirrors has inspired contemporary Passover ritual, the placing of mirrors on the seder plate. This practice originated with Judith Kates after a gift from Gail Twersky Reimer of two mirrors facing one another on a small stand (conversation with Judith Kates, June 2018). The gift was inspired by Avivah Zornberg's

reading of the redemptive work of the "mirror drama" in the Tanhuma. See Avivah Gottlieb Zornberg, *The Particulars of Rapture: Reflections on Exodus* (New York: Schocken, 2011), 220.

51. Levinson, *Twice Told Tale*, 304–5. MS Oxford 2675.2 reads *yoreid mi-shemei marom* (descended from heaven), eliminating the intermediary, with God acting directly as midwife. See also Deuteronomy Rabbah 15: "Said R. Hiyya ha-Gadol: The angels did not do this but rather the Holy Blessed One in his glory, as it says, 'And I bathed you [Ezekiel 16:10].' If it had said, 'I caused you to be bathed,' I might have said perhaps it was done by an angel. But since it is written, 'And I bathed you' and not by an angel, May the name of the Blessed One be praised, He in His glory did this for them" (ed. Lieberman 14). On the different variants found in Exodus Rabbah, later ones of which include the word *mal'akh* (angel), see Shinan's notes in Shinan, *Shemot Rabbah Chapters I–XIV*, 55, and Shinan, "Aggadic Motifs," 207n14. On angels in T. Sotah, see Ahuvia, *On My Right Michael*, 86–90.

52. B. Sotah 22a mentions a woman named Yohani bat Retivi as an example of a "gadabout widow" who destroys the world. Rashi (s.v. *ke-gon yohani bat retivi*) describes her as a witch and a midwife who would utilize her witchcraft to hinder a woman's labor. At the appropriate time, she would also utilize her witchcraft to enable a woman's labor to progress and for her to give birth. It is worthwhile to consider the hypothesis that Rashi mentions this story in B. Sotah because of the tractate's mention of midwives. On Rashi's stories, see Lewis Landau, "Sippurei rashi ha-nidpas be-talmud ha-bavli," *Eshel Beer-Sheva* 3 (1986): 101–17.

53. See also the same use of the verb (*sh.r.b.b.*) to describe the spies' tongues in their gruesome deaths.

BIBLIOGRAPHY

Adelman, Rachel. *The Female Ruse: Women's Deception and Divine Sanction in the Hebrew Bible*. Sheffield, UK: Phoenix Press, 2015.

Ahuvia, Mika. *On My Right Michael, on My Left Gabriel: Angels in Ancient Jewish Culture*. Oakland: University of California Press, 2021.

Albeck, Hanoch. *Introduction to the Talmud Bavli and Yerushalmi*. Tel Aviv: Devir, 1987 [Hebrew].

Albeck, Hanoch, ed. *Shishah Sidrei Mishnah: With New Commentary, Introductions, Additions, and Completions*. Jerusalem: Mossad Bialik, 1978.

Alexander, Elizabeth Shanks. *Gender and Timebound Commandments in Judaism*. New York: Cambridge University Press, 2013.

Alexander, Elizabeth Shanks. *Transmitting Mishnah: The Shaping Influence of Oral Tradition*. New York: Cambridge University Press, 2006.

Amsler, Monika. *The Babylonian Talmud and Late Antique Book Culture*. Cambridge: Cambridge University Press, 2023.

Baker, Cynthia M. *Rebuilding the House of Israel: Architectures of Gender in Jewish Antiquity*. Stanford: Stanford University Press, 2002.

Balberg, Mira. *Blood for Thought: The Reinvention of Sacrifice in Early Rabbinic Literature*. Oakland: University of California Press, 2017.

Balberg, Mira. *Purity, Body, and Self in Early Rabbinic Literature*. Berkeley: University of California Press, 2014.

Balberg, Mira. "'The Vows That He Annuls': The Definition and Classification of Annullable Vows in Rabbinic Literature." Master's thesis, Hebrew University, 2005 [Hebrew].

Balberg, Mira, and Haim Weiss. *When Near Becomes Far: Old Age in Rabbinic Literature*. New York: Oxford University Press, 2021.

Baumgarten, Elisheva. *Biblical Women and Jewish Daily Life in the Middle Ages*. Philadelphia: University of Pennsylvania Press, 2022.

Belser, Julia Watts. *Power, Ethics, and Ecology in Jewish Late Antiquity: Rabbinic Responses to Drought and Disaster*. New York: Cambridge University Press, 2015.

Belser, Julia Watts. *Rabbinic Tales of Destruction: Gender, Sex, and Disability in the Ruins of Jerusalem*. New York: Oxford University Press, 2017.

Benatar, David. "Obligation, Motivation and Reward: An Analysis of a Talmudic Principle." *Journal of Law and Religion* 17, no. 1/2 (2002): 1–17.

Benjamin, Mara H. *The Obligated Self: Maternal Subjectivity and Jewish Thought*. Bloomington: Indiana University Press, 2018.

Benjamin, Mara H. "On Teachers, Rabbinic and Maternal." In *Mothers in the Jewish Cultural Imagination*, edited by Marjorie Lehman, Jane L. Kanarek, and Simon J. Bronner, 359–76. Liverpool: Littman Library of Jewish Civilization, 2017.

Berggrün, Nissan. *Studies in the Hebrew Language*. Jerusalem: Academy of the Hebrew Language, 1995 [Hebrew].

Berkowitz, Beth A. *Execution and Invention: Death Penalty Discourse in Early Rabbinic and Christian Cultures*. New York: Oxford University Press, 2006.

Berkowitz, Beth A. "The Limits of 'Their Laws': Ancient Rabbinic Controversies about Jewishness (and Non-Jewishness)." *Jewish Quarterly Review* 99, no. 1 (2009): 121–57.

Berkowitz, Beth A. *Defining Jewish Difference: From Antiquity to the Present*. New York: Cambridge University Press, 2012.

Bohak, Gideon. "Jewish Magic in the Middle Ages." In *The Cambridge History of Magic and Witchcraft in the West*, edited by S. J. David J. Collins, 268–99. Cambridge: Cambridge University Press, 2015.

Bonfil, Robert. *History and Folklore in a Medieval Jewish Chronicle: The Family Chronicle of Ahima'az Ben Paltiel*. Leiden: Brill, 2009.

Boxel, Piet van. "Johann Christoph Wagenseil: From Scholar to Missionary." In *The Mishnaic Moment: Jewish Law among Jews and Christians in Early Modern Europe*, edited by Piet van Boxel, Kirsten Macfarlane, and Joanna Weinberg, 215–34. Oxford: Oxford University Press, 2022.

Boyarin, Daniel. *Carnal Israel: Reading Sex in Talmudic Culture*. Berkeley: University of California Press, 1993.

Boyarin, Daniel. *Unheroic Conduct: The Rise of Heterosexuality and the Invention of the Jewish Man*. Berkeley: University of California Press, 1997.

Boyarin, Daniel. "Women's Bodies and the Rise of the Rabbis: The Case of Sotah." In *Jews and Gender: The Challenge to Hierarchy*, edited by Jonathan Frankel, 88–100. New York: Oxford University Press, 2000.

Bregman, Marc. "Midrash Rabbah and the Medieval Collector Mentality." *Prooftexts* 17, no. 1 (1997): 63–76.

Bregman, Marc. *The Tanhuma-Yelammedenu Literature: Studies in the Evolution of the Versions*. Piscataway: Gorgias Press, 2003 [Hebrew].

Brody, Robert. *Mishnah and Tosefta Studies*. Jerusalem: Magnes Press, 2014.

Brown, Peter. *The Body and Society: Men, Women, and Sexual Renunciation in Early Christianity*. Twentieth Anniversary Edition with a New Introduction. New York: Columbia University Press, 2008.

Brüll, N. "Die Entstehungsgeschichte des babylonischen Talmuds als Schriftwerk." In *Jahrbücher für Jüdische Geschichte und Literatur II*, edited by N. Brüll, 1–123. Frankfurt, 1876.

Buber, Solomon, ed. *Midrash Tanhuma*. Jerusalem, 1964.

Cohen, Abraham. "An Edition and Comprehensive Commentary on Chapters II & III of Tractate Sotah in the Babylonian Talmud." PhD diss., Bar-Ilan University, 2013 [Hebrew].

Cohen, Jeremy. *Be Fertile and Increase, Fill the Earth and Master It: The Ancient and Medieval Career of a Biblical Text*. Ithaca, NY: Cornell University Press, 1989.

Cohn, Naftali S. *The Memory of the Temple and the Making of the Rabbis*. Philadelphia: University of Pennsylvania Press, 2012.

Cover, Robert M. "Obligation: A Jewish Jurisprudence of the Social Order." *Journal of Law and Religion* 5, no. 1 (1987): 65–74.

Cribiore, Raffaella. *Gymnastics of the Mind: Greek Education in Hellenistic and Roman Egypt*. Princeton, NJ: Princeton University Press, 2001.

Dalton, Krista. "Teaching for the Tithe: Donor Expectations and the Matrona's Tithe." *AJS Review* 44, no. 1 (2020): 49–73.

Destro, Adriana. *The Law of Jealousy: Anthropology of Sotah*. Atlanta, GA: Scholars Press, 1989.

Diamond, Eliezer. *Holy Men and Hunger Artists: Fasting and Asceticism in Rabbinic Culture*. New York: Oxford University Press, 2004.

Ebner, David Yechiel. "The Composition and Structure of Mishnah 'Sotah.'" PhD diss., Yeshiva University, 1980.

Epstein, J. N. *Introduction to Amoraic Literature: Bavli and Yerushalmi*. Jerusalem: Magnes Press, 1962 [Hebrew].

Epstein, J. N. *Introduction to Tannaitic Literature: Mishna, Tosephta and Halakhic Midrashim*. Jerusalem: Magnes Press, 1957 [Hebrew].

Epstein, J. N. *Introduction to the Mishnaic Text*. Jerusalem: Magnes Press, 2001 [Hebrew].

Fishbane, Michael A. "Accusations of Adultery: A Study of Law and Scribal Practice in Numbers 5:11–31." *Hebrew Union College Annual* 45 (1974): 25–45.

Fishman, Talya. *Becoming the People of the Talmud: Oral Torah as Written Tradition in Medieval Jewish Cultures*. Philadelphia: University of Pennsylvania Press, 2013.

Flatto, David C. *The Crown and the Courts: Separation of Powers in the Early Jewish Imagination*. Cambridge, MA: Harvard University Press, 2020.

Fonrobert, Charlotte Elisheva. *Menstrual Purity: Rabbinic and Christian*

Reconstructions of Biblical Gender. Stanford: Stanford University Press, 2000.

Fonrobert, Charlotte Elisheva. "The Place of Shabbat: On the Architecture of the Opening Sugya of Tractate Eruvin (2a–3a)." In *Strength to Strength: Essays in Honor of Shaye J. D. Cohen*, edited by Michael L. Satlow, 437–54. Providence, RI: Brown Judaic Studies, 2018.

Fraade, Steven D. "Before and after Babel: Linguistic Exceptionalism and Pluralism in Early Rabbinic Literature and Jewish Antiquity." *Diné Israel* 28 (2011): 31–68.

Fraade, Steven D. "Nomos and Narrative before Nomos and Narrative." *Yale Journal of Law & the Humanities* 17, no. 1 (2005): 81–96.

Fraenkel, Yonah. *Darkhe ha-ʾaggadah ve-ha-midrash*. Givʿatayim: Yad la-Talmud, 1991.

Friedman, Shamma. "Ha-baraitot ba-talmud ha-bavli ve-yahasan le-makbiloteihen she-ba-tosefta." In *Atara l'haim: mehkarim ba-sifrut ha-talmudit veha-rabanit li-khevod professor haim zalman dimitrovsky*, edited by Daniel Boyarin et al., 163–201. Jerusalem: Magnes Press, 2000.

Friedman, Shamma. "Perek ha-ʾishah rabbah ba-bavli." In *Mehkarim u-mekorot*, edited by H. Dimitorovsky, 277–441. New York: Jewish Theological Seminary of America, 1977.

Friedman, Shamma. "Sorting out the Wages of Adultery: Execution, Ordeal, or Divorce." In *Shoshannat Yaakov: Jewish and Iranian Studies in Honor of Yaakov Elman*, edited by Shai Secunda and Steven Fine, 77–109. Leiden: Brill, 2012.

Frymer-Kensky, Tikva. "The Strange Case of the Suspected Sotah (Numbers V 11–31)." *Vetus Testamentum* 34 (1984): 11–26.

Fuchs, Ilan. *Jewish Women's Torah Study: Orthodox Religious Education and Modernity*. London: Routledge, 2014.

Gardner, Gregg E. *The Origins of Organized Charity in Rabbinic Judaism*. New York: Cambridge University Press, 2015.

Gray, Alyssa M. *A Talmud in Exile: The Influence of Yerushalmi Avodah Zarah on the Formation of Bavli Avodah Zarah*. Providence, RI: Brown Judaic Studies, 2005.

Green, Arthur. *Keter: The Crown of God in Early Jewish Mysticism*. Princeton, NJ: Princeton University Press, 2014.

Greenberg, Moshe. *Ezekiel 1–20*. New York: Doubleday, 1983.

Gribetz, Sarit Kattan. "Consuming Texts: Women as Recipients and Transmitters of Ancient Texts." In *Rethinking 'Authority' in Late Antiquity: Authorship, Law, and Transmission in Jewish and Christian Tradition*, edited by A. J. Berkovitz and Mark Letteney, 178–206. London: Routledge, 2018.

Gribetz, Sarit Kattan. *Time and Difference in Rabbinic Judaism*. Princeton, NJ: Princeton University Press, 2020.

Gribetz, Sarit Kattan. "Women's Bodies as Metaphors for Time in Biblical, Second Temple, and Rabbinic Literature." In *The Construction of Time in Antiquity: Ritual, Art, and Identity*, edited by Jonathan Ben-Dov and Lutz Doering, 173–204. New York: Cambridge University Press, 2017.

Grushcow, Lisa. *Writing the Wayward Wife: Rabbinic Interpretations of Sotah*. Leiden: Brill, 2005.

Haberman, Bonna Devora. "The Suspected Adulteress: A Study of Textual Embodiment." *Prooftexts* 20, no. 1–2 (2000): 12–42.

Hacham, Noah. "Rabban Simeon Son of Gamaliel in Beitar." *Tarbiz* 74 (2005): 547–64 [Hebrew].

Halbertal, Moshe. *Interpretive Revolutions in the Making*. Jerusalem: Magnes Press, 1997 [Hebrew].

Halivni, David Weiss. *The Book and the Sword: A Life of Learning in the Shadow of Destruction*. Boulder, CO: Westview Press, 1998.

Halivni, David Weiss. *The Formation of the Babylonian Talmud*. Translated by Jeffrey L. Rubenstein. New York: Oxford University Press, 2013.

Halivni, David Weiss. *Mekorot u-mesorot: nashim*. Tel Aviv: Devir, 1968.

Hallewy, E. E. "Concerning the Ban on Greek Wisdom." *Tarbiz* 41, no. 3 (1971): 269–74 [Hebrew].

Harari, Yuval. "The Scroll of Ahimaʿaz and Jewish Magical Culture: A Note on the Ordeal of the Adulteress." *Tarbiz* 85, no. 1–2 (2006): 185–202 [Hebrew].

Harris, Robert A. "Sexual Orientation in the Presentation of Joseph's Character in Biblical and Rabbinic Literature." *AJS Review* 43 (2019): 67–104.

Hasan-Rokem, Galit. *Tales of the Neighborhood: Jewish Narrative Dialogues in Late Antiquity*. Berkeley: University of California Press, 2003.

Hauptman, Judith. "A New View of Women and Torah Study in the Talmudic Period." *Jewish Studies, an Internet Journal* 9 (2010): 249–92.

Hauptman, Judith. *Rereading the Mishnah: A New Approach to Ancient Jewish Texts*. Tübingen: Mohr Siebeck, 2005.

Hauptman, Judith. *Rereading the Rabbis: A Woman's Voice*. Boulder, CO: Westview Press, 1997.

Hauptman, Judith. "Women's Voluntary Performance of Mitzvot from Which They Are Exempt." *Proceedings of the World Congress of Jewish Studies* (1993): 161–68 [Hebrew].

Hayes, Christine Elizabeth. *Between the Babylonian and Palestinian Talmuds: Accounting for Halakhic Difference in Selected Sugyot from Tractate Avodah Zarah*. New York: Oxford University Press, 1997.

Hezser, Catherine. *The Social Structure of the Rabbinic Movement in Roman Palestine*. Tübingen: Mohr Siebeck, 1997.

Horovitz, H. S., and I. A. Rabin, eds. *Mekhilta de-rabbi ishmael*. Jerusalem: Shalem Books, 1997.

Ilan, Tal. *Jewish Women in Greco-Roman Palestine*. Peabody, MA: Hendrickson, 1996.

Ilan, Tal. *Massekhet Hullin: Text, Translation, and Commentary*. Tübingen: Mohr Siebeck, 2017.

Ilan, Tal. *Massekhet Ta'anit: Text, Translation, and Commentary*. Tübingen: Mohr Siebeck, 2008.

Ilan, Tal. *Mine and Yours Are Hers: Retrieving Women's History from Rabbinic Literature*. Leiden: Brill, 1997.

Ilan, Tal. "'Yerushalayim shel zahav' ve-ha-gar'in ha-histori be-siporei eishet r. akiva." In *Woman in Jerusalem: Gender, Society, and Religion*, edited by Tova Cohen and Joshua Schwartz, 33–46. Ramat-Gan: Bar-Ilan, 2002.

Israeli, Anat, Esther Fisher, and Inbar Raveh. *Massekhet Qiddushin Chapter 4: Text, Translation, and Commentary*. Tübingen: Mohr Siebeck, 2021.

Jaffee, Martin S. "A Rabbinic Ontology of the Written and Spoken Word: On Discipleship, Transformative Knowledge, and the Living Texts of Oral Torah." *Journal of the American Academy of Religion* 65, no. 3 (1997): 525–49.

Jaffee, Martin S. *Torah in the Mouth: Writing and Oral Tradition in Palestinian Judaism, 200 BCE–400 CE*. New York: Oxford University Press, 2001.

Jaffee, Martin. "Writing and Rabbinic Oral Tradition: On Mishnaic Narrative, Lists and Mnemonics." *Journal of Jewish Thought and Philosophy* 4 (1994): 123–46.

Jastrow, Marcus. *A Dictionary of the Targumim, Talmud Bavli, Yerushalmi, and the Midrashic Literature*. New York: Judaica Press, 1996.

Johnson-DeBaufre, Melanie. "'Gazing upon the Invisible': Archaeology, Historiography, and the Elusive Wo/men of 1 Thessalonians." In *From Roman to Early Christian Thessalonike: Studies in Religion and Archaeology*, edited by Charalambos Bakirtzis, Laura Nasrallah, and Steven J. Friesen, 73–108. Cambridge, MA: Harvard Theological Studies, 2010.

Kahana, Menachem, ed. *Sifrei Bemidbar*. Jerusalem: Magnes Press, 2011.

Kahana, Menahem. "The Arrangement of the Orders of the Mishnah." *Tarbiz* 86 (2007): 29–40 [Hebrew].

Kalmin, Richard. "The Formation and Character of the Babylonian Talmud." In *The Cambridge History of Judaism*, vol. 4, *The Late Roman-*

Rabbinic Period, edited by Steven T. Katz, 840–76. New York: Cambridge University Press, 2006.

Kalmin, Richard. *The Sage in Jewish Society of Late Antiquity*. London: Routledge, 1999.

Kamholz, Rebecca. "Virginity in the Babylonian Talmud: Sex, Identity, and Epistemology." PhD diss., Yale University, 2019.

Kanarek, Jane L. *Biblical Narrative and the Formation of Rabbinic Law*. New York: Cambridge University Press, 2014.

Kanarek, Jane L. "Rewriting ʿArakhin: Women and Tannaitic Vows of Valuation." *AJS Review* 40, no. 2 (2016): 261–77.

Kanarek, Jane. "A Tale of Two Women: Standing At the Center of the Talmud." *Sources: A Journal of Jewish Ideas* (Fall/Winter 2024): 141–51.

Kanarek, Jane L. "Thinking Gender through Grammar: B. Qiddushin 2a–3b." In *Jewish Culture and Creativity: Essays in Honor of Professor Michael Fishbane on the Occasion of His Eightieth Birthday*, edited by Eitan P. Fishbane and Elisha Russ-Fishbane, 123–36. Boston: Academic Studies Press, 2023.

Kiel, Yishai. *Sexuality in the Babylonian Talmud: Christian and Sasanian Contexts in Late Antiquity*. New York: Cambridge University Press, 2016.

Kugel, James L. *In Potiphar's House: The Interpretive Life of Biblical Texts*. Cambridge, MA: Harvard University Press, 1994.

Labovitz, Gail. "A Man Spinning on His Thigh: Gender, Positive Time-Bound Commandments and Ritual Fringes; Mishnah Moʿed Katan 3:4." *Nashim: A Journal of Jewish Women's Studies & Gender Issues* 28 (2015): 75–87.

Labovitz, Gail. "'These Are the Labors': Constructions of the Woman Nursing Her Child in the Mishnah and Tosefta." *Nashim: A Journal of Jewish Women's Studies & Gender Issues* 3 (2000): 15–42.

Landau, Gilad. "An Edition and Comprehensive Commentary on Chapter IX of Tractate Sotah in the Babylonian Talmud." PhD diss., Bar-Ilan University, 2016.

Landau, Lewis. "Sippurei rashi ha-nidpas be-talmud ha-bavli." *Eshel Beer-Sheva* 3 (1986): 101–17 [Hebrew].

Lavee, Moshe. "Like Mother Like Daughter: Mother-Daughter Relations in Babylonian Talmudic Stories." In *Mothers in the Jewish Cultural Imagination*, edited by Marjorie Lehman, Jane L. Kanarek, and Simon J. Bronner, 105–28. Liverpool: Littman Library of Jewish Civilization, 2017.

Lehman, Marjorie. *Bringing Down the Temple House: Engendering Tractate Yoma*. Waltham, MA: Brandeis University Press, 2022.

Lehman, Marjorie. *The En Yaaqov: Jacob Ibn Habib's Search for Faith in the Talmudic Corpus*. Detroit: Wayne State University Press, 2011.

Lehman, Marjorie. "Examining the Role of Gender Studies in the Teaching of Talmudic Literature." *Journal of Jewish Education* 72, no. 2 (2006): 109–21.

Lehman, Marjorie. "Imagining the Priesthood in Tractate Yoma: Mishnah Yoma 2: 1–2 and Bt Yoma 23a." *Nashim: A Journal of Jewish Women's Studies & Gender Issues* 28 (2015): 88–105.

Lehman, Marjorie. "Rabbinic Masculinities: Reading the *Ba ʿal Keri* in Tractate Yoma." *Jewish Studies Quarterly* 22, no. 2 (2015): 109–36.

Lehman, Marjorie. "Searching for Redemptive Readings: Grappling with Homophobia." *Journal of Textual Reasoning* 10, no. 1 (2018): 53–71.

Lev, Sarra. "Sotah: Rabbinic Pornography?" In *The Passionate Torah: Sex and Judaism*, edited by Danya Ruttenburg, 7–23. New York: NYU Press, 2009.

Levine, Baruch A. *The JPS Torah Commentary: Leviticus*. Philadelphia: Jewish Publication Society, 1989.

Levine, Baruch A. *Numbers 1–20: A New Translation With Introduction and Commentary*. New York: Doubleday, 1993.

Levinson, Joshua. "An-Other Woman: Joseph and Potiphar's Wife: Staging the Body Politic." *Jewish Quarterly Review* 87, no. 3/4 (1997): 269–301.

Levinson, Joshua. *A Twice Told Tale: A Poetics of the Exegetical Narrative in Rabbinic Midrash*. Jerusalem: Magnes Press, 2005 [Hebrew].

Lewin, B. M., ed. *ʾIgeret rav sherira gaon*. Jerusalem: Makor, 1971.

Lewis, Richard S. *"And before Honor—Humility": The Ideal of Humility in the Moral Language of the Sages*. Jerusalem: Magnes Press, 2013 [Hebrew].

Lieber, Laura S. "An Unholy Spectacle: The Ordeal of the Accused Adulteress in the Early Synagogue." *Jewish Studies Quarterly* 29, no. 2 (2022): 135–62.

Lieberman, Saul. *Greek in Jewish Palestine/Hellenism in Jewish Palestine*. New York: Jewish Theological Seminary of America, 1994.

Lieberman, Saul. *Midrash Debarim Rabbah: Edited for the First Time from the Oxford Ms. No. 147 with an Introduction and Notes*. Jerusalem: Shalem Books, 1992.

Lieberman, Saul. *Tosefta ki-fshutah: A Comprehensive Commentary on the Tosefta*. Vols. 6–7. New York: Jewish Theological Seminary of America, 1962.

Lieberman, Saul. *Tosefta ki-fshutah: A Comprehensive Commentary on the Tosefta*. Vol. 8. New York: Jewish Theological Seminary of America, 1973.

Lieberman, Saul, ed. *The Tosefta: According to Codex Vienna, with Variants from Codices Erfurt, Geniza Mss. And Editio Princeps (Venice 1521)*. Volume *Nashim*. New York: Jewish Theological Seminary, 1973.

Liss, Abraham, ed. *The Babylonian Talmud with Variant Readings Collected from Manuscripts, Fragments of the "Genizah" and Early Printed Editions.* Jerusalem: Institute for the Complete Israeli Talmud, 1977.

Margulies, Mordekhai, ed. *Midrash Wayyikra Rabbah: A Critical Edition Based on Manuscripts and Genizah Fragments with Variants and Notes.* New York: Jewish Theological Seminary of America, 1993.

Marks, Susan. "Follow That Crown: Or, Rhetoric, Rabbis, and Women Patrons." *Journal of Feminist Studies in Religion* 24, no. 2 (2008): 77–96.

Marmorstein, A. *The Doctrine of Merits in Old Rabbinical Literature.* London: Oxford University Press, 1920.

Mayse, Ariel Evan. "Expanding the Boundaries of the Holy: Hasidic Devotion, Sacred Speech, and Early Modern Jewish Thought." *Jewish Social Studies* 25, no. 1 (2019): 45–101.

Miles, Tiya. *All That She Carried: The Journey of Ashley's Sack, a Black Family Keepsake.* New York: Random House, 2021.

Milgrom, Jacob. *The JPS Torah Commentary: Numbers.* Philadelphia: Jewish Publication Society, 1990.

Milgrom, Jacob. "The Case of the Suspected Adulteress, Numbers 5:11–31: Redaction and Meaning." In *The Creation of Sacred Literature*, edited by Richard P. Friedman, 69–75. Berkeley: University of California Press, 1981.

Milikowsky, Chaim. "Gehenna and 'Sinners of Israel' in the Light of Seder ʿOlam." *Tarbiz* 55 (1986): 311–43 [Hebrew].

Milikowsky, Chaim. "Which Gehenna? Retribution and Eschatology in the Synoptic Gospels and in Early Jewish Texts." *New Testament Studies* 34, no. 2 (1988): 238–49.

Moscovitz, Leib. *The Terminology of the Yerushalmi: The Principal Terms.* Jerusalem: Magnes Press, 2009 [Hebrew].

Neis, Rachel. *The Sense of Sight in Rabbinic Culture: Jewish Ways of Seeing in Late Antiquity.* New York: Cambridge University Press, 2013.

Neusner, Jacob. *A History of the Mishnaic Law of Purities.* Leiden: Brill, 1977.

Neusner, Jacob. "The Mishnah's Generative Mode of Thought: Listenwissenschaft and Analogical-Contrastive Reasoning." *Journal of the American Oriental Society* 110, no. 2 (1990): 317–21.

Neusner, Jacob. *The Reader's Guide to the Talmud.* Leiden: Brill, 2001.

Noam, Vered. "Why Did the Heavenly Voice Speak Aramaic? Ancient Layers in Rabbinic Literature." In *The Face of Torah: Studies in the Texts and Contexts of Ancient Judaism in Honor of Steven Fraade*, edited by Michal Bar-Asher Siegel, Tzvi Novick, and Christine Hayes, 157–68. Göttingen: V&R Academic, 2017.

Pardes, Ilana. *The Biography of Ancient Israel: National Narratives in the Bible.* Berkeley: University of California Press, 2000.

Pardes, Ilana. *Countertraditions in the Bible: A Feminist Approach.* Cambridge, MA: Harvard University Press, 1993.

Peskowitz, Miriam. "Spinning Tales: On Reading Gender and Otherness in Tannaitic Texts." In *The Other in Jewish Thought and History: Constructions of Jewish Culture and Identity,* edited by Laurence J. Silberstein and Robert L. Cohn, 91–120. New York: NYU Press, 1994.

Peskowitz, Miriam B. *Spinning Fantasies: Rabbis, Gender, and History.* Berkeley: University of California Press, 1997.

Plaskow, Judith. *Standing Again at Sinai: Judaism from a Feminist Perspective.* San Francisco: Harper & Row, 1990.

Pomeranz, Jonathan Aaron. "Ordinary Jews in the Babylonian Talmud: Rabbinic Representations and Historical Interpretation." PhD diss., Yale University, 2016.

Radwin, Ariella Michal. "Adultery and the Marriage Metaphor: Rabbinic Readings of Sotah." PhD diss., University of California Los Angeles, 2007.

Rich, Adrienne. *Of Woman Born: Motherhood as Experience and Institution.* New York: W. W. Norton, 1995.

Rosen-Zvi, Assaf. "'Even Though There Is No Proof to the Matter, There Is an Indication of the Matter': The Meaning, Character and Significance of the Phrase in the Tannaitic Literature." *Tarbiz* 78, no. 3 (2009): 323–44 [Hebrew].

Rosen-Zvi, Ishay. *Demonic Desires: "Yetzer Hara" and the Problem of Evil in Late Antiquity.* Philadelphia: University of Pennsylvania Press, 2011.

Rosen-Zvi, Ishay. "Hyper-Sexualization in the Bavli: An Initial Survey." In *Midrash and the Exegetical Mind,* edited by Lieve Teugels and Rivka Ulmer, 181–205. Piscataway, NJ: Gorgias Press, 2010.

Rosen-Zvi, Ishay. "Measure for Measure as a Hermeneutical Tool in Early Rabbinic Literature: The Case of Tosefta Sotah." *Journal of Jewish Studies* 57, no. 2 (2006): 269–86.

Rosen-Zvi, Ishay. *The Mishnaic Sotah Ritual: Temple, Gender and Midrash.* Leiden: Brill, 2012.

Rosen-Zvi, Ishay. "The Ritual of Suspected Adulteress (Sotah) in Tannaitic Literature: Textual and Theoretical Perspectives." PhD diss., Tel Aviv University, 2004 [Hebrew].

Rosenblum, Jordan. "'Blessings of the Breasts': Breastfeeding in Rabbinic Literature." *Hebrew Union College Annual* 87 (2016): 145–77.

Rosenthal, David. "ʿAricot kedumot ha-meshukaʿot ba-talmud ha-bavli." In *Mehqerei Talmud: Talmudic Studies 1,* edited by David Rosenthal and Yaacov Sussman, 155–204. Jerusalem: Magnes Press, 1990.

Rubenstein, Jeffrey L. *The Culture of the Babylonian Talmud.* Baltimore: Johns Hopkins University Press, 2003.

Rubenstein, Jeffrey L. "Social and Institutional Settings of Rabbinic Literature." In *The Cambridge Companion to the Talmud and Rabbinic Literature*, edited by Charlotte Elisheva Fonrobert and Martin S. Jaffee, 58–74. New York: Cambridge University Press, 2007.

Rubenstein, Jeffrey L. *Stories of the Babylonian Talmud*. Baltimore: Johns Hopkins University Press, 2010.

Rubenstein, Jeffrey L. *Talmudic Stories: Narrative Art, Composition, and Culture*. Baltimore: Johns Hopkins University Press, 1999.

Saks, Jeffrey, ed. "'Rupture and Reconstruction' Reconsidered: A Symposium." *Tradition: A Journal of Orthodox Jewish Thought* 51, no. 4 (2019).

Sarna, Nahum M. *The JPS Torah Commentary: Genesis*. Philadelphia: Jewish Publication Society, 1989.

Satlow, Michael L. *Tasting the Dish: Rabbinic Rhetorics of Sexuality*. Atlanta, GA: Scholars Press, 1995.

Satlow, Michael L. "'Texts of Terror': Rabbinic Texts, Speech Acts, and the Control of Mores." *AJS Review* 21, no. 2 (1996): 273–97.

Schäfer, Peter. *The History of the Jews in the Greco-Roman World*. London: Routledge, 2003.

Schäfer, Peter. *Jesus in the Talmud*. Princeton, NJ: Princeton University Press, 2007.

Schäfer, Peter. "Jewish Liturgy and Magic." In *Geschichte—Tradition—Reflexion: Festchrift für Martin Hengel zum 70. Geburtstag*, edited by Hubert Cancik, Hermann Lichtenberger, and Peter Schäfer, 541–56. Tübingen: Mohr Siebeck, 1996.

Schäfer, Peter, and Shaul Shaked, eds. *Magische Texte aus der Kairoer Geniza*. Tübingen: Mohr Siebeck, 1994.

Schofer, Jonathan Wyn. *The Making of a Sage: A Study in Rabbinic Ethics*. Madison: University of Wisconsin Press, 2005.

Schremer, Adiel. *Male and Female He Created Them: Jewish Marriage in the Late Second Temple, Mishnah and Talmud Periods*. Jerusalem: Zalman Shazar Center, 2003 [Hebrew].

Schwartz, Joshua. "Once More on the Nicanor Gate." *Hebrew Union College Annual* 62 (1991): 245–83.

Schwartz, Seth. "Language, Power and Identity in Ancient Palestine." *Past & Present* 148 (1995): 3–47.

Seidman, Naomi. *Sarah Schenirer and the Bais Yaakov Movement: A Revolution in the Name of Tradition*. London: Liverpool University Press, 2019.

Septimus, Zvi. "Trigger Words and Simultexts: The Experience of Reading the Bavli." In *Wisdom of Bat Sheva: The Dr. Beth Samuels Memorial*

Volume, edited by Barry S. Wimpfheimer, 163–85. Jersey City: Ktav, 2011.

Shectman, Sarah. "Bearing Guilt in Numbers 5:12–31." In *Gazing on the Deep: Ancient Near Eastern, Biblical, and Jewish Studies in Honor of Tzvi Abusch*, edited by Jeffrey Stackart, Barbara Neverling Porter, and David P. Wright, 479–93. Bethesda, MD: CDL Press, 2010.

Shields, Mary E. "Multiple Exposures: Body Rhetoric and Gender Characterization in Ezekiel 16." *Journal of Feminist Studies in Religion* 14, no. 1 (1998): 5–18.

Shinan, Avigdor. "Aggadic Motifs between Midrash and Story." *Jerusalem Studies in Hebrew Literature* 5 (1984): 203–20 [Hebrew].

Shinan, Avigdor, ed. *Midrash Shemot Rabbah Chapters I–XIV: A Critical Edition Based on a Jerusalem Manuscript with Variants, Commentary and Introduction*. Jerusalem: Devir, 1984.

Siegal, Michal Bar-Asher. *Early Christian Monastic Literature and the Babylonian Talmud*. New York: Cambridge University Press, 2013.

Small, Jocelyn Penny. *Wax Tablets of the Mind: Cognitive Studies of Memory and Literacy in Classical Antiquity*. New York: Routledge, 1997.

Smelik, Willem F. *Rabbis, Language and Translation in Late Antiquity*. Cambridge: Cambridge University Press, 2013.

Sokoloff, Michael. *A Dictionary of Jewish Babylonian Aramaic of the Talmudic and Geonic Periods*. Ramat-Gan: Bar Ilan University Press, 2002.

Soloveitchik, Haym. "Rupture and Reconstruction: The Transformation of Contemporary Orthodoxy." *Tradition: A Journal of Orthodox Jewish Thought* 28, no. 4 (1994): 64–130.

Strack, Hermann Leberecht, and Gunter Stemberger. *Introduction to the Talmud and Midrash*. Minneapolis: Fortress Press, 1996.

Sussmann, Yaacov. "'Torah she beʿal peh'—peshutah ke-mashmaʿah: koho shel kotzo shel yod." In *Mehqerei Talmud: Talmudic Studies Dedicated to the Memory of Professor Ephraim E. Urbach*, vol. 3, edited by Yaacov Sussman and David Rosenthal, 209–384. Jerusalem: Magnes Press, 2005.

Swartz, Michael D. "Sacrificial Themes in Jewish Magic." In *Magic and Ritual in the Ancient World*, edited by Paul Mirecki and Marvin Meyer, 303–15. Leiden: Brill, 2001.

Talmud Yerushalmi: According to Ms. Or. 4720 (Scal. 3) of the Leiden University Library with Restorations and Corrections. Jerusalem: Academy of the Hebrew Language, 2001.

Tigay, Jeffrey H. *The JPS Torah Commentary: Deuteronomy*. Philadelphia: Jewish Publication Society, 1996.

Trifon, Dalia. "A Mishnah Fragment as Evidence of the Status of King

Agrippa." *Cathedra: For the History of Eretz Israel and Its Yishuv* 53 (1989): 27–48 [Hebrew].

Turan, Sinai (Tamas). "'Wherever the Sages Set Their Eyes, There Is Either Death or Poverty'—on the History, Terminology and Imagery of the Talmudic Traditions about the Devastating Gaze of the Sages." *Sidra: A Journal for the Study of Rabbinic Literature* 23 (2008): 137–205 [Hebrew].

Urbach, Ephraim E. "When Did Prophecy Cease?" *Tarbiz* 17 (1946): 1–11 [Hebrew].

Vidas, Moulie. "Greek Wisdom in Babylonia." In *Envisioning Judaism: Studies in Honor of Peter Schäfer on the Occasion of His Seventieth Birthday*, edited by Raʿanan S. Boustan, Klaus Hermann, Reimund Leicht, Annette Yoshiko Reed, and Giuseppe Veltri, 287–306. Tübingen: Mohr Siebeck, 2013.

Vidas, Moulie. *Tradition and the Formation of the Talmud*. Princeton, NJ: Princeton University Press, 2016.

Walfish, Avraham. "The Measure of Tractate Sotah: Justice beyond the Bounds of Human Jurisdiction." TheGemara. Accessed May 7, 2025. https://thegemara.com/article/the-measure-of-tractate-sotah/.

Walfish, Miriam-Simma. "Upending the Curse of Eve: A Reframing of Maternal Breastfeeding in BT Ketubot." In *Motherhood in the Jewish Cultural Imagination*, edited by Marjorie Lehman, Jane L. Kanarek, and Simon J. Bronner, 307–25. Liverpool: Liverpool University Press, 2017.

Wasserman, Mira Beth. *Jews, Gentiles, and Other Animals: The Talmud after the Humanities*. Philadelphia: University of Pennsylvania Press, 2017.

Wegner, Judith Romney. *Chattel or Person? The Status of Women in the Mishnah*. New York: Oxford University Press, 1988.

Weisberg, Dvora E. *Levirate Marriage and the Family in Ancient Judaism*. Waltham, MA: Brandeis University Press, 2009.

Weisberg, Dvora E. *Massekhet Menahot: Text, Translation, and Commentary*. Tübingen: Mohr Siebeck, 2020.

Weiss, Avraham. *The Literary Activities of the Saboraim*. Jerusalem: Magnes Press, 1953 [Hebrew].

Weiss, Haim, and Shira Stav. *The Return of the Absent Father: A New Reading of a Chain of Stories from the Babylonian Talmud*. Translated by Batya Stein. Philadelphia: University of Pennsylvania Press, 2022.

Wimpfheimer, Barry Scott. *Narrating the Law: A Poetics of Talmudic Legal Stories*. Philadelphia: University of Pennsylvania Press, 2011.

Wimpfheimer, Barry Scott. *The Talmud: A Biography*. Princeton, NJ: Princeton University Press, 2018.

Wolf, Sarah. "'Between Her and Others': The 'Spirit of Jealousy' in Numbers 5:14 and Its Ancient Jewish Reception." In *Making History: Studies in*

Rabbinic Literature, History, and Culture in Honor of Richard L. Kalmin, edited by Carol Bakhos and Alyssa Gray, 461–75. Providence, RI: Brown Judaic Studies, 2024.

Wollenberg, Rebecca Scharbach. *The Closed Book: How the Rabbis Taught the Jews (Not) to Read the Bible*. Princeton, NJ: Princeton University Press, 2023.

Yahalom, Joseph. "Angels Do Not Understand Aramaic: On the Literary Use of Jewish Palestinian Aramaic in Late Antiquity." *Journal of Jewish Studies* 47 (1996): 33–44.

Zornberg, Avivah Gottlieb. *The Particulars of Rapture: Reflections on Exodus*. New York: Schocken, 2011.

Zuckermandel, M.S., ed. *Tosefta*. Jerusalem: Wahrmann Books, 1970.

INDEX